— *Also by* —

DIANA BUTLER BASS

Grateful

Grounded

Christianity After Religion

Christianity for the Rest of Us

A People's History of Christianity

Freeing Jesus

Freeing Jesus

REDISCOVERING JESUS
AS FRIEND, TEACHER, SAVIOR, LORD,
WAY, *and* PRESENCE

DIANA BUTLER BASS

HarperOne
An Imprint of HarperCollinsPublishers

Scripture quotations, unless otherwise noted, are from the New Revised Standard Version of the Bible, copyright © 1989 by the Division of Christian Education of the National Council of the Churches of Christ in the USA. All rights reserved.

HarperCollins books may be purchased for educational, business, or sales promotional use. For information, please email the Special Markets Department at SPsales@harpercollins.com.

FIRST HARPERCOLLINS PAPERBACK EDITION PUBLISHED IN 2022

Library of Congress Cataloging-in-Publication Data is available upon request.

ISBN 978-0-06-265953-8

23 24 25 26 27 LBC 9 8 7 6 5

To my sister, Valerie

That's the best thing about little sisters:
they spend so much time wishing they were elder sisters
that in the end they're far wiser than the elder ones
could ever be.

—*Gemma Burgess*

It is just mortifying to be a Christian,
except for the Jesus part.

—*Anne Lamott*

Whoever feels attracted to Jesus cannot adequately explain why.
We must be prepared to be always correcting our image of
Jesus for we will never exhaust what there is to know.
Jesus is full of surprises.

—*Adolf Holl*

Jesus teaches but requires more of a listener. We are invited to
join the journey, wrestle with our assumptions, confront our
spiritual bigotry and struggle with the humbling mystery
and profound profundity of God.

—*Otis Moss Jr.*

Contents

Liberate Jesus

Who do you say that I am?

—*Matthew 16:15*

My knees hurt. The cushion at the marble altar almost did not matter. I could feel the cold in my legs, the ache of unanswered prayers. "Where are you, God?" I asked.

Silence.

I looked up at Jesus in full triptych glory, surrounded by angels, robed in cobalt blue against a gilt background, shimmering sanctity. The small chapel in the great cathedral was one of my favorite places to pray, mostly because of this Jesus. Today, however, I was restless as I gazed intently at the massive icon of Christ. Usually, the image drew me deeper toward God, and the railing where I knelt was a place of awakening and wisdom. "Where are you, God?" I asked again. Silence.

"God?" A quiet plea, really, the most incomplete of prayers.

"Get me out of here," a voice replied.

Was someone speaking to me? I looked behind, around.

"Get me out of here," the voice said again.

I stared up at the icon. "Jesus? Is that you?"

"Get me *out of here*," I heard again, more insistent now.

"But Lord . . ."

The chapel fell silent, but I know I heard a divine demand for freedom. I was not sure what to think, but I also did not want to tell the priest who was wandering up the aisle. I doubted the Washington National Cathedral would take kindly to the Son of God looking for the exit. And I was not sure what to do. Smuggling an altarpiece out of the building was not going to happen. Instead, I got up and nearly bolted out, all the while envisioning how I might rescue Jesus from the cathedral. I felt bad leaving him behind.

Jesus spoke to me almost a decade ago. It was not completely unusual, as I have heard whispers from the sacred in prayer, walking along the beach, in the wind, or while meditating. Having God or the universe or my own inner voice speak to me in such ways is really no big deal. Until that day at the cathedral, however, I had never heard an out-loud, clear God-voice arising from something other than my own spiritual intuitions, especially one issuing a completely un-expected directive like "Get me out of here." My husband still laughs about "that time Jesus asked you to spring him from the slammer." I rarely share the story because, well, you just never know how people will respond to a voice from heaven—or a talking painting—requesting parole from church. Truthfully, I did not know how to respond.

It makes a bit more sense now, however. During the intervening years, millions of Americans have left church behind, probably many more have left emotionally, and countless others are wondering if they should. One of the most consistent things I hear from those who have left, those doubting their faith, and those just hanging on is that church or Christianity has failed them, wounded them, betrayed them, or maybe just bored them—and they do not want to have much to do with it any longer. They are not unlike novelist Anne Rice, who in 2010 declared, "I quit being a Christian. I'm out. I remain committed to Christ as always but not to being 'Christian' or to being part of Christianity."[1] She was not the first to make this negative confession, nor was she the last. It is a common refrain in these times: "I don't consider myself Christian anymore, but I love Jesus, and I still want to follow him" or "I'm not a church person; I follow Jesus."

The theologically trained and professional religious types roll their eyes at comments like these. One of the main tenets of faith is that the church is the body of Christ and that Jesus cannot really be known (at least fully) outside of the life of the church. Ecclesiastically approved theology will not let you separate Jesus and the church. But the millions of those who have done so beg to differ. They are more than content to have fled institutional Christianity, deconstructing their faith and disrupting conventional notions of church. Even while exiting the building, however, some of those religious refugees seem to have heard the same voice I did at the altar, "Get me out of here," and are trying to free Jesus that he might roam in the world with them.

There are, of course, those who stay within church and hear Jesus pleading for release from the constraints often placed on him. During a recent Christmas season, a Methodist minister actually put the baby Jesus in a cage on her church's front lawn. This congregation's point was political: by identifying Jesus with refugee children being held at the border, they were attempting to pressure authorities to release them. It was a dramatic illustration equating the captive Jesus with the poor, the weak, the voiceless, all those held in bondage.

Those Methodists wanted to free Jesus too, as both a political and theological point. The story made national news. Many people came to the display, leaving notes, ribbons, and signs of support: "Set the prisoners free!" But the church and the pastor also received death threats saying it was irreverent, even blasphemous, to imprison Jesus. I commented to my husband, "It is odd that the physical fence bothers them. If only they noticed the invisible fencing they've already placed around him."

What does it mean to set Jesus free?

The Jesus of History and the Christ of Faith

The question of freeing Jesus was first posed to me in the early 1990s. Then, the question did not come from those fleeing church; rather, the query arose in a group of friends who were returning to church. They had left church once— they had grown up with religion, but stepped away in the 1970s as teenagers or young adults. They were among the first "leavers," what one sociologist of religion dubbed "a generation of seekers." Although those seekers never returned to church in the same numbers that they left, some portion of them made their way back to Christianity in the 1990s, filling pews long empty and bringing new energy to declining churches.[2]

These were not fundamentalist or evangelical congregations, but mostly liberal mainline churches finding new life. I was a parishioner at one such church—Trinity Episcopal in Santa Barbara, California, a congregation that went through a genuine rebirth in the decade before the millennium's end. On a sunny Sunday afternoon, I remember standing outside the building talking to a friend who had just returned to church; she was speaking of how glad she was to be back in faith community, how she loved the liturgy, and how grateful she was to speak of God.

"But," she said in a confiding tone, "I don't really know what to say about Jesus. He's important, the center of everything. But I don't know how to think about him, how to explain him. Who is he, really?"

She was not alone in wondering about Jesus. As the 1990s unfolded, Jesus topped the religion book charts, including several blockbusters that landed on the *New York Times* bestseller list. This was the heyday of the Jesus Seminar, a group of scholars who were dedicated to uncovering the historical Jesus and whose work was communicated to millions through television, radio, national magazines and newspapers, and a vast network of churches and conferences. They looked at Jesus in new ways: as a rabbi, prophet, teacher, miracle worker, itinerant mystic, political rebel, and rabble-rousing Jewish peasant—nothing like the Jesus surrounded by angels at the altar in the Washington National Cathedral. "Who is Jesus, really?" proved a powerful question as Western society moved toward 2000, his biggest birthday celebration of all time.

Of course, not everyone liked the Jesus of the 1990s, the one stripped of glory and rediscovered in the dust of ancient Israel. Those opposing the historical Jesus wrote books too. Lots of them reasserted the miraculous God-Jesus, emphasizing his divinity, making sure Jesus Christ stayed on his throne in heaven—or, at the very least, remained the One to whom all praise songs were directed. For them, what mattered was neither Roman political history nor Jewish cultural background, but the theology of the church as the infallible guide to knowing Jesus the Christ. Those books made it to the bestseller lists too. If nothing else, the 1990s could well be described as a battle for Jesus.

It was, however, not a new conflict. The arguments may have been shaped by new questions and circumstances in

American religion and fought by new combatants, but the sides had taken shape a century earlier. In 1892, the German scholar Martin Kähler made a distinction between the "Jesus of history" and the "Christ of faith" and set the trajectory of arguments over Jesus to the present day.[3] The Jesus of history needed to be recovered, reclaimed, and reinterpreted as the man Jesus who had a radical ministry and life; the Christ of faith needed to be renewed, reasserted, and reembraced as the Jesus Christ of orthodox doctrine. Some authors, teachers, and pastors tried to integrate the two, but, for the most part, people took sides, as Christians have been wont to do for the better part of the last one hundred years.

Since my friend posed the question, "Who is he, really?" much has changed. Instead of the earlier generation of leavers who returned to church and did not understand the Jesus they encountered there, those who are leaving the church today want to take Jesus out into the world with them. But whether coming in or going out, the question remains, "Who was Jesus, really?" When I bolted for the exit at the Washington National Cathedral, I think I heard both voices: "Who was Jesus, really?" and "Get me out of here," simultaneously, almost like a polyphonic monastic chant.

Understanding the Jesus of history has proved helpful (and even life-giving) for me; and I appreciate the theological traditions surrounding the Christ of faith. Yet neither historical scholarship nor conventional doctrine quite captures who Jesus is for me—the skepticism bred by one and the submissiveness inculcated by the other do not fully tell the story of the Jesus I know: the *Jesus of experience*. Well before I studied Jesus the Jewish peasant or worshipped Christ the King, I *knew* Jesus. Even as a small child, I knew his name. I had a sense of his companionship. I knew he was the heart of Christian faith. Although I now understand both history and theology, neither intellectual arguments nor ecclesial authority elucidates the Jesus I have known.

Jesus has always been there, a memory, a presence, and a person. We grew up together, Jesus and me.

I hesitated to write a book about Jesus. Part of my hesitation arose from the vastness of the subject. What can a writer say that hasn't already been said? And I didn't want to exclude anyone, because not everyone has a "Jesus and me" story. That is as it should be. We are all different people, with different stories, differing religious traditions, from different cultures and places. But these days, Christians shy away from telling their stories of Jesus, perhaps for fear of offending others or perhaps not knowing what to say. There is no denying that Christians often speak of Jesus badly—in exclusive, hurtful, and triumphal ways. Despite the reticence of some and the hubris of others, Jesus remains central to the lives of millions of Christians, however awkward it has become in a pluralistic world to talk of him.

Yet, I love sharing stories; and I love listening to others' stories. There is a way—maybe even the way—we can live together in this diverse and divided world—learning from each other's stories. Even stories of Jesus. My story can never be your story (that is called colonization—something I hope we are leaving behind). But my story might inform yours, or be like yours, or maybe even add depth or another dimension to yours. If nothing else, sharing our stories might lead to greater understanding, tolerance, appreciation, and perhaps even celebration of our differences.

As I thought of Jesus and me, I came to understand that few people grasp the significance of the "Jesus Christ of experience." I worry that people are stuck, not knowing how to talk about Jesus without sounding dogmatic, narrow, or pietistic. Christians often seem inauthentic when we mimic creeds even we do not understand, using words drawn from theologians long gone instead of our own. Our language about Jesus confines both him and us—and may well have been part of his complaint when he asked to be freed from above the altar.

Whether you are coming into a church for the first time, or whether you are running out the door with your hair on fire; whether you are a Jew or a Muslim, a humanist or a Buddhist who is curious about Jesus, I am glad you have taken the time to be with me, a Christian, as I share the stories of the Jesus I have known. And to my fellow Jesus followers in particular, I invite you into your own memory and experience, where I trust Jesus can be found.

The Jesus Question: "Who Are You?"

It feels odd to write the words "Jesus question," because Jesus has never been much of a question for me. Over the years, when quizzed why I am still a Christian, I have always responded, "Because of Jesus. I know it sounds corny, but I love Jesus." If you love Jesus, if you somehow believe in and believe Jesus, that comes pretty near the definition of what it means to be a Christian. Although I'm not quite at the end point yet, my eulogy might say I was a "cradle to grave" Jesus person.

That does not mean I have not questioned Jesus. There are lots of questions when it comes to Jesus. Nine out of ten Americans (not just Christians, but Americans) believe that Jesus was a real person, and six of ten say they have made some sort of personal commitment to Jesus.[4] Two thousand years after he lived, "Jesus" may still be one of the most recognized names on the planet, making for myriad questions from all sorts of people. Those who are not Christians have questions; those who are no longer Christians have questions; people who are trying to stay Christian have questions; Christians have questions. I have questions about Jesus still. And many friends and acquaintances regularly ask me their questions about Jesus.

The most typical questions from people of other religions involve basic queries about Jesus—things like who he was, what he taught, and whether Christians actually believe he rose from the dead. Questions from those who are no longer

Christian often involve skepticism regarding doctrines, especially those about the Trinity, miracles, or some particular teaching that makes no sense, and are the core reason for their rejection of the faith. But the struggling question too. Recent surveys show that even among churchgoers, belief in classic dogma about Jesus—such as his having lived a sinless life, his virgin birth, and his divinity—has eroded significantly in recent years.[5]

Most of these surveys devise their questions on the basis of Christian creedal statements, the ancient formulations outlining orthodoxy, or "right belief," as determined by certain early church authorities. That is actually odd, given that people in the United States are leaving religion in droves and only about one in four (or five, depending on the research) Americans attend a religious service on a regular basis.[6] Quizzing people on material when they have not attended class does not seem quite fair. Some may vaguely remember what their church told them to believe about Jesus and manage to check the correct box, but many more fail the test. And that is the real problem: thinking that belief is an exam, that there are right or wrong answers.

A few years after the Romans killed Jesus, a man named Saul was persecuting Jesus's early followers, known as those who belonged to the Way. When he was traveling to Damascus, a light from heaven struck Saul to the ground as a voice thundered, "Saul, Saul, why do you persecute me?" Saul, a zealous Jew, knew the voice of God when he heard it. "Who are you, Lord?" he asked. The voice replied, "I am Jesus, whom you are persecuting" (Acts 9:3–5). In a life-changing second, Saul—later known as Paul—became a believer. But not because of a creed or any idea about Jesus, because creeds did not exist yet and the ideas he held about Jesus were not particularly helpful. He believed because he experienced Jesus as a blinding light, as the risen Christ, as healer of his own broken soul. He would have gotten every question on the doctrine test wrong.

In the decades that followed, however, Paul would reflect on his experience of Jesus—and his many experiences of Jesus yet to come—sharing those reflections and insights in letters to his friends and co-workers in small Christian communities throughout the Roman Empire. Those letters, Paul's ruminations on his Christ experience, were loved and treasured by the church; eventually they would make up about a third of the New Testament and form the theological spine of much of Christian doctrine.

Each letter struggles with Paul's very first question—"Who are you?"—as he contends with faith, personal travails, and conflicts in the little churches he founded. Through the letters, we do not meet a single Jesus. Rather, Paul introduces many Jesuses: gift-giving Savior, egalitarian radical, Wisdom of God, Merciful One, Light of the World, Joy of All Hearts, mystical insight, deliverer from sin and guilt, cosmic vision. From his first encounter on the Damascus road, along the paths of his missionary journeys, to his own imprisonment and execution, Paul met Jesus over and over again, and Jesus was always new.

Paul's first question intrigues me. He asked, "Who are you?" not "What are you doing?" or "Why are you talking to me?" "Who" is a relational question, a question that opens us toward companionship, friendship, and perhaps even love. It is the question we try to answer whenever we meet someone new; if we find out "who" is sitting across from us, we might know how to proceed with whatever comes next. To know "who" is an invitation into a relationship that can—if we let it—change us, often sending our lives onto a completely unexpected path.

If we think that being with Jesus means getting the right answers from a creed or remembering points of doctrine from a sermon, we probably will not manage to truly know Jesus. We will only succeed in keeping the right responses scribbled on some back page of our memory. "Who are you, Lord?" is the question of a lifetime, to be asked and experienced over and over again. That query frees Jesus to show up in our lives over and over again, and entails remembering where we first met, how we struggled with each other along the road, and what we learned in the process.

I just passed a "big" birthday, having completed the sixth decade of my journey with Jesus. Like Paul so many centuries before, I have not known just one Jesus—I have met many. But there are six who stand out, the Jesuses who have been with me: friend, teacher, Savior, Lord, way, and presence. At each part of the journey, I met Jesus primarily in these ways, with the particular understanding appropriate to that stage— from childhood, through the teen and young adult years, to adulthood, wherever I was on life's time line. Jesus as my friend was my earliest experience. Although I am well past the Sunday school room, I still understand Jesus as friend, but it is different now than it was then. The same goes for each Jesus in turn.

This book is an exercise in memory—remembering *then*, with all the nostalgia, sorrow, and joy memory summons. It is also an exercise in *now*, taking the lessons once learned and applying them to the present. And it is an exercise in what *can be*, having a certain confidence to keep on the way in the midst of even radical challenges. We live in a time of disruptions, deconstruction, and dislocations, of political chaos, climate crisis, and global pandemic. Yet we are still called to go on journeys to unexpected places, get lost, get found, and continue farther down the road.

As I collected the memories of Jesus assembled in these pages, I realized how profoundly the past shapes our spiritual lives. A verse in the New Testament says: "Jesus Christ is the same yesterday and today and forever" (Heb. 13:8). Sometimes Christians interpret that to mean that Jesus is static, almost like a pillar of stone, ever reliable, never changing. But *we*, of course, do change, and because of that Jesus goes with us in and through change, growing with us as we grow, a surprising companion who never ceases to be who we need at any given time, showing up recognized but ever new. This is not a story about a fundamentalist, liberal, orthodox, unconventional, demythologized, or liberationist Jesus (even though some of those Jesuses show up in this tale). Instead, this is a story of the Jesus of experience, who shows up consistently and when least expected. Freeing Jesus means finding Jesus along the way.

Your six Jesuses may be different, or they may be the same but in a different order. Perhaps you have known eight or ten Jesuses. Or maybe you have only known one and are looking to know that Jesus more deeply or anew. Whatever the case, you are welcome here—to this story of Jesus, a rediscovery of the Jesus who is liberated from constraint and whose company releases the possibility of peace, healing, and compassion in our lives and for the world.

Friend

The Son of Man has come eating and drinking,
and you say, "Look, a glutton and a drunkard,
a friend of tax collectors and sinners!"

—*Luke 7:34*

Miss Jean, my favorite Sunday school teacher, held up a picture of Jesus surrounded by children. He seemed to be laughing, and boys and girls were sitting next to him or on his lap and hanging around his neck. A girl, whom I imagined to be me, leaned her head on his arm. "Jesus loves little children," Miss Jean said reassuringly. "He will always be your friend." She put down the poster and read from the Bible: "Jesus said, 'Let the children come to me, and do not hinder them; for to such belongs the kingdom of heaven'" (Matt. 19:14, RSV).

About fifteen of us sat in a circle. Miss Jean again said, "Jesus is your friend," before we sang:

Jesus loves me, this I know,
for the Bible tells me so.
Little ones to him belong;
they are weak, but he is strong.

Yes, Jesus loves me.
Yes, Jesus loves me.
Yes, Jesus loves me.
The Bible tells me so.

If Miss Jean said Jesus was my friend, then Jesus was my friend.

That song was the first theology I learned. Jesus loved children, and he was a loyal friend, one who protected those he loved. We sang that song in Sunday school and at bedtime. I sometimes sang it in the bath or while walking to school. "Jesus Loves Me" was the soundtrack of my early life. I was the little girl in the picture, and Jesus was my friend.

❧

"Friend" seems a gentle way of understanding Jesus, yet it is often mocked. Atheists sometimes ridicule Christians as having an "invisible friend." But the criticism is not limited to atheists. I have heard famous preachers and theologians explicitly attack the idea of Jesus as friend as juvenile and instead argue for a more "mature" Jesus. Even churchgoers dismiss certain worship songs as "Jesus is my boyfriend" music. Those who engage in such mockery might be surprised to learn that much of this goes back to Sigmund Freud, who concluded that God, the "invisible friend," was an illusion, a fairy tale, a projection, "an infantile prototype," and a neurosis.[1]

The Bible tells a different story about friendship with God, especially in the Hebrew scriptures. Friendship is anything but immaturity; it is a gift of wisdom: "In every generation [wisdom] passes into holy souls and makes them friends of God, and prophets" (Wisd. of Sol. 7:27). Two of Israel's greatest heroes, Abraham, the father of faith, and Moses, the liberating prophet, are specifically called friends of God. In Isaiah 41:8, God refers to Abraham as "my friend," a tradition that carries into the New Testament (James 2:23). Of Moses, Exodus says: "The Lord used to speak to Moses face to face, as one speaks to a friend" (33:11), a very rare intimacy, for such close proximity to the divine usually meant death (33:20).

Despite the uniqueness of seeing "face to face," sacred friendship also appears in other places and to other biblical characters. Indeed, Moses married into a clan whose family name was Reuel, meaning "friend of God." The point is that friendship with God establishes the covenant—and that Israel is freed from bondage into a new family forged by friendship through the law given by Moses. Friendship with God is not a biblical side story; rather, it is central to the promises and faithfulness of being a called people, in which all are friends, companions, intimates, siblings, and beloved.

Early Christians, most of whom were Jews, knew all of this and extended the idea of divine friendship to Jesus. The New Testament vividly recounts the closeness of Jesus's circle of friends, women and men transformed through their relationship with him. The only episode in which Jesus cries is at the tomb of Lazarus, whom he referred to as "our friend." Indeed, Jesus instructed his friends to pray to "Abba" (as we can assume he himself prayed), a term most often rendered as "Father" in English, but one that contains shades of meaning denoting intimacy and familiarity, including that of fraternal relations like "brother" or "companion," and is related to the Hebrew word for "friend" (*ahab*), used to describe Abraham.

Thus, Jesus introduces his friends (the disciples) to his other friend (God) in the daily prayer known as the "Our Father," perhaps the spirit of which is better captured by "Our Father-Friend" or just "Our Friend." This idea of "Our Friend in heaven" was a revolutionary one, as Jesus, acting as a mediator of divine companionship, collapsed the sacred distance between God and us. That thread of insight is found scattershot in the tradition, appearing in comments of theologians like St. Gregory of Nyssa, who linked the tradition of Moses as God's friend with Jesus when he wrote, "Christ is our true friend."[2]

With due respect to critics and Dr. Freud, in my experience, that is exactly who Jesus was to me as a child: my friend. I had one close childhood friend who moved to Ohio shortly before kindergarten. Otherwise, I was a fairly isolated girl. There was an empty lot across the street from our house, the last stand of trees in a Baltimore neighborhood that had once been a great wood. I played there, alone except for Jesus, acting out fairy tales and Bible stories, making art of rocks and twigs. He was my first companion as I noticed moss and watched birds, as I lay on the ground and looked up through autumn leaves to the bright blue sky.

At church, Miss Jean told the story of God walking around with Adam and the pair naming all the animals, "The Lord God formed every beast of the field and every bird of the air, and brought them to the man to see what he would call them; and whatever the man called every living creature, that was its name" (Gen. 2:19, RSV). The wooded lot was my own private Garden of Eden, and Jesus walked with me there, just as the grown-ups sang in the big church on Sundays:

And he walks with me, and he talks with me,
And he tells me I am his own,
And the joy we share as we tarry there,
None other has ever known.

There were no divisions between the worlds for me—neighborhood and family and church and world existed together, all mixed up with the Bible. When I was three, I remember the adults speaking reverently about a man who lived in a white house (I thought they said he rode a "white horse"), and, when he was killed, I wondered if he might rise from the dead like Jesus. A preacher on television spoke about having a dream of children playing together—that sounded nice to me—but my uncle said the man was a Communist. I asked Miss Jean what a Communist was and if they were in the Bible.

One December, figurines went missing from our manger scene. After a frantic search, my mother found the Blessed Virgin and her baby behind the wheel of my orange toy convertible conversing with a bikini-clad Barbie. I had moved the Holy Family into the spare bedroom at Barbie and Ken's house, thinking that a suburban two-story was better for Jesus than growing up in a barn. Jesus lived easily in all these worlds—the woods, in the White House, on the television news, and with my dolls. "I do not call you servants any longer," Jesus said to his followers, "but I have called you friends" (John 15:15). *Yes, Jesus loves me.* And Jesus was the best invisible friend any little girl could ever have.

In the Beginning

In the film *Miracle on 34th Street*, a bitter Doris Walker raises her little girl, Susan, to never believe in fairy tales. Although the story focuses on Doris's eventual conversion from cynicism to love, young Susan's transformation is just as interesting. Susan seems old before her time, like a world-weary adult. She has no friends her own age and even sneers that the other children she knows are immature. Once Kris Kringle befriends Susan, however, her world opens to the power of imagination and, in a very real sense, she becomes a child. The point is not that she comes to believe in Santa Claus or fairy tales; rather, it is that Susan herself now became the child her mother forced her to deny.

We often associate friendship with children and even arrange "playdates" to encourage it in them. Go to your local library or bookshop and look at the children's section. Scores of books are about finding a friend, being a friend, welcoming others into friendship, crossing boundaries to be friends, befriending outsiders, overcoming loneliness through friendship, working with friends, and treating friends well. Children's literature is a world of friendship, one populated by boys and girls from all ethnicities and races, animals and pets of all kinds, and even elements of nature. In addition to all the general books about friendship, there are dozens of books from specific faith traditions about it—stories of friendship from the Bible, the life of Jesus, Jewish history, and the lives of Islamic heroes.

If the books we read to children are any indication, friendship may well be the very first virtue we teach and the highest value for which we wish them to strive. Certainly, stories of friendship are the earliest stories many of us hear, and their resonance stays with us through life. The lessons learned from those first words remain compelling: be yourself, welcome others, practice kindness, and play well together.

When my daughter was young, I read to her all the time—and I would wind up crying over the stories. I think I loved some of the books more than she did; I remember marveling at the wonders of a playground détente, the joy of a new girl moving in to the empty house next door, the awkwardness of an elephant and a pig being friends, and the change in the rainbow fish who learned to share. And it is not just books—it is the entire world we create for children in film, video, and animation and through games and play.

My daughter accepted the lessons easily; I cried when reading because I knew how hard it would be. We teach our children to be friends and then we ourselves forget the teaching. Surely the playground is not Eden, but it may well be one of the few places where we still strive to create a community of friends who know freedom, trust, and mutual joy. We think friendship is juvenile, but it is not. Friendship may well be the hardest thing of all. Maybe that is why we encourage friendship in the youngest in our midst, hoping against hope that they may do a better job with it than we did.

It is not, perhaps, surprising that the first story in the Bible is about friendship. In the opening chapters of Genesis, God is lonely and wants a friend. Of course, it does not say that directly, for most theologies depict God as perfect and complete, with no need for anything beyond God's own self. But when I read those pages, God, at the very least, seems bored by divine isolation. So God creates, almost as if at play in the cosmos. All sorts of things come forth: day and night; water and sky; oceans and earth; plants and trees; sun, moon, and stars; all the fish and animals and creatures of every kind. The last artistic flourish is humankind; God made male and female to be friends, companions, and lovers and to bring forth children, just so no one will ever be lonely again. What was a brooding, chaotic universe becomes a realm at play, one in which everything and everyone is harmonious, a circle of friends caring for and with all, and God said it was very good.

Friendship is an important theme in the biblical creation stories. In the beginning, God walks with Adam and Eve in mutual delight. These friends share the same spirit—the breath of God—and a common vocation to tend and attend creation. Often religious people read Genesis as deadly serious, maintaining that it is about sin and punishment, but when I read those first pages, I always laugh. God makes man from the dust of the ground, watered by a spring, and gives him everything. But the man is not happy even when he has all of creation at hand. To keep boredom at bay, he names all the animals—rather like an only child naming stuffed toys—a venture that winds up being deeply unsatisfying. It is hard to imagine feeling somehow incomplete when one has God's total attention and the entire animal kingdom as companions, but Adam must have been a uniquely needy guy.

So God makes a new friend for him, the woman Eve, whose name means "life." When he sees her, Adam proclaims, "Bone of my bones and flesh of my flesh!" (2:23), a pronouncement that may be the best description of true friendship ever. Adam was incomplete without a partner, the one whose friendship finally gave him life. Thus, Adam and Eve become spouses, but this is always a story about more than an exclusive friendship of two. In Genesis, a sacred circle of friends forms within the circle of creation, in the delight of uncomplicated trust; the first act in biblical history is oneness of three, mutual vulnerability with no shame. Kindred souls, playmates, friends. Man, woman, God.

We are pretty far from Eden, but we see the qualities that make for friends most often in children. Although it is more than possible to romanticize children and friendship (and to forget the indignities of the playground), we remember our own childhood friendships and marvel at the capacity of the children in our lives to make friends. As one writer says simply, "A friend is someone fun to play with—and someone you can trust."[3] Children get that. By adulthood, however, most people, bullied and wounded by betrayal, have forgotten how to play. But imagine Jesus in that way—playful and trustworthy.

When we consider friendship one of the primary spiritual purposes of creation, other biblical stories emerge in new ways. The lovely story of Jesus and children that Miss Jean showed us a picture of in Sunday school is told in the gospels of Mark, Luke, and Matthew (where the incident is actually told twice!). As word of the loving rabbi Jesus spreads through Israel, people begin to bring their children to Jesus that he might bless them. The disciples rebuke them, but Jesus, in turn, rebukes them: "Let the little children come to me, and do not stop them; for it is to such as these that the kingdom of heaven belongs" (Matt. 19:14). Most scholars interpret this text on the basis of the low social standing of children in the ancient world—children ranked only slightly higher than slaves with regard to status and rights. That Jesus invited them to his side is not particularly unusual given his propensity to welcome all sorts of outcasts and marginalized people, as he envisioned an upside-down world where those who were last would be first.

But when we combine the creation story's emphasis on friendship with Jesus's welcome of children, something else comes to the fore. Does Jesus welcome children only because of their low status? Perhaps Jesus is welcoming them because they somehow understand all this, intuit it, better than older people. In the ancient world, friendship between adults became caught up in labyrinthine structures of patronage, debt, kinship, and moral obligation. People prized friendship as a virtue, but friendship was also treacherous territory filled with potential rivalries and betrayal. It was assumed that friendship was political—you helped your friends and you hurt your enemies.

Even in the ancient world, however, friendship between children was a carefree state uncomplicated by worldly realities. Although most ancient philosophers did not consider children capable of deep friendship, since they lacked virtues like wisdom and judgment, others, like Plutarch, noticed that children possessed something called "first friendship," a quality endued to them by "Nature." This "brotherly love" was a desirous trait, but however noticeable it was in children, it appeared lost to most adults.[4]

"Truly I tell you," said Jesus, "unless you change and become like children, you will never enter the kingdom of heaven" (Matt. 18:3). Perhaps we could render his words afresh: "Truly

I say to you, unless you return to first friendship—the way of trusting love and playfulness—you won't know anything about the life God promises." Apparently, Jesus sees friendship in childhood as something to aspire to, not look down upon. We may shake our heads in Calvinist disagreement or argue against such notions with modern psychological maturity, knowing full well that the stark realities of original sin or the theories spun by Freud better express the selfishness and brutality of childhood. Jesus, however, goes on to say that if you inhibit the natural propensity of children toward friendship with him, "it would be better for you if a great millstone were fastened around your neck and you were drowned in the depth of the sea" (Matt. 18:6).

And therein is the problem of assigning friendship to children: everybody grows up. There are stumbling blocks aplenty. Friendship gets cast aside in favor of more important tasks, to be recovered only in our leisure time if at all. Meanwhile, the picture from Sunday school hangs in the clouded corners of memory. And Jesus's welcome of children points us toward the friendship for which we were created, even as we mourn that we do not know how to get back there. But Jesus is still waiting on the playground, wanting to be our friend.

"You Are My Friends"

In August 2019, at the beginning of the school year in the United States, a photo showing two little boys holding hands went viral. Conner, an autistic boy entering the second grade, was going to school alone for the first time. Although the bus trip went well, when he arrived at the school, he froze with fear and started to cry; he hid in a corner, unable to walk into the building. Christian, another boy, saw Conner and went to comfort him. Then he took Conner by the hand and led him inside the building. "He found me and held my hand, and I got happy tears," Conner later told a reporter when asked about Christian. "He was kind to me. I was in the first day of school, and I started crying. Then he helped me, and I was happy." Conner's mother said, "Christian is Conner's first real friend." And Christian's mother explained, "They have an inseparable bond."[5]

Like millions of others who saw the photograph and read this story, I felt verklempt, unable to hold back small tears of joy. I also laughed—because who would believe it without a picture? A white boy named Conner huddled in a corner, a Black boy named Christian—Christian!—reaching out to help him. It was an updated American parable, a rewrite of *The Pilgrim's Progress* for an age of racial anxiety and political division. As I looked at the photograph, it seemed an icon for these days, a Jesus tenderly leading a frightened boy toward a new world. "This is my commandment," said Jesus, "that you love one another as I have loved you. . . . You are my friends if you do what I command you" (John 15:12–14).

I am not sure if I ever knew what to make of those words of Jesus: "You are my friends *if* you do what I command you." It all sounded so conditional. What kind of friendship was that? The story of Conner and Christian clarified it, though.

Friendship is contingent on love—real love: compassion, empathy, reaching out, going beyond what we imagine is possible. That is the command: love. And *if* we reach out in love, friendship is the result, even friendship with God. Friendship is mutual, a hand extended and another reaching back.

When I think of friendship with Jesus, I imagine that hand extended. It happens in different ways, of course. Sometimes, the hand is part of an ancient story, the hand of Jesus outstretched to embrace little children or to invite us to follow him. But more often it is the hand of another person. When I feel afraid, huddled in a corner, unable to move forward, it is the hand that reaches out to comfort me, remind me that I am not alone, or guide me toward the next step on my journey. St. Teresa of Ávila once said, "God has no hands but yours. . . . Yours are the hands with which he blesses all the world." Sometimes, I am the one who needs the hand; at other times, mine is the hand that reaches. Friendship is an eternal circle, the ceaseless reaching toward one another that strengthens us and gives us joy.

"I do not call you servants," Jesus said, "but I have called you friends." Astonishing.

Imagine how Jesus's close followers felt when they heard those words for the first time. Of course, he was their friend. They had been through so much together, years of wandering homeless in Israel, learning from and teaching each other, sharing meals and prayers. They had come to suspect their companion was something more than a regular friend—a great rabbi, a spiritual healer, a mystical prophet, the Son of God. That last one made no intellectual or doctrinal sense to them. They were Jews, and there was only one God. Yet this friend of theirs knew and loved God more intimately and more uniquely than they had ever imagined possible.

Jesus brought them to the very heart of God and then revealed that God's heart longed for friendship. They had heard this story before—Abraham, Moses, and Miriam were friends of God, as were the prophets and seers of ancient times and the great heroes of Israel like Ruth and Naomi, Esther, and David and Jonathan. They were more than servants to God. God was their friend; and they were friends of God. Servanthood, although admirable, is the lesser thing. Friendship, the knowing, loving, and free and joyful giving to another, is the passionate desire of God.

And now Jesus is saying, "I have called you friends," not just to special people of the past whose names were recorded in sacred memory, but to the ragged fishermen and curious women, sitting around him listening to his tales, trusting for the first time that the God of Israel had not forgotten them, souls broken under the weight of Roman oppression, suffering under imperial slavery. They were not slaves, not even servants. They were friends of Jesus, friends of God.

In that world, Caesar was a god. Everyone feared him. He had no friends. The Egyptians and Persians had gods. None of those gods were friends to regular people. They were to be satisfied, their wrath appeased. There were gods aplenty, all awaiting your servile sacrifices and terrified loyalty, cold and isolated and distant in their marble and gold temples. The gods demanded so much of you, craving blood to prove obeisance, even your own if and when the whim suggested itself.

Jesus calls us friends. God reaches toward us, not as a fearsome master or judge, but a friend, beckoning us to reach back. Memories of Eden flood the heart, that ancient longing for friendship with God. The exile is ended, the embrace endures. Once, we were created by that hand that reached to dust and rib; now that same hand joins ours again and again, the clasp of the unfailing friend.

We might not stop to think about what makes for a friend, but one professor says close friendship is made up of three simple things: "Somebody to talk to, someone to depend on, and someone to enjoy."[6] Children, of course, know the ease of this, and it underscores how important freedom is in the exchange: God freely reaches, and we freely reach back. The great Christian theologian Dietrich Bonhoeffer likened friendship to wildflowers:

> No one has planted, no one watered it;
> it grows, defenseless in freedom,
> and in cheerful confidence
> that no one will grudge it
> life
> under the broad sky.[7]

Adults make friendship hard, almost as if it is a burden on our time, taking our attention away from more pressing matters. We have forgotten the effortless and winsome aspects of friendship, how the best of friends often show up when least expected. Perhaps we have become too cultivated in modern life. Researchers have found that most Americans have only two friends they consider "confidantes," a number that has fallen from three friends in the mid-1980s.[8] Younger people tend to have more friends than older adults. By midlife, however, Americans often consider friendship optional, especially when raising families and pursuing careers. For older adults, making friends is difficult, as issues such as living alone and health concerns limit opportunities for new connections. One theologian, who writes powerfully about friendship, notes, "Authentic friendship is notoriously different [from relationships we can control or manipulate] and inescapably risky."[9]

In an age of risks, the last thing most of us think we need is yet another uncertainty, no matter the potential rewards. The social, technological, and economic pressures of contemporary life have made us all Conner—we might have been brave enough to get on the bus, but when we arrive at school, we fear that someone will hurt us, we will not be accepted, or we cannot walk through the door into an unknowable future. Overcoming one risk opens up more risks. And, revealing my inner Conner for a moment, the honest truth is that I just want to go home.

The picture of Christian taking Conner's hand is, of course, an image of love. But it is also an image of risk. Clearly it was a risk for Conner, in view of whatever he imagined awaited him in that scary school building. But Christian risked as well. He did not know how Conner might respond. Would Conner use a racial slur against him, hit him, or reject his hand? But Christian went ahead anyway, regardless of the consequences, in freedom and (what Bonhoeffer called) "cheerful confidence" that love—uncultivated, uncalculated—was greater than the risk. "True friendships are not," muses one author, "relationships we control but adventures we enter into."[10] If friendship is risky, then it is the risk of a shared journey. Better to go together than alone.

The story of the New Testament is that the risk of friendship is *the* risk that frees us from fear and reshapes our lives—it is better to go together than to go alone. Jesus befriends us, opening our hearts to genuine love and the capacity to forgive each other, welcome all, and act justly in the world. Friendship with Jesus may begin on the playground, in the Sunday school class, while wandering in the woods, or pretty much anywhere, but it becomes an adventure, a journey, as the relationship grows and changes over a lifetime. That is what friendship is, the field where the wildflowers grow, where the unpredictable, beautiful things of being human come forth from the soil, where we flourish with others.

Friendship makes us different from the person we would be if we were alone, and, I daresay, it makes Jesus different as well, for friendship is mutuality, shared vision, and affection. Some versions of Christianity insist that Jesus is immutable, but if Jesus invites us into friendship, how can that be? As Jesus risks with outstretched hand toward a world of potential friends, does not every hand that is returned—in some way—transform Jesus as well? It is not friendship if it is not mutual: no sharing, no friendship.

Conner and Christian both changed, something impossible without mutual risk and mutual response. It is just that simple. When Jesus extends the hand of friendship and we reach back, everything changes with the clasp. And that is the stunning, mind-bending, soul-expanding truth of the words that thunder beyond an ancient page toward every trembling "Conner" moment of our lives: *I have called you friends.*

Then comes the other surprise. Jesus tells us to go be the other boy at school; we are to be Christian: "Go and bear fruit, fruit that will last. . . . I am giving you these commands so that you may love one another" (John 15:16–17). Jesus befriends us so we can befriend others. That is the odd thing about friendship. Sometimes we are Conner, but we always aspire to be Christian, who takes the risk, knowing that Jesus risked when reaching toward us.

Friends to Each Other

There is a thread that runs through Western philosophy and theology that defines friendship as a potentially exclusive and selfish relationship. In ancient thought, friendship was needed to make oneself a better person; it ennobled virtue and was necessary for the good life. While commentators praised friendship as a glorious thing, many also fretted that

friendship is preferential and private (not to mention the continued undercurrent of homophobic concern about the lines
being crossed from male friendship to erotic love). We choose
our friends because we like them, feel kinship toward them,
and perhaps even perceive their similarity to us. The Danish
theologian Søren Kierkegaard actually scorned friendship
on these grounds as morally inadequate and even anti-
thetical to Christianity. "Friendship belongs to paganism," he
wrote.[11]

Although Kierkegaard was partial to theological extremes,
it is true that nearly everything written about friendship in
Western history has been written by men and maintains certain misunderstandings based in hierarchy and privilege. I
have wondered if this line of thinking inspires some contemporary criticism of Jesus as friend, an insult often directed at
those deemed theologically immature, "childish," or, more
overtly, "feminine."

But there is another thread in the history of Western
spirituality that weaves friendship into practices of justice
and equality. A few years ago, I discovered—much to my
surprise—that my first ancestors to come to America were
Quakers. Although we mostly think of that tradition through
old-fashioned stereotypes, "Quakers" is the nickname for the
Society of Friends, and that group, founded in the mid-1600s,
has never been quaint. Quakers believed that every human
being was filled with the "inner light," or the presence of
God. Because of this, there was no need for clergy or even a
church. The Friends met to encourage one another to listen
to and experience the light. As a result, they formed distinc-

tively egalitarian communities, with shared responsibilities between men and women, and rejected class divisions. They called themselves "Friends of the Truth" or "Friends of the Light." They were friends of God and to one another.

The idea that Quakers were quaint came from their practice of addressing people as "thou" or "thee," words we consider old-fashioned today. However, "thou" and "thee" were once the familiar forms of address, used for intimates and friends in place of the more formal "you." Thus, when a Quaker walked down a road in England, crossed paths with the local squire, and addressed his higher-ranking neighbor as "thou" instead of the more formal, expected "you," it was akin to calling a member of the local nobility "mate" or "buddy," a greeting to which the Quakers' lordly superiors did not take kindly.

Such practices of friendship—based on the belief that since we are friends of God, we are all friends of one another— were deemed radical, heretical, and a threat to the good order of society. Thus, the Quakers found themselves at odds with authorities, sentenced to prison, and exiled for the crime of being friends. As the movement spread, Friends advocated for all sorts of social justice causes, including abolition and women's rights. It all seemed pretty obvious to them: friends do not let friends be held in slavery. Friendship expanded naturally from the most profound inner experiences to the world of social relations and politics, as friendship with God meant a more just, loving, and egalitarian society.

Friendship is not just for friends. Friendship is for the good of the world.

The radical, inclusive friendship of God shows up in the New Testament, where Jesus is accused of being a friend of sinners and tax collectors (Luke 7:34), as many of his closest associates—his friends—were outcasts and marginal people. It was an odd group of friends, one that went well beyond convention and included "the poor, the crippled, the lame, and the blind" (Luke 14:13). Perhaps the simplest thing to understand in the entire New Testament is that Jesus invites his friends to dinner—all of them, respectable and not. The earliest followers of Jesus gathered at table, making the meal or feast the focus for the new community, causing one scholar to refer to the whole Jesus movement as "a banquet of unusual friends," men and women together, who turned the social order of table relations on its head.[12] Unlike the vision of heroic "virtue" friendship of the ancient world, a relationship between individual men seeking valor and the good life, Jesus's friendship is known in community, a wide-open invitation to mutual love, care, and sharing. "It is not a friendship of one or two," proclaimed a preacher more than a century ago, "but of many."[13]

Friends do things together. When we are children, we play. As we grow up, we might share a hobby or interest. When we are adults, we may find ourselves working side by side for a cause or at a protest march. If a friend is in trouble, we do whatever we can to help. But something else happens as well. Instead of just rejoicing in the private relations between friends, we turn outward and invite others to come along. We do not just please ourselves or work to serve others, we invite them to the table, to sit and enjoy the companion-ship of all. We give up false notions of friendship—notions of exclusivity and preference—and instead set a table where everyone is welcome, where strangers become friends, and where every person is an honored guest.

But what about Jesus's comment: "No one has greater love than this, to lay down one's life for one's friends" (John 15:13)? For far too long, Christians have interpreted this to mean that we have to die for our friends. Of course, there are rare moments when a friend might save another's life by putting their own self in danger—like a hostage situation, pushing a friend out of oncoming traffic, or rushing into a burning house. More typically, we "lay down" other things in friendship, surrendering isolation, burdens, despair, and self-delusion. We lay down the lives we had when we accept the invitation to Jesus's dinner party. There, Jesus does not assign new arrivals to the dishwashing crew or the group wiping down the tables. Instead, as soon as we enter the banquet hall, he waves at us, calling out, "Friend, move up higher!" and points to a place marked by name (Luke 14:10).

Friends do not just work together to make a better world; even the best of such friendships are too often based in a common self-interested vision. Jesus as friend does not offer a plan; instead, he extends a hand that guides us into a new reality. Here friendship itself is the embodiment of a more just and loving world. Like Christian and Conner on the school playground. Like many saints and wise ones through-out history.

This is what Howard Thurman, the African American mystic and activist, knew in 1935 when he made a "pilgrimage of friendship" to India to meet Gandhi. He traveled half-way around the planet to make friends with the great teacher of nonviolence, intuiting that sitting together, listening, and learning could change the world. Gandhi explained that the soul force of nonviolence was beneath and through all things, and this force, and this force alone, could break through the unjust structures of racism, poverty, and class and allow broken humanity to find true oneness. The joining of friends unleashed the nonviolent energy present throughout the cosmos, and that would bring forth genuine freedom and equality for all in beloved community. The friendship of two changes little; the friendship of many changes everything.[14]

I have called you friends.

Sometimes the first thing is the most important thing, in this case, the Sunday school lesson long ago. "Jesus kept on telling us we should try to be like children," said Dorothy Day shortly before she passed away, "be more open to life, curious about it, trusting of it; and be less cynical and skeptical and full of ourselves, as we so often are when we get older."[15] Know that Jesus is your friend. Be a friend.

A couple years ago, Rev. Dr. Eric Elnes, a friend of mine, preached a sermon series on friendship.[16] Eric holds a PhD in Old Testament and is pastor of a well-educated, culturally sophisticated congregation. At the end of the first sermon, he invited the church into a simple practice to imagine themselves as friends of God:

> If you want to experience a fraction of God's love for you, I have a suggestion for the next time you approach God in prayer. I invite you to imagine that your very best friend is before you—someone who is no less loving or gracious, or endearing, or wise than your very best friends on earth. If you will treat God like your very best friend, you will eventually come to know the God whom Jesus and Abraham knew as Friend. This is a promise I make to you. More importantly, it is a promise the Scriptures make.

We forget what was promised, what we knew to be true before we knew anything else. We have to be reminded when we grow up. All that cynicism and skepticism—those are easier to believe than the promise. I have to remind myself of Miss Jean, of walking and talking with Jesus in the woods. It is hard to remember the woods.

We do, of course, grow up. And the world changes. One day, in the spring after I turned five, a bulldozer arrived and mowed down all the trees across the street. A small ranch house arose in place of the woods. My arboreal playground disappeared overnight, but a new family moved in. Their daughter became a classmate when we started school—and my friend.

Teacher

You call me Teacher and Lord—and you
are right, for that is what I am.

—John 13:13

In autumn 1964, I started kindergarten. The first day was
unlike any other day of my life. My mother walked me
to school with my baby sister in a carriage and my toddler
brother holding her hand. I led the familial parade, determined as always, unwilling to let my fear show, toting a pink
Barbie lunch box and a small book bag.

When we approached the classroom, Miss Kinersley, my
new teacher, came out and welcomed me, as another teacher
had welcomed my father to that same classroom twenty-five
years earlier. I felt suddenly shy and hid behind my mother's

skirt. But Miss Kinersley took my hand, instructed me to place my things in the cubby marked "Diana," and told me to take my seat.

When all the students were sitting in neat rows of tiny desks, she announced: "These are the classroom rules." She read us a list of "dos" and "don'ts," so we would know how to behave. On the wall hung a big chart with each student's name, along with places for little checks and stars to track our progress in following the rules. And thus school began.

That fall, Sunday school changed too. We still sat on a carpet in a circle and sang songs about Jesus while Miss Jean read to us during Bible story time. But there were little desks in the new room, not just blocks and toys. In addition to stories about Jesus, we now had lessons about what Jesus taught. There were Sunday school worksheets and coloring assignments, all to help us learn things about the Bible, about being Methodist, and about Jesus. And there was a chart with checks and stars on the wall—very like the one in Miss Kinersley's room—to track our progress in church school. Suddenly, my world was filled with desks, charts, and homework.

One other thing changed at church. For the first time, I was allowed to go upstairs to the big church with my mother. The sanctuary was a bit like a schoolroom—with people sitting in rows on hard seats so they would pay attention. But it was different too. The windows were colored glass and, when light fell through them, it made rainbow patterns on the red carpet. We sang, a choir sang, and we said prayers. At the center of grown-up church was a preacher. He seemed a bit like a teacher, even though he insisted that Jesus was really the Teacher. At grown-up church, there were fewer stories involving Jesus. Instead, the minister gave short lectures about what Jesus taught. This was new to me. Life was a school, and there was much to learn.

❧

Although Christians call Jesus by many names, those who knew him best mostly called him "teacher." Of the ninety or so times Jesus is addressed directly in the New Testament, roughly sixty refer to him as "teacher," "rabbi," "great one," or "master" (as in the British sense of "schoolmaster"). In the gospels, the preponderance of action that occurs is Jesus teaching. He teaches at the Temple, on a hillside, by a lake, in a field, by a campfire, at a dinner table, while at a wedding, and in the center of the city. He teaches individuals, his disciples, large crowds, small groups, his friends, and his foes.

The only biblical story we have of Jesus's childhood is one in which he is teaching. When he was merely twelve, his parents took him to Jerusalem, where they promptly lost him. They searched for their son for three days and finally found him in the Temple, "sitting among the teachers, listening to them and asking them questions," causing these learned ones to be "amazed at his understanding and his answers" (Luke 2:41–50).

We hear nothing else of him until more than a decade later when his cousin John baptized him, and in the aftermath of that spiritually transforming event Jesus walked into a local synagogue and began to teach. His words so upset his neighbors that they ran him out of town. Following this unhappy pedagogical debut, Jesus was forced into his ultimate profession as an itinerant rabbi. Jesus was a born teacher and a born-again one, and he was still teaching on the night before he was arrested and even while being tortured by the Romans. He lived and died a teacher.

Many years after Sunday school, I learned that some Christians dislike calling Jesus "teacher," citing the term as inadequate and the source of tepid moralism over against a more robust understanding of who Jesus was in view of his divinity. But that misses the point. The word typically translated as "teacher" was the title "rabbi" or "rabbouni," a fairly new—and even revolutionary—term in the first century. The word "rabbi" did not mean a Jewish clergyperson, as it does today, nor did the title appear in the Hebrew Bible. Indeed, it was just coming into use during Jesus's time for one whose teachings bore spiritual authority—a sage, a storyteller, an insightful interpreter of the Law, or a particularly wise elder.

Oddly enough, the Christian scriptures may contain some of the most ancient evidence of this Jewish development, and Jesus himself was the "earliest attested person in literature to bear the title 'Rabbi.'"[1] To be a rabbi in the first century was to be a teacher who was crafting a new approach to Hebrew texts, traditions, and interpretations. And, sadly, both Christians and Jews have forgotten how completely innovative and challenging Jesus was as a rabbi. Jewish scholar

Amy-Jill Levine calls both to account for missing the point of Jesus: "He must, in the Christian tradition, be more than just a really fine Jewish teacher. But he must be that Jewish teacher as well."[2]

About a decade ago, a rabbi reminded me of Jesus the Jewish teacher. I had been asked to address a group of rabbis on retreat, an invitation that both honored and humbled me. The days together were wonderful. After a particularly beautiful time of prayer and song, I blurted out to one of the rabbis, "I want to be Jewish!"

He looked at me with a glimmer of laughter in his eyes and inquired, "You follow Jesus, right?"

"Yes," I responded.

"He was a rabbi, you know," he said. "Follow him. Listen to his teaching, and you'll do just fine."

From that day on, I understood that Jesus was indeed my rabbi. He had been for a long time. Follow his teachings— the rules and commands—listen to the stories, embrace the word, and live his wisdom. Rabbi Jesus shows the way.

The Rules

If you had asked me as a child where Jesus lived, I might have replied that he lived on the flannel board in the Sunday school classroom. Sometimes, sheep or birds would accompany him. Perhaps he was on a boat or at the edge of a lake. He might have been holding bread. But mostly he stood in front of a small group listening intently to him—teaching.

I imagined him telling people what they should and should not do, just like my parents or my teachers at school and in church. Jesus instructed us on how we should treat people and how to follow him. Like all teachers, he made sure we knew the rules. Miss Jean said that although Jesus taught many things, being Christian came down to a single tenet called the Golden Rule: "Do to others as you would have them do to you" (Luke 6:31).

When you are little, rules make sense. Life was made up of rules, like "Hang up your jacket," "Brush your teeth before you go to bed," "Pick up your toys," and "Don't fight with your brother." There were school rules and rules at home. There were lists of instructions to follow each day; if I did certain things, I got a check mark from my teacher or gold star from my mother. The Sunday school gave gold stars too, for attendance, mostly. There were also stars for reading from the Bible, cleaning up after the snack, and for nice artwork. But Sunday school teachers could not give gold stars for "Do unto others." How would you check that off a list? The Golden Rule was quite unlike any other rule in my six-year-old life. Okay, so Jesus had a rule, but his was, well, weird. Surely, this was going to take some explaining.

And explain the church did. The Golden Rule was twinned with something called the Great Command: Love God and love your neighbor as yourself (Luke 10:27). Oh! I was to be nice to others, as I wanted others to be nice to me. The Golden Rule was tied up with loving my family and friends, and that love was somehow part of loving God. Most of the rules in my young life seemed based on capricious adult demands (why, after all, must a girl put away her toys every night?), but Jesus's rule made some sense—love makes for more love. This was surprisingly logical even if there were no gold stars. The Golden Rule explained the "neighbor part" of the Great Command.

I noticed, however, the church added its own rules to being a Christian. Church rules were more like those of home or school: don't talk in worship; don't wiggle in the pew; don't run in the "big" church when the preacher is talking; don't snack on the crackers and grape juice. At times, the adults would laugh about breaking church rules—about going to dances, drinking martinis, or smoking cigarettes. When I asked about this, my mother replied that there were Jesus's rules and there were Methodist rules. The first set, apparently, were inviolate; and the second, not so much. She said that Methodist rules were "old-fashioned." This was confusing and made me wonder what other rules could be ignored or were out-of-date and who got to decide.

Since I was six, I did not have to worry about the dancing, drinking, and smoking rules yet, so I paid attention to Jesus's rules. Eventually, some of Moses's rules got added to Jesus's list, rules about not killing people or stealing things or doing something called adultery, which no one would explain to me. For the most part, these rules seemed based on love too and made sense. Except for the rule about honoring my parents. There were lots of days I did not want to do that and secretly felt mad at my mother and father. I hoped nobody noticed. I was a rule breaker too.

When I was a bit older, I asked grown-ups—either a Sunday school teacher or my parents—who Jesus was. They all agreed: Jesus was a good moral teacher. The best. Better than any other teacher who ever lived. We should do what he taught, follow his example. Early on, however, I noticed a problem—the people around me did not seem to heed their own advice except on Sundays. No one would ever party on a Sunday or light up in the sanctuary. They kept the Methodist rules one day a week. I began to wonder if the same was true for Jesus's rules about love and doing nice things for others. Did grown-ups keep the rules in church and play by a different set the rest of the time?

There wasn't much following of the Methodist rules, and I began to notice that following of Jesus's rules was sort of rare too. As I became more aware of the world beyond school and church, I could not figure out how it was loving to the Black people who came into my grandfather's store to make them use the back door. I could not figure out how it was loving to cheer a cruel sheriff on the news using water cannons on kids my own age. I could not figure out how it was loving to insult women with opinions and tell them to get back into the kitchen. I could not figure out how it was loving to shoot people in some far-off place named Vietnam. I did not think Jesus taught any of this. Yet the good Methodists around me either did these things or supported others who did them. Children are logical, if nothing else. They pay attention to teachers. They notice when grown-ups break their own rules. If there had been gold stars for Jesus's rule of love, some of the adults I knew failed to earn them.

In 1963, just a couple years before my childhood observations about rules and teachers, John A. T. Robinson, the Bishop of Woolwich in the Church of England, published a book called *Honest to God*, one of the bestselling and most widely read religion books of the twentieth century. Among many things the bishop criticized about Christianity was the church's view that Jesus was a great spiritual teacher, a view, he said, that would result in powerless faith and always devolve into moralism (following a list of dos and don'ts). Instead, Robinson claimed that Jesus did not merely teach love; he embodied it. "Christ was utterly and completely 'the man for others,'" he wrote, "because he *was* love."[3] Jesus did not issue rules to be ticked off on a list; Jesus embodied the rule of love, a way of life to be followed, and to *be* fully, completely human.

The Golden Rule is not a "rule" as we generally think of laws. Instead, it is the "utter openness in love to the 'other' for his own sake."[4] Robinson went on to claim "nothing" is prescribed "except love."[5] Jesus did not only teach an ethics of love to follow; he embodied the love that he spoke of in his stories and sermons. Jesus, who was complete love, the man for others, taught us to go and *be* likewise. He did not teach rules. He taught that love ruled. He lived what he taught.

It would be years before I read *Honest to God*. I have always wondered if some brave young preacher proclaimed these ideas at the church. I think I would have heard them if he did—because I liked going to the grown-up church to listen to the sermons. Jesus was, indeed, a teacher, one who taught from his heart and whose words and deeds were completely coherent. Sort of like Miss Jean. He did not tell us what to do. Instead, he asked us to be love, as he had been. I had to learn more, and I knew I wanted Jesus to be my teacher always.

The Commands

In Sunday school, we learned about Jesus and the New Testament, but we also learned about the Old Testament. The only gold star I ever received for memorization was successfully learning the names and the right order of the first five books of the Bible: Genesis, Exodus, Leviticus, Numbers, and Deuteronomy. For fun, I threw in Joshua, Judges, and Ruth as well. I'm pretty sure that's what earned me the star.

The Bible presented to me in September 1967, "On the Occasion of Promotion to Elementary III," was a confusing book. We learned about Jesus, who seemed the most important character in the book, long before I actually had a copy in hand. As I turned the pages of my new Bible, it was vaguely shocking to see that Jesus did not actually show up until page 757 of its nearly 1,000 pages. Three-quarters of the Bible was not about Jesus at all. There were other stories, other teachers. There was Jesus's Great Command. And, even though I was not sure where those Methodist rules were in the Bible, it became clear in short order that there were other rules in the Bible—those rules of Moses that had been added to Jesus's rules—ten big ones found in the book of Exodus and repeated in the book of Deuteronomy: "You shall have no other gods before me; you shall make no graven images; you shall not take the Lord's name in vain; remember the Sabbath; honor your father and mother; you shall not kill; you shall not commit adultery; you shall not steal; you shall not bear false witness; you shall not covet."

Years later, I would find out that Jesus's Great Command—the New Testament's one big rule—was actually a summary of those ten commands and that Jesus himself was quoting from both Deuteronomy and Leviticus in his own version of a theological remix when he said, "Love God, and love your neighbor as yourself." But at the time, I was confused. A few months before receiving my third-grade Bible, my mother had taken me to the movies to see *The Ten Commandments*. In full Technicolor glory at the local theater, Sunday school unfolded before my eyes. The flannel board had nothing on this—pyramids and Pharaoh's army, the miracle of the Red Sea, Moses on the mountain, the Golden Calf. But one thing bothered me. I may have gotten a gold star for memorizing the books of the Old Testament, but for the life of me, at eight years old, I could not tell the difference between Jesus and Moses. As far as I could figure, Charlton Heston and Jesus were the same character—robes, rules, commandments, and all.

I was not the first or the last Christian to notice the similarity between Moses and Jesus. Indeed, the gospel of Matthew, written between 80 and 90 CE, makes an explicit comparison between the two. In its opening chapters, the gospel presents Jesus's birth by echoing the birth of Moses in Exodus 1–2. In both cases, an evil king is bent on destroying the intended savior of God's people by killing all the firstborn Jewish male babies and young children. In the stories of Moses and Jesus, each boy is protected by divine directive and savvy parental resistance. "From the very beginning of his life," writes New Testament scholar Marcus Borg, "Jesus was already the new Moses and Herod was the new Pharaoh . . . a new Moses leading a new exodus from a new pharaoh into a new way of life."[6]

Moses was, of course, more than the liberator of the Jews. He was also the giver of the Law, the one who handed down the Torah, the teachings from God contained in the first five books of the Hebrew scriptures, the names of which I memorized in Sunday school. In the same way that Matthew compares Moses and Jesus as liberating saviors, the gospel also makes a direct comparison between Moses and Jesus as teachers, the ones who speak on behalf of God's law and interpret it for a freed people. In the Old Testament, Moses's teaching is shared in five books; in the gospel of Matthew, Jesus's teaching is structured into five discourses, five short "books" on different themes. The fivefold form clearly echoes that of the law of Moses, a point that Matthew intends to make.

The most substantial teaching section is found in Matthew 5–7, chapters commonly known as the Sermon on the Mount.

This section opens with Jesus going "up the mountain," a deliberate choice that ancient Jewish Christians would have recognized as aligning Moses and Jesus. The Sermon on the Mount opens with blessings—on the poor, those who mourn, the meek, and those who hunger—in the same way that Moses pronounces blessings on the people of Israel as they prepare to enter the land of milk and honey in Deuteronomy 28; the blessings are a result of following the commandments. The blessings of Moses and those of Jesus are an interesting contrast, Moses's clearly aimed at an Israel whose people would prosper in their own land, and Jesus's directed at an Israel whose people were oppressed by Rome in an occupied land.

Yet Jesus's first hearers would have understood what he was doing. Jesus was restating the written Torah, the passed-down law of Moses, in the words of his own "oral Torah," a practice common in Judaism. In Matthew, Jesus places himself in the line of authoritative voices in the Hebrew tradition. Although this was done throughout the history of Israel by teachers, scribes, and prophets, including the most revered leaders, when Jesus claimed to join the ranks of these teachers, it was a pretty gutsy thing to do.

Thus, the Sermon on the Mount opens with a specific comparison between Moses on the mountain and Jesus on the mountain, with each proclaiming blessings as a result of following the way of God. Jesus goes on to say that he loves the law and considers that his teaching fulfills it, carefully explicating specific directives in the law of Moses on murder, adultery, false witness, and other issues of Jewish law like divorce, vengeance, love of neighbor, prayer, fasting, and dealing with money. Near the end of the sermon, Jesus states the Golden Rule, the foundation of all the commandments: "In everything do to others as you would have them do to you; for this is the law and prophets" (7:12). Upon the conclusion of the sermon, Matthew relates: "Now when Jesus had finished saying these things, the crowds were astounded at his teaching, for he taught them as one having authority, and not as their scribes" (7:28–29). Or, as Amy-Jill Levine puts it, "He spoke without citing his teachers and without always offering scriptural precedent or justification."[7] The crowds got it—Jesus the rabbi was at work renewing and reinterpreting the law and, in the process, claiming the divine authority to do so: a teacher *and* a prophet.

The identification of Moses and Jesus is a common confusion of Sunday school children, a deliberate theological choice on Matthew's part, and created a deadly problem in Christian history. Too many Christians argue that Jesus as teacher was also the Son of God, which, from their perspective, means that Jesus *replaced* Moses. Somehow, Jesus's law was superior, and perhaps even contrary, to the law of Moses, and these two great figures, however much one might have thought them the same after watching *The Ten Commandments*, offered competing visions of truth. This twisted understanding birthed Christian anti-Semitism, with its thousands of persecutions, pogroms, and crusades against the Jews.

Jesus, however, as eloquently maintained by Levine, was a teacher within a tradition and in a community in which one "argues with the text and with fellow Jews about the text, and . . . in some cases multiple meanings are possible."[8] As a teacher, Jesus is not contradicting Moses or demeaning other Jewish teachers. He is offering his interpretation of the law, teachings that surprised his followers with their originality and insight. To understand Jesus as a teacher in this sense— even if one does consider him divine—is to remember that teachers, even those with great authority, teach within a long line of communal interpretation, something that Jesus himself would have known. Jesus does not replace. Jesus reimagines and expands, inviting an alternative and often innovative reading of Jewish tradition.

Jesus's teaching, like the teaching of Moses, includes commands, a big list of dos and don'ts. Although I have sometimes heard Christians say that Christianity is not about rules and commands, the Sermon on the Mount has quite a few, things like: be reconciled to your brother or sister; do not look at a woman with lust; do not get divorced; do not swear at all; let your yes be yes and your no be no; if someone wants your coat, give him your cloak as well; give to everyone who begs from you; pray in secret; do not store up treasures on earth; you cannot serve God and wealth; do not worry about tomorrow; do not judge; and ask and it will be given to you.

As a rabbi, Jesus was remarkable, challenging, and inventive. His teachings remain compelling, influencing people throughout the ages and well beyond Christianity; and those teachings stand on their own as beautiful without needing to diminish others. "I saw that the Sermon on the Mount was the whole of Christianity for those who wanted to live a Christian life," recalled Mahatma Gandhi. "It is that Sermon which has endeared Jesus to me."[9] Perhaps, even as Gandhi himself bemoaned, if Christians really followed the one they claimed as Teacher, the world would be a more just and loving place.

The Stories

The New Testament recounts many stories about Jesus, but it also contains many stories *by* Jesus. Christian Sunday school lessons are replete with them, these memorable stories about all sorts of seemingly mundane things—seeds, baking bread, lost coins, bad bosses, equal pay, lighting lamps, weddings, and parties. The stories are often like this one:

> With what can we compare the kingdom of God . . . ?
> It is like a mustard seed, which, when sown upon the
> ground, is the smallest of all the seeds on earth; yet when
> it is sown it grows up and becomes the greatest of all
> shrubs, and puts forth large branches, so that the birds of
> the air can make nests in its shade. (Mark 4:30–32)

Although I cannot remember when I first heard this story, I do remember the teacher passing out tiny seeds to us. I looked at them in my palm, marveling that these small things would become large plants, so that birds would make nests in their branches. As I listened to the story, I felt surprised, sensing something just beyond my ability to name or explain. Later, I would learn the words that captured how I felt: mystery, wonder, and awe.

Jesus's stories are called parables. They are not rules, commands, or doctrine. Instead, they are open-ended tales that invite us to struggle with their meaning, to wonder, to see the world from unexpected angles. Amy-Jill Levine says they are "mysterious," in that parables "challenge us to look into the hidden aspects of our own values, our own lives. They bring to the surface unasked questions, and they reveal the answers we have always known, but refuse to acknowledge."[10] Parables are fiction, as Levine says, "short stories by Jesus," or, as New Testament scholar John Dominic Crossan puts it, "*fictional* events about *fictional* characters."[11]

As stories go, I particularly love mysteries. When I was a girl, my favorite books were the Nancy Drew mysteries. Containing puzzles, riddles, and challenges, they were stories that beckoned me to look beneath the surface and discover the truth of the thing. Youthful mysteries are full of morals and meanings, opening up ways of thinking about the world and encouraging critical exploration that sharpen both the mind and the heart.

No wonder I loved the biblical parables; they are mini mysteries. Jesus teaches through detection. In the Nancy Drew books, everyday things like old clocks, secret doors, and lost wills prompted the imagination to see beyond the shape of things; parables do the same. Yet unlike those Nancy Drew books, whose hidden facts always add up to a familiar solution to the mystery—the good person did not commit the crime; the rightful heir to a fortune could be found—Jesus's detective tales layer surprises and twists leading to a myriad of different potential endings.

In Nancy Drew, the old clock's secret will always reward the kind relatives; in the New Testament, the tale of the persistent widow or the Good Samaritan has no similar ending. Nancy Drew always has a clear resolution; at the end, we know that truth has won, that justice has been done, and we breathe easy. Jesus's detective fiction gives us no neat solutions; instead, it asks us to dive more deeply into the questions, to wrestle with the parable again and again. The kingdom of God is like that—a different kind of mystery, one that invites listeners to be part of the story.

Many Christians are under the misimpression that the parables are like Nancy Drew mysteries—that they bear one meaning, that there is a single solution to these gospel puzzles. During a recent fall, I preached for six weeks on the parables from the gospel of Luke and posted bits of those sermons on Twitter. Those tweets came to be the bane of my existence, especially when I tweeted about Jesus's story of a Pharisee and a tax collector. The standard interpretation (and the one too many church people seem to think is the only legitimate one) is that Jesus criticizes the Pharisee as a hypocrite and praises the tax collector as a true saint. For years I thought the same. But when I looked at the story anew, it struck me that both Pharisee and tax collector are accepted and loved, one as a faithful believer, the other as a repentant sinner. The tale of the Pharisee and tax collector was not an "either-or" choice, but a "both-and" mystery.

I learned something from that sermon, an exciting possibility that challenged my understanding of piety and grace, of how God loves and whom God accepts. When I shared it on social media, however, my Twitter feed blew up. Three or four days of attacks ensued (mostly from clergy!) about how wrong I was, how the parable was as clear as a bell, how I had violated the whole of Christian tradition. "You can't say that!" "Don't you read the Bible?" "Block the heretic" (which is, I suppose, a bit gentler than the medieval alternative of burning heretics). And those were the nice tweets.

"Parable" comes from two Greek terms, *para*, meaning "to come alongside," and *ballein*, meaning "to throw," and is itself a paradoxical word. A parable is intended to be a story that comes alongside our regular understanding and, frankly, upsets it. It uses ordinary things to draw us to extraordinary ones and crafts understanding using the seen to explain the unseen. In effect, the parables are Jesus coming alongside us and ripping off our cozy theological comforters. Parables should leave us gasping, out in the doctrinal cold, and shaking with anger, awe, or surprise. Nothing is as we thought. The whole point of a parable is to disturb and perplex us, shaking up what we believe to be true, all without providing an easy answer or simple moral to fall back upon.

The parables are neither Nancy Drew nor Aesop's fables. Ultimately, they are more like the koans of Eastern religions, for example:

Once a monk made a request of Joshu.
"I have just entered the monastery," he said. "Please give me
  instructions, Master."
Joshu said, "Have you had your breakfast?"
"Yes, I have," replied the monk.
"Then," said Joshu, "wash your bowls."
The monk had an insight.[12]

Jesus's stories are more like that, but in the context of the
Hebrew Bible and Jewish practice. "Wash your bowls" sounds
remarkably like, "The kingdom of heaven is like yeast that a
woman took and mixed in with three measures of flour until
all of it was leavened" (Matt. 13:33), engendering a response
like "WTF" or an almost unfathomable "Aha."

If you grew up in Sunday school, you might think you
understand the parables. There is a reason for that. Teachers
and preachers not only taught the parables, but they also
gave students and congregants an approved interpretation,
a way of understanding the story, one often passed down
through generations, that we have come to accept as the
only interpretation. Thus, if you are a Christian, the familiar
parables you think you know are subjected to conventional
interpretations, almost like a Rosetta Stone of secret knowledge: the persistent widow is always about faithfulness in
prayer; parables about Pharisees are always about hypocrites;
when the rich are condemned, it is always a metaphor.

Imposing interpretations on the parables is an ancient
practice. Indeed, Luke employed it when he reported the

original Jesus stories in his gospel. For almost every parable, Luke prefaces the story with what he wants you to think about it, he recounts the story told by Jesus, and then he finishes by restating what he (that is, Luke) thinks the story means. Throughout the gospel of Luke, the same pattern occurs: Luke, Jesus, Luke. In other words, the parables were so upsetting and so uncontrollable that even the disciples worked to neaten them up so early audiences would understand. To experience the parable as it was first told, however, one needs to lift the frame from the story and set Jesus's words free to do their wilding work of imagination, without the gospel writer's editorial intrusion.

Children seem to like parables, because when we are little, we have no fixed ideas to defend. When I preached about the Pharisee and the tax collector, I asked the congregation: "Who does God love in this story?"

A little boy shouted back, "Both of them!"

"Well, you just preached my entire sermon," I responded.

Children appreciate a great mustard tree and do not question a God who loves both Pharisee and tax collector. But grown-ups? Not so much. We have to explain that the mustard tree really is not the biggest tree in the world and that it is fine to exclude those we deem hypocrites. The mystery, after all, has to be solved, the puzzle unpacked, all tension resolved. We have to arrive at the right answer. The possibility of multiple meanings is hard to imagine, especially for those schooled in the notion that texts can only be interpreted in one way, usually by employing some test of source criticism or demanding submission to a particular authoritative tradition. Because pastor says.

But being one who "comes alongside" and "throws down" is a perfect description of both a great mystery writer and a great guru. Jesus, the teller of parables, is both. And that makes Jesus the teacher pretty hard to take.

The Bible

At the end of elementary school, my parents insisted that both my brother and I be confirmed. In churches that practice infant baptism (like the Methodists), Confirmation is the ritual whereby young people "take on" the vows that their parents made for them at baptism. Most churches invite children around twelve to participate, to explore what it means to be a Christian and a church member and adopt the responsibilities of such for oneself. I was in eighth grade, and my brother in sixth. Confirmation class lasted many weeks, a semester, if I rightly recall.

Two particular moments stand out for me. The first was learning that we were called Methodists as an insult. John Wesley, the founder of our church, prayed and studied the Bible methodically, and his opponents took to calling him and his followers "those Methodists" with a sort of sneer. I laughed at that. I rued it as well, knowing that I had never been able to follow any sort of method or program (much less one of prayer). Thus I feared I might have been born into the wrong church.

The second thing I remember was the minister teaching us about the Bible. My parents were, if it is to be told truthfully, vaguely secular Methodists in the early 1970s. They went to church and fulfilled certain religious duties, including making sure their children went to church, but that seemed the extent of it. Conversations about faith, prayer, or the Bible were rare. My parents, however, developed a particularly unique approach to the Bible—they hid it. Yes, the family Bible lived in a cabinet under a bookshelf behind a recliner in the living room. You had to make a real effort to get to it, pull it out, and read it. There were a few smaller Bibles around the house, but somehow they wound up in that bottom cabinet as well. Apparently we had a Bible hider in our family, who took great pains to disappear the Word of God.

As a result, I would search out the Bible and sneak away to read it. There is nothing like a forbidden book to entice a child. Once, when I was in sixth grade, sitting in the warm Maryland woods reading the book of Acts about the coming of the Holy Spirit, a bird pooped on my head. No fire, just feces. I suppose that might have persuaded another person to become an atheist, but it only made me more persistent in my secret sacred reading sessions—and it made me wear a hat when doing so.

I loved reading the Bible, and I knew it was important. But I did not understand what it was or where it came from. In Confirmation class, our pastor said, "God gave us the Bible."

I asked, "But how? How does God give the Bible?"

He replied, "From his hand in heaven."

This was less than satisfactory. I felt puzzled. Did God write the Bible? Was that even possible? I wanted to pursue these issues.

I noticed that my brother was scribbling something down. I thought he was taking notes. A few minutes later, he nudged me and passed me a piece of paper. It was a drawing. At the top there was a cloud with a big disembodied hand coming out of it. A book—HOLY BIBLE—was falling from the sky toward a boy who was ducking to avoid being pelted by the heavenly volume. We both giggled.

The pastor frowned. "What's wrong?" he quizzed us.

We stuffed the artwork in my brother's class folder. I felt as if we had done something wrong, something oddly sacrilegious. God wrote the Bible, the Hand dropped it. No questions allowed. This was the Word of God.

Most of the pastors in my childhood churches were not fundamentalist Christians of any sort. From the pulpit, they preached some form of biblical criticism, incorporating historical and cultural contexts of scripture into practical messages of either piety or doing good. My parents took pride in being part of a church with an educated clergy—in the mid-twentieth century there were still plenty of churches without seminary-trained ministers—and the intellectual sermons they offered, even when they disagreed with the pastor's conclusions (especially regarding politics). In those years, most of the Methodist clergy in our area went to either Wesley Seminary, in Washington, DC, or Yale Divinity School, both of which taught ministers in traditions of Protestant liberalism or the newer theologies of Karl Barth or Reinhold Niebuhr. A few of our pastors even raised provocative questions; in fact, one caused quite a stir in 1966 when he held up *TIME* magazine emblazoned with "Is God Dead?" on its cover.

But all those things were for the grown-ups. In Sunday school and Confirmation classes, our teachers still taught us God dropped a handwritten, leather-bound, red-letter version of the book from the sky. Looking back, I think that at least some of them were uncomfortable with this. Even Sunday school teachers skirted around questions about a seven-day creation story, a literal Adam and Eve, a flood that engulfed the world, a boat holding a single pair of every animal in the world, and a Jesus who walked across a lake. When some brave student attempted to raise a question, teachers would retreat to safer territory like reviewing the Ten Commandments, having us memorize the kings of Israel, or pointing out Paul's journeys on the Bible land maps in the classroom. I once asked my own mother how, if Moses wrote the first five books of the Bible, he could write that he died at the end of Deuteronomy. Wouldn't he have been dead? She quickly handed out pictures of Moses and the burning bush for us to color. I wondered if the grown-ups even knew how to answer the questions, if they were even listening to sermons burnished in the traditions of Protestant historical criticism.

And therein was the problem. It was pretty clear that we were not fundamentalists, who took the Bible literally, but we did not really know who we were (other than something called "Methodists") or how to engage questions about the Bible. Because of this lack of clarity, all the churches of my childhood reflected a more general cultural understanding of the Bible as a book literally written by God and delivered from heaven to a surprised people below. Americans are de facto biblical literalists, whether they are Christians or atheists or some other religion.

American folk religion—Protestant fundamentalism—calls itself "Bible believing" and takes every iota of scripture as literal, factual, scientific truth, from a snake with legs who tempts Eve to sin in a garden four thousand years ago to the four horseback riders who will gallop down from the heavens to destroy humankind at some point in the apocalyptic future. But you do not have to be a fundamentalist to place the Bible on a golden pillow on a special stand in church, allow it to be read in worship only by specially trained people, designate ordained ministers to preach from it, or have a robed clergyperson hold it high above a bowing congregation intoning "the word of the Lord" as it processes down the aisle. Most American Christians are bibliolaters of a sort.

Understanding the Bible is key to understanding Jesus. The writings of the Hebrew Bible formed him as teacher, and the writings of the New Testament contain his teachings and the earliest Christian interpretations of those teachings. When the Bible is worshipped and taken literally, however, problems arise—many people do not know what to do with the Bible, whether they are inclined to accept it or dispute it.

Part of the misconstrual of Jesus and the Bible comes from the Bible itself, from an often-quoted verse from of the gospel of John: "In the beginning was the Word, and the Word was with God, and the Word was God" (1:1). Like millions of Christians before me, when I first heard that text—most likely during a childhood Christmas—I thought it referred to the Bible. After all, we were taught that the Bible was the word of God.

And there it was: John's magisterial and mystical opening— the Word was God. Somehow, God and the Bible were indeed one. Maybe, I mused, that is why my parents hid the Bible. It was so special, so holy, and so sacred that it should not sit on a shelf or coffee table with any other book. It needed to be hidden, like the face of God, behind a veil, gazed upon by only those ordained to do so. The Bible was with God, and the Bible was God. It is almost as if the Bible itself were a fourth member of the Trinity, which is peculiar in every way possible.

That is completely wrong. Much of what we think about the Bible is the result of a horrible theological mix-up based on the English translation, "Word." The Greek term that John used was *logos*. *Logos* means "ground" or "speech" or "expectation," among other things. It does not mean "word" as a part of speech made up of alphabetic letters, like the words I am writing on this page or the words in a book. The Greek term for that sort of "word" was *lexis*, not *logos*. John said, "In the beginning was the *logos*, and the *logos* was with God, and the *logos* was God." Not *lexis*, but *logos*—the very ground of divine being, the breath of God, the presence of the holy in and through all things.

John equated Jesus with the *logos*. If John had meant for us to conflate Jesus and God and the Bible, John should have made himself much clearer and simply called Jesus the *biblion*, the "book" or "scroll," of God: "In the beginning was the *biblion*, and the *biblion* was with God, and the *biblion* was God." But *logos* is neither *lexis* (a word on the page) nor *biblion* (a book made up of words). Rather, John's statement is a radical, mystical philosophical claim: the God who breathed the whole of the cosmos into existence has been embodied in the human Jesus.

So that begs that question: What is the Bible anyway? Scholars have been arguing about the nature of the Bible for centuries, using terms like "inerrant," "infallible," "authoritative," and "God-breathed" to describe it. Some say that these terms apply to "everything" in its pages, while others insist that these adjectives pertain only in matters of "faith and salvation" found therein (leaving science and history to scientists and historians). Still others argue it is a collection of wisdom and historical texts from ancient Israel and early Christian communities imbued with meaning through centuries of liturgical and ethical engagement. Others still insist that it is a book of books, a variety of genres to be read and understood in a myriad of literary ways, offering a wide range of spiritual insights over time and space. It has a narrative arc, or maybe it has many. It is full of contradictions; some maintain every inconsistency can be reconciled.

Over the years I have wrestled with scripture, argued and learned from different colleagues, preachers, and scholars, and settled into an understanding of the Bible as a collection of inspired and extraordinary texts that rehearse the spiritual experiences of two ancient faith communities—Jews and Christians—and all the tensions, conflicts, and struggles within and between them. My friend Bible scholar Peter Enns describes this much more simply: "The Bible is ancient, ambiguous, and diverse." Like him, I have come to experience the Bible as "an invitation to join an ancient, well-traveled, and sacred quest to know God, the world we live in, and our place in it."[13] I wish someone had told me that in Confirmation class. I am certain I would have understood that at thirteen.

A month or two after the theological shame of laughing at God dropping the Bible on my brother's head, I stood in front of the congregation as the pastor posed a Confirmation question: "Do you receive and profess the Christian faith as contained in the scriptures of the Old and New Testaments?"

It was not framed as an invitation. It sounded a bit like a threat, but it was intended as a vow. At least the authorities did not ask if the Bible was the Word of God. They wanted an answer, however, not an RSVP.

"I do," was my solemn response.

I had no idea what he meant or where such a promise would take me. What I wanted to say was that I would keep showing up. And keep learning from the Word.

The Sage

Confirmation was important to me. Unlike some of my peers who went through the rite and then left church, I became more interested in spiritual things. About a year after being confirmed, I had an argument with a friend at school. My friend, a conservative evangelical, found my Methodist theological education wanting.

"Who is Jesus?" he asked me.

"Well," I replied, "Jesus was a great teacher. The Golden Rule. You know."

The next day, he brought me a book, *Evidence That Demands a Verdict*, by Josh McDowell. First published in 1972, it was a work of popular apologetics, intended to make the case to an increasingly skeptical world that Jesus was God. The evangelical magazine *Christianity Today* would eventually place it at number 13 on its list of "most influential" Christian books of the twentieth century.

"Read this," he instructed. He pointed to a section with a long quote from C. S. Lewis, a British author I had not heard of until then:

I am trying here to prevent anyone saying the really foolish thing that people often say about Him: "I'm ready to accept Jesus as a great moral teacher, but I don't accept His claim to be God." That is the one thing we must not say. A man who was merely a man and said the sort of things Jesus said would not be a great moral teacher.

He would either be a lunatic—on the level with the man who says he is a poached egg—or else he would be the Devil of Hell. You must make your choice. Either this man was, and is, the Son of God, or else a madman or something worse. You can shut Him up for a fool, you can spit at Him and kill Him as a demon, or you can fall at His feet and call Him Lord and God. But let us not come with any patronizing nonsense about His being a great human teacher. He has not left that open to us. He did not intend to.[14]

Why was it so wrong, I wondered, to think of Jesus as a "great moral teacher"? The Golden Rule, the commands about love, the parables, the New Testament itself? So much teaching, so many challenging ideas. I did not understand.

I had, of course, stumbled into an argument that I did not know existed. Although I had an inkling of some sort of rift in Protestant Christianity, I was unaware that "Jesus as teacher" triggered strong theological reactions, one of the ideas that had for nearly a century driven a wedge between conservative and liberal Protestants. My Methodist upbringing emphasized Jesus as the model teacher—and this was intellectually and morally important. Jesus as teacher did not stop us from singing hymns about his being born in a manger or celebrating the Resurrection on Easter. It did not seem to contradict other things the church taught about Jesus or recited in creeds. Rather, the teacher Jesus somehow existed alongside the Son of God Jesus without much of a second thought. To diminish "teacher" in favor of, say, "Lord," made little sense to me.

But my friend was mad—mad—that I thought of Jesus as teacher. He wanted to correct my bad theology, make sure I knew the right doctrine about Jesus. Jesus was Lord, and that was it. "Teacher" was weak, incomplete, and dangerous. He pressed on me Lewis's logic of Lord, liar, or "lunatic" (Lewis's word). Those were the choices. Moral teacher was not on the list. Jesus as teacher was what liberals thought, what heretics believed. He continued, "You don't want to be one of those, do you?"

When you are fifteen and someone you desperately want to impress asks such a question, there is only one way to answer. No, I did not want to be a liberal or a heretic. I wanted to be part of his group, to go to his church, where another boy I had a crush on went, to sit in the circle and hold hands while singing, "They will know we are Christians by our love." It must be bad, I thought, to be Christian and a liberal or a heretic. This C. S. Lewis fellow thought it was bad, as Josh McDowell so logically explained. If I had three choices—Lord, liar, or lunatic—and Jesus the great moral teacher has been crossed off the list, it was not hard to choose. I said goodbye to the Jesus I had known. Holding hands with the cute boy in Bible study beckoned.

Although I had grown from child to teenager with Jesus the teacher, I had limited notions of what a teacher was. As far as I knew, a teacher was a rule keeper, a tool giver, and a content provider, maybe a sort of third parent or good storyteller. Perhaps my friend was right. Jesus was much more than a teacher, and it diminished him to call him such. Over the years, however, I have come to understand that the problem was more in my definition of "teacher" than with Jesus.

Like many others, I mostly thought of teachers as guardians of a set of middle-class values and civic virtue, as those who instilled conventional ideas about citizenship and history. This is not a particularly bad designation, but it inhibits creativity and questioning, often reducing education to a set of fairly benign principles about conformity and acceptability. That was a real problem when I was growing up in the 1960s— when what happened in the schoolroom echoed morals in books from decades earlier instead of the chants for peace and justice in America's streets. As one friend of mine quipped, "The problem with 'Jesus as teacher' is not that it's wrong, but that it's shallow."[15] At least it was for a couple generations of Americans who found themselves in classrooms in the mid- to late-twentieth century.

As I made my way through high school, college, seminary, and graduate school and finally into classrooms where I stood in front of the students, I learned that teachers were far more than dispensers of information or guardians of civic orthodoxy. The best ones did not teach to anybody's test. Instead, they taught from the heart by raising questions and presenting material in surprising ways. Great teachers opened their homes and tables and modeled a generosity of knowledge and spirit that transformed the lives of their students. Indeed, the best teachers I have ever known—as well as the teacher I aspired to be—nurtured a way of being in the world, a way that treasured questions and logic, research and study, critical thinking, and a love of words. I heard it said of one such master teacher, a professor whose dinners with students were legendary, at his memorial service: "He gave us instructions and he set us free."[16] That is what it means to teach: to instruct and liberate.

In *Jesus: A New Vision*, Marcus Borg wrote:

> Jesus was a sage, a teacher of wisdom. Regularly addressed as "teacher" during his lifetime by followers, opponents, and interested inquirers alike, he has been hailed by subsequent generations of Christians as more than a teacher, as indeed he was. Nevertheless, he was not less than a teacher.

Then, to the point, Borg added an important question: "But what was he a teacher of?"

Borg was not asking about Jesus's subject matter. As a teacher himself, Professor Borg was aware that great teachers go well beyond ideas and morals:

> Jesus was not primarily a teacher of either correct beliefs or right morals. Rather, he was a teacher of a way or path, specifically a way of transformation.[17]

The definition of a sage is a "profoundly wise" person, "one distinguished for wisdom." A sage is a certain kind of teacher, one who upsets convention by offering a different way of understanding and living, a way that embodies wisdom. Sages teach justice, with compassion. Sages set people free.

Jesus was that sort of teacher. He taught radical interpretations of the Hebrew scriptures and Jewish practice that inspired people to actually leave their homes and follow him. He invited them into a way of life based on a vision of a wildly gifting God, who created everything, who turns authority upside down, who shatters the pretenses of power, who proclaims a kingdom of the heart, and who brings the poor, the outcast, the forgotten, and the mourning to a table set with an endless feast. And he taught this by holding forth the rule of love, extending the purview of divine commands, and speaking in proverbs, poetry, paradox, and parables to confound the learned and compel the curious. With all due respect to C. S. Lewis and Josh McDowell, it was, to use their term, "mad." There is nothing really logical about it. Instead, this teacher called followers into a way that promised loss and self-sacrifice and the possibility of the cross in his revolution of love. He was a teacher, yes. And a sage. Jesus, the wisdom teacher.[18] And people followed. He had lots of students.

❦

Teachers are often our first heroes. They give us the tools to read and write and do math; they introduce us to the basics of history and science. They stand up for us when we are bullied, encourage us when we feel the sting of failure, and open our imaginations to a bigger and better world. Without good teachers, those grown-up guides on a path toward work and adulthood, most of us would not be the people we have become.

My grandmother wanted to be a teacher, but she never made it beyond eighth grade. My mother wanted to be a teacher, but she did not know how to apply to college. By the sheer good luck of being born when I was and armed with the insistence and persistence of the older women in my life, I became a teacher, a college professor. I taught for several years in the formal academy, and for the last fifteen years I have been in alternative settings, as an itinerant teacher.

Wherever I found myself, no matter the classroom, I remember the privilege of bearing the title of teacher. It bewilders me that teachers are so undervalued, even ridiculed in our society. At every level, they are overworked, underpaid, and taken for granted. Although teaching is a great responsibility and (I think) a deeply spiritual calling, it is also hard, often gut-wrenching, work to accompany students on a journey of learning, especially when your profession is made a scapegoat for all of society's ills by angry parents or greedy politicians. We have forgotten the honor of the title "teacher."

When I get down about the fact that teachers fail to get the respect they deserve, I remember a story reminding me that being called "teacher" is a holy thing. In July 2016, I was worshipping at Foundry United Methodist Church in

Washington, DC. When the senior pastor, Rev. Ginger Gaines-Cirelli, called the little ones forward for the children's sermon, about a dozen preschoolers gathered on the chancel steps.

The pastor asked, "Where is the candle? Do you see the candle?"

The children looked around. One sharp-eyed boy said, "There it is."

"Would you get it?" the pastor asked. The boy retrieved the candle and handed it to her.

"Where is the white bowl?" she then asked. It was located and retrieved.

"Where are the silver and gold beads?" Same thing again.

"Where is something that reminds you of Christmas?" Also gotten.

Finally she asked, "Where is God?"

The children looked about—up, down, all around. There were a few bewildered looks, some shrugged shoulders. Then a small boy in a plaid shirt, about three years old, said, "I know!"

The pastor said, "You do?"

The little boy looked excited, insisting, "Yes! Yes!"

"Where?" asked the pastor.

And the little boy replied, "I'll go get God!"

He jumped up from the chancel stairs and ran down the center aisle. His father, obviously worried about the open doors at the back of the sanctuary, leaped out of his pew to fetch his son.

Before he got very far, however, the little boy had returned. He was holding the hand of a kind-looking woman in her sixties or seventies, literally pulling her down the aisle. "Here!" he cried, "Here's God! She's here!"

The pastor looked puzzled. "Miss Jean?"

The boy pointed at her. "There she is! God! God!"[19]

She was his Sunday school teacher.

At the time, there was not a dry eye in the congregation. Since then, I have wondered if this was how people responded to Jesus—pointing at their beloved teacher, the one who instructed them in a way of love, and crying out, "Here! Here's God! God!"

We so often forget how beautiful that is, until the mystery of it overtakes us again. Jesus the Teacher.

I would miss him in the coming years.

Savior

Do not be afraid . . . : to you is born this day in the city
of David a Savior, who is the Messiah, the Lord.

—*Luke 2:10–11*

Every night, my mother sat on the edge of my bed, held my hand, and said, "Let us pray." Together we recited:

Now I lay me down to sleep,
I pray thee, Lord, my soul to keep;
If I should die before I wake,
I pray thee, Lord, my soul to take.

Evening after evening, with the dusk falling about us, it was the one prayer she taught me. It was not a prayer about blessing food or welcoming the day. No, in my family, the maternal theology lesson was about death. The words, intoned for generations, were handed down through the Puritans' *New England Primer* to myriads of American children, even those raised by typically sunny Methodist mothers: a prayer of protection against death in the night and, if death should come, a prayer to go safely into the arms of Jesus.

In many ways, the outlook of the prayer was deeply countercultural. My mother's other bible was Dr. Spock's *Baby and Child Care*, that revolutionary manual of parental love, permissive child-rearing, and common sense, a book far more in tune with postwar optimism and advances in health care and longevity. It was hard to reconcile the nightly prayer with the Flintstones, in their weekly antics to leave the Stone Age behind, or the Jetsons, with their flying cars and robot maid, much less the advice of Dr. Spock.

I was born in the age of metallic Christmas trees, neon nightscapes, and Sputnik chandeliers. My parents were relentlessly modern, as they married young and were in their early twenties when I was born. They strove to be cool, even if saddled with a suburban mortgage and a couple of kids. They were always first among their friends with the latest gadgets in kitchen and living room, inviting guests to sit on sleek furniture and pouring martinis to those oohing and aahing over the sound of the latest records playing on the stereo console. It was a bit like growing up with a working-class version of Don Draper, sans the false identity and multiple affairs. Tradition was not their thing.

"Now I lay me down to sleep" were odd words in this world, a world that was chasing fears of death away. My parents seemed part of a generation molding a plastic future where nothing would ever grow old, decay, or die.

But impermanence snuck in. The nightly news broadcast how many Americans were killed in Vietnam. One of my mother's cousins died of an overdose when I was six or seven, and people spoke of the episode in hushed tones. About the same time, a neighbor shot himself in order to avoid the draft. And then there were the assassinations of John F. Kennedy and Martin Luther King and the riots that ensued. One edged close to us, and we could smell the fires and hear gunshots. My grandfather died from lung cancer. All the neon and plastic in the world could not cover up the fact that modernity veiled morbidity and death waited nearer than anyone wanted to admit.

Thus it came to be that one night when I was twelve, a few years after the evening prayer ritual with my mother had ceased, I woke up screaming. The idea of the Lord taking my soul in sleep resulted in terrors of the night.

My mother ran to my bed. "What's the matter? What's the matter?"

"I don't want to die!" I could barely choke out the words. "I don't want to die."

"Well, I doubt that you are going to die tonight," she replied. "What scares you?"

"I don't know. Endless nothing," I said. "I'll be nothing, there will be nothing. Forever. Nothing. Emptiness."

I might have missed my calling as a philosopher.

But my mother laughed. "Don't be afraid," she assured me. "You won't know it when it happens. Now go back to sleep."

I don't think it occurred to her to pray.

At twelve, at the edge of adolescence, I was crying out for certainty. In the night, I felt the first fright of mortality, the longing for meaning. The friendly Jesus of earliest memory and the instructive teacher Jesus who helped me understand the commands seemed absent in the dark. I wanted to believe that whatever this life was that I had been given, the consciousness I experienced, was more than a brief sojourn through time. I wanted to believe that life meant something. I wanted to be remembered. I wanted to believe—anything. Not endless nothing. Anxiety surrounded me, forming nightmare clouds before sleep.

Even in bright daylight, I sometimes asked my mother, "Why are we here?"

She replied, "To help others."

I followed up. "Why are they here?"

And her answer: "To help even more people, I suppose. You ask too many questions."

So questions haunted the night and dogged the day. Whatever the case, when it came to this death and life business, this pondering of meaning and purpose, it became increasingly clear that I was on my own.

❦

A neon sign hung outside a storefront church at the edge of our neighborhood. Two words formed a glowing red cross: JESUS SAVES.

"Savior" may well be the most ubiquitous term that Christians use to describe Jesus. This is especially true in Western Christianity, and Protestant churches in particular, where the emphasis on Jesus as the One who saves us from sin and death is a primary focus of both preaching and piety. Whether one prays before a crucifix, recites vows of baptism and Confirmation, goes forward for an altar call, or falls to the floor with ecstatic utterance, "Jesus saves" is understood as the central and continued meaning of his work for both individual Christians and the life of the world.

Yet, oddly enough, "Savior" appears only twice in the gospels to describe Jesus. One is at the beginning of the gospel of Luke, and the other is in John 4:42, where neighbors of a Samaritan woman proclaim, "This is truly the Savior of the world." Other titles, like "teacher" and "rabbi," appear far more frequently. Additional theological titles, like "Christ" ("anointed one") and "Lord," are also more prevalent than "Savior." If, however, you ask random Christians who Jesus is, I am willing to bet the answer "Jesus is my Savior" would be high on the list, and perhaps the top reply.

Although the neon cross grabbed my attention, "Savior" was not a term I typically heard as a child. I suspect that my Methodist clergy friends will not be glad to hear that. Other than in the lyrics of Wesley hymns, ours was not a congregation that spoke easily of Jesus as Savior. Instead, Jesus was truly friend and teacher, who inspired us to goodness and love of neighbor.

My first recollection of hearing Jesus called "Savior" comes from a much more mundane source—*A Charlie Brown Christmas*, the classic holiday cartoon, first aired on television in 1965. I was six, my little brother four, and my sister a toddler. We gathered around the new color television, turned to CBS, and watched. Poor Charlie Brown! No one remembered the true meaning of Christmas. He was so depressed! At the climax of the show, he cried out in frustration, "Isn't there anyone who knows what Christmas is all about?" His friend Linus stepped on stage and recited verses from Luke 2: "And the angel said unto them, Fear not . . . for unto you is born this day in the city of David, a Savior which is Christ the Lord."

I looked over to the manger scene, newly purchased from Sears, that was set up in the living room. Mary, in her blue cloak, was on her knees leaning reverently toward her infant son, who was lying in a cradle of straw. Baby Jesus the Savior? My family did not talk this way, quoting scripture like that. People at my church would have shied away from expressing such religious sentiment in prime time—these words belonged in a pulpit or Sunday school classroom. I had no idea what I needed to be saved from and no clue what it meant, but it was a mysterious-sounding word, mesmerizing even. I liked it—"Savior"—and somehow I intuited what Linus was saying. This was the true meaning of Christmas. Born this day, a Savior. Born to Mary, born into each heart.

To understand at six and to understand when you are older are, of course, two different things, but learning a single word is often an invitation into a deeper faith, to go on a journey with an insight, an idea. At six, "Savior" invited me to wonder, to love Christmas. Eventually, "Savior" would prove the door into a much more encompassing faith, a way of belief that would, for a time at least, answer my questions.

Getting Saved

"Maybe we should sing?" a girl in the Bible study asked tentatively. "Something we all know?"

I expected one of the new songs I had recently learned at the church I was attending in Scottsdale, Arizona. I liked "Pass It On." The words started playing in my mind:

> It only takes a spark
> to get a fire going . . .
> That's how it is with God's love
> once you've experienced it.
> You spread his love to everyone,
> you want to pass it on.

The song comforted me. It resonated with everything I had learned in Sunday school back in Baltimore.

Other than familiar theological sentiments, however, much had changed. In 1972, when I was thirteen, my parents uprooted us and moved to Arizona, leaving behind—

and cutting ties with—family and community almost as completely as their ancestors had done a couple hundred years before when they left Europe and landed in the New World. And new world it was. Arizona is *not* Maryland. Everything was different: weather, food, landscape, people, and history—you name it. We didn't even have grass in the yard to run around or roll downhill in. We had rocks.

And that is the perfect way to describe those first years in Arizona—a rocky adjustment. At first, Mom and Dad took us to the Methodist church in the neighborhood, where my brother and I were duly confirmed. After that, they lost interest in religion and stopped attending. On Sunday, my mother took to sleeping in; my father would take the Jeep out to the desert. She was depressed; he was increasingly distant. Sometimes, I would follow my mother's lead; other times, I would join Dad.

Jesus might still be my teacher, but increasingly I skipped class. My new classmates and friends hailed from all over the United States, and a few from farther abroad; some of their parents had come from places like Jordan, Mexico, Austria, Cuba, and Argentina. And surprise! They were not all Methodists. They were Catholics, Jews, Presbyterians, Baptists, Episcopalians, and Mormons. We lived a scant mile from the Pima Indian community, and we encountered people who held ancient ideas about the land and practiced tribal rites. More intriguing than formal labels, perhaps, were other words people used to describe themselves: "charismatic," "holy," "agnostic," "Bible-believing," and "nondenominational."

I missed Jesus, and I started tagging along with my friends to their worship services. By the time I was fifteen, I was attending on an ad hoc basis a Catholic charismatic Mass, Mormon "release time" for teens to study their holy book, Presbyterian youth events (with my first boyfriend), occasional bar and bat mitzvahs, Christian rock concerts, and more revival meetings than I can even remember. Fun, yes, but a bit theologically confusing.

Eventually, I settled in with some friends who went to Scottsdale Bible Church, then a small congregation that emphasized the Bible and Jesus and took faith very seriously. They never talked of Jesus as a teacher; instead, he was their Savior. They quoted the Bible constantly, especially John 3:16, their favorite verse: "For God so loved the world that he gave his only Son, so that everyone who believes in him may not perish but may have eternal life." My friends spoke easily of sin, guilt, and freedom and confidently asserted that they would go to heaven and be with Jesus forever. Salvation meant being rescued from this world by Jesus, and they really looked forward to it, almost as if they wanted to die.

At my Methodist Confirmation, the minister had asked: "Do you confess Jesus Christ as your Savior?" I had learned that meant trusting in his grace and serving others. We had not really talked about sin and guilt or going to heaven in Confirmation class. When asked if I confessed Jesus as my Savior in the liturgy, I had happily answered, "I do." The Methodist pastor who confirmed me talked more about service in this world than being saved in the next. Death, judgment, hell, and heaven—these were minor chords in my childhood church.

At the Bible Church, the order was reversed: nearly every question wound up being a question about sin and dying, and Jesus was the only answer. My new friends rarely spoke of doing good or serving others; their only worldly concerns were to become pastors, missionaries, or teachers in order to get others saved from the fire of eternal judgment.

"I know what we should sing," one teen in the Bible study said. And then she started to hum the melody to "Jesus Loves Me." I was still learning the Bible Church hymns and songs, but this one I knew. "Jesus loves me . . ." I began and then suddenly stopped. Everyone else in the circle was singing, "Jesus saves me, this I know, for the Bible tells me so." Not "loves," but "saves." I quickly switched lyrical gears and hoped nobody had noticed my rookie mistake.

In this circle of teens, Jesus was not a tender friend or moral teacher. Instead, he was their Savior and the Savior of the world, the one who would reward them with heaven and punish all who did not believe in him. He died on the cross to cleanse them from sin, to take their place when God rightly judged them sinners. Jesus saved them from God's eternal wrath. They trusted in him. They believed him. They put their lives in his hands. And they would be with him forever in heaven, not consigned to eternal nothingness.

Their faith burned as brightly as the neon cross back on Harford Road in Baltimore: Jesus saves.

Born Again

"Have you been born again?" my friend Phil asked me several weeks later. "Confessed your sins and given your life to Jesus? Is Jesus your Savior?"

"Yes," I replied, somewhat sheepishly.

"Where? When?" he wanted to know.

I knew he would want a place and time. You had to have a "testimony" to fit in. I hesitated telling him that I had not confessed my sins—for I was not convinced that I was a sinner in the ways my new friends seemed to expect. There were heartbreaking stories about drugs and sex, about hating parents and pride, about cheating on tests and shoplifting, about lying to teachers and beating up "sissies" in the locker room. I had no idea that high school was such a soap opera and I had studiously avoided all those sins.

Sure, I had broken some rules, including getting in some bad arguments with my brother and, rather shamefully, having stolen quarters from my mother's dressing table. Maybe I was overly proud of my good grades and a bit judgmental about my friends' parties and drinking. But these things did not seem to qualify as the sorts of Big Sins the Bible Church seemed to expect. Maybe I was not bad enough to get saved. I was a good girl, obedient, generally kind, helpful, aghast when people were not nice, and always wanting to do the right things.

"Y-e-s. Yes," I replied again, thinking about his question. I might not have a litany of sins to confess, but I did trust that Jesus was my Savior. Sin was not my problem as much as feeling lost. Dislocated, separated from everyone and everything I knew and loved, cut off from my roots. Unsure what to believe, even if the ground under my feet was hard and unyielding. I did not tell Phil how my uncle, after he arrived from Baltimore to visit, used to invade my bedroom at night.

No, I did not sin. I was sinned against. Even at fifteen, however, I was smart enough to figure out that Phil would say that my lack of forgiveness was a sin.

Years later, I would come across these words from Jesus scholar Marcus Borg: "Some people do not feel much guilt . . . guilt is not the central issue in their lives. Yet they may have strong feelings of bondage, or strong feelings of alienation and estrangement."[1] For such people, the conventional rendering of Jesus as Savior, the one who takes away whatever is sinful and unclean in their lives, makes no sense. Borg insists, however, that there are other things from which one needed to be saved: victimization, meaninglessness, suffering. Jesus offers the "good news of 'coming home'" from exile in the wilderness. He continues, "For some, the need is liberation; for others, the need is homecoming; and for still others, the need is acceptance."[2] No matter our experience or our deepest needs, Jesus saves. Homecoming. Yes, I needed a home, a safe and familiar home.

We often think of being "saved" as being rescued, and when it comes to Jesus as Savior, the popular conception is one of Jesus snatching believers from the perils of hell. Jesus saves us by taking us to heaven. That is not, however, what the word "salvation" means. The word "salvation" comes from the Latin *salvus*, which originally referred to being made whole, uninjured, safe, or in good health. *Salvus* was not about being taken out of this life; it was about this life being healed. In this sense, *salvus* perfectly describes the biblical vision of God's justice and mercy, peace and well-being, comfort and equanimity. This is the dream of a saved earth—one where oppression ends, mercy reigns, violence ceases to exist, and all live safely under their own "vine and fig tree." Jesus the Savior is the one who brings this dream to reality: he is peacemaker, light of justice, and the good physician.[3] Jesus saves in all these ways and more.

But even in this strange and rocky land, Jesus had found me. Or I had found Jesus again. He was consistent and present—my friend, my teacher of love. Yet he was also becoming something more, offering safety and the possibility of wholeness. Yes, Jesus saved me. From the desert wilderness. I did not think lostness qualified as a sin at Scottsdale Bible Church, but Jesus certainly was a guide and companion here and now, the one who wept with me at night. My savior.

Had I realized this during Communion at church? While walking to school? At Bible study? Around a backyard campfire at youth group? I really did not know. But I sensed that Phil and I were not speaking quite the same language.

"At youth group in August," I replied to his question. "When we were singing 'I Wish We'd All Been Ready.'"

I *had* felt something there, a warmth, the same warmth I knew in Sunday school or when walking in the woods. Always when singing hymns. No sense telling him I had known Jesus my whole life. A day and a time were necessary to be saved. It was the sort of answer they expected, an answer guaranteeing that I fit in, that I could be part of the group. It was not really a lie, or maybe just a little white one. Had I just fibbed about being saved?

But Phil smiled. I had passed the test. "May I pray with you?" he asked.

There, sitting at his house, he prayed me through the "Sinner's Prayer," just to make sure I got the words right. Lost, found, saved. I went from a sad and lonely teen, missing home, to Jesus girl. I stopped attending all those other churches. Not only had I found Jesus, but a new family came with the deal. I had a brand-new Bible covered in a quilted cozy, an "I Found It!" bumper sticker on my car, and Christian music blaring on my record player. I sang along:

Now my life is changed, it's rearranged.
When I think of my past I feel so strange,
Wowie, zowie, well he saved my soul.
He's the rock that doesn't roll.[4]

Stability. Certainty. The surest of all foundations. I memorized John 3:16, passed out tracts, and witnessed to my parents and non-Christian friends. I read every Christian book I could, prayed more, studied the Bible, and learned stories of great missionaries and preachers. The youth pastor told me that it was "too bad" that I was a girl—because if I were a boy, I could go to seminary. He assured me that I would become a great pastor's wife. If, of course, I learned to play the piano. This was a whole new world, a new life. Born again. I was sure of that.

And I fixed the bedroom door. Yep, Jesus saved me—with a little help from Yale locks.

Sin and Death

My new church friends loved to talk about theology. In order to keep up, I had to learn a new vocabulary of faith. There were all sorts of mysterious-sounding words, most of which started with either *pre-* or *omni-*. Like "predestination" (which came in one of two forms, single or double; who knew?) and "premillennialism," the first having to do with free will, the latter with judgment. It was hard to keep them straight. And big terms about God: "omnipresence," "omnipotence," and "omniscience," meaning God was everywhere, all-powerful, and all-knowing. There were other new words too, like "inerrancy," "submission," and "dispensationalism" (about the Bible, women, and the end times). They sounded crisp and authoritative, words that demanded attention and allegiance, and they beckoned to a world of knowledge I did not know existed.

Sometimes I wondered if my Methodist Sunday school education had been totally worthless, for I had no clue what my Bible Church friends were saying. If nothing else, I was glad to be a quick study. When some of my friends joined Scottsdale Bible Church, they gave away—or destroyed—their secular rock albums. Divesting oneself of such worldly distractions and replacing the devil's music with good Christian rock were considered almost as important as being baptized.

For me, it was not albums. It was novels. Long-loved books like *Little Women*, *Jane Eyre*, *A Wrinkle in Time*, *The Witch of*

Blackbird Pond, and *Anne of Green Gables* disappeared from my shelves and were slowly replaced with cheap grocery-store editions of books by evangelical pastors like Chuck Smith, Tim LaHaye, Hal Lindsey, Bill Gothard, and Josh McDowell. Seeing that I was theologically precocious, the youth pastor recommended C. S. Lewis and John Stott for their more intellectual takes on tough questions. Clearly, being born again meant reading a lot of books, and I busily set myself to proving that I was up to the task. I read myself into a new universe of faith, one dominated by a great savior, a Jesus who hated sin and delivered the world from death.

This theological world was, if nothing else, orderly and internally logical. It was a lot like figuring out a puzzle. Somehow, all these words fit together and created a new picture of Jesus, of church. And the key piece to the whole was sin. The Bible Church loved talking about sin, worrying about sin, fighting sin, confessing sin, and forgiving sin. Of course, most Christians care about sin. Honestly, many—if not most—religions are concerned with it. But these particular Christians were consumed by it. And, despite the fact that my Methodist upbringing had taught me about sin, I quickly learned that the way the Bible Church understood sin and what I thought to be sin were not exactly the same.

Growing up, I thought sin was doing naughty things. Sinning meant breaking commandments or bending rules—not loving your neighbor, not doing what Jesus would want you to do. There were little sins and big ones. We might look askance if someone committed a big sin, but we were equally confident that somehow Jesus forgave everyone. With mended lives, trying to do better, we moved on.

But my new friends did not share these ideas. To them, all sin was the same. If you sinned, even a tiny little sin only once, you deserved hell. The consequence of sin was death. Period. No excuses. No bargaining with God, no getting off the hook. I may not have felt terribly guilty, but I was afraid of death. Even though I suspected I was more sinned against than sinner, the sermons at the Bible Church drove the point home week after week. No one was without sin, not one. God hates sin, and anyone who sinned would be banished from God's sight forever. Hell threatened.

Nearly every sermon, every Bible study, every conversation included some variation on this theme. I asked, "Even if I am only mad at my brother?" The answer came swiftly in the form of a Bible verse that likened anger to murder: "I say to you that if you are angry with a brother or sister, you will be liable to judgment" (Matt. 5:22). Maybe I *should* feel guilty, I thought. Maybe I *was* awful. Maybe I *deserved* hell. Although the church promised the Good News of salvation, I began to feel as though it really preached the bad news of being human. "All have sinned and fall short of the glory of God" (Rom. 3:23) was the refrain. I learned that verse by heart because people quoted it all the time.

I heard this referred to as "original sin," a term to describe the state of corrupted human nature. Why do human beings do bad things? Where did evil originate? These are basic questions of human experience, concerns that religion and philosophy have attempted to answer for thousands of years. Christianity responds that sin is nearly as old as the human race itself: Adam and Eve disobeyed God when tempted by Satan. That act, the first rebellion, shattered the harmony of creation and ushered in violence and death. From one sin came all sin, cosmic consequences that none can escape.

Despite the near universality of questions about sin and evil, early Christians were not overly concerned with these ideas. In the New Testament, there is only one major passage teaching that human beings are totally sinful (Rom. 5:12–21). And even the first creeds and councils (in the 300s) are far more focused on God and the nature of Jesus than they are about the human predicament.

Eventually, some prominent Christian thinkers sensed there was a connection between how we understand Jesus and how we understand ourselves. In the 200s, almost two centuries after Jesus died, theologians like Irenaeus wrote about the sacredness of the universe, creation, and human bodies. Irenaeus, a Greek who had studied in Turkey in the East, lived in Gaul (now France). As the conversation regarding human nature developed, a rift emerged between Christians in the eastern and western parts of the Roman Empire. Eastern theologians understood creation as good and maintained that the original goodness had been disordered and obscured—but not destroyed—by sin. Adam's sin revealed the human propensity to sin, and we are each guilty when we, like our first parents, choose sin.

But Western thinkers crafted a different approach, arguing that sin was literally passed from parent to child and that sin was an inescapable inherited condition of a fallen world. The Western idea was expressed most fully by Augustine (354–430), who believed that the entire human race was a *massa damnata*, a "condemned mass," mired in self-gratification, pride, and lust, as guilty for their sins as Adam had been for his because Adam's stain was imprinted on each and every human ever born. We are completely helpless to ever choose the good, and the penalty for sin is death and hell. And thus we all deserve the ultimate consequence for sin: physical death and eternal separation from God. This stark view shaped Roman Catholicism and Protestantism, spawning ideas that went on to be rehearsed by generations of Western Christians in catechisms, prayers, and primers: "In Adam's fall sinned we all."

The people at Scottsdale Bible were not terribly interested in what Augustine thought—or if there were different ideas in the ancient church. They were opposed to tradition, seeing it as a Catholic thing, and a human invention. Tradition itself was a product of sin. If some in the past may have gotten things right, it was because they read the Bible, not because they followed teachings of church councils. They believed the Bible taught that Adam and Eve sinned, and they passed sin down to the rest of us through sex. And they believed that Paul taught that. Case closed.

"All have sinned and fall short of the glory of God." After all, Paul said it, right there in the letter to the Romans. Those at the Bible Church never imagined they were heirs of a long line of interpretation of those scriptures, a line that stretched back to an ancient argument won, in Western Christianity at least, by Augustine. Years later, I would hear a seminary professor—the only female professor I had—refer to Augustine as the "long shadow" over the West.

I was a tenderhearted teenage girl, very willing to believe elders who insisted I was a sinner from birth, a miserable offender, rightly condemned to death. No one, of course, informed me that there was a big fight in early Christianity about these ideas, and that to this day Eastern Orthodox Christians think their Western kin are far too pessimistic about human nature.

No one mentioned that in Romans Paul was writing to a church where Gentile Christians and Jewish Christians had become estranged, mostly through external politics of the Roman Empire, and that the apostle was trying to reconcile the two groups. "All have sinned and fall short of the glory of God" is part of Paul's polemic making the point that both Gentile Christians and Jewish Christians hold wrongheaded views of one another and each is guilty of hypocrisy. He is mostly concerned with maintaining that the two groups are one—that they "are equals in the solidarity of failure and in the solidarity of grace."[5]

Indeed, the idea that everyone sins all the time runs contrary to other parts of scripture, including Paul's own self-description of being both righteous and blameless (Phil. 3:6). As one commentary puts it, "Paul's argument [about human sinfulness] should not be universalized but understood as a polemical diatribe against hypothetical accusers."[6] The freedom Paul described in Romans is more like the liberation of slaves, harkening back to the oppression of the Israelites in

Egypt, surely not a fate they deserved. According to Paul, God frees all humanity—Gentile and Jew—from such slavery, and together those who follow Jesus are transformed through faith.[7] The emphasis is not that we are all terrible sinners through and through. Rather, the emphasis is that human beings are equals, all capable of both messing up and living faithfully. And God provides a way through Jesus to heal what is broken and make it whole, liberating human beings from wounded lives.

In 1983, as I was sitting in a classroom at an evangelical seminary, the professor was holding forth on the doctrine of sin in American theology. Early New England theology was in the line of Augustine, as interpreted by John Calvin and Jonathan Edwards, complete with sophisticated arguments about the nature of the will but still maintaining a doctrine of utter human depravity. In the 1820s, however, Yale theologian Nathaniel William Taylor dared to question these ideas and, as my professor said with more than a hint of malice in his tone, taught that "sin is in the sinning" and human beings were not corrupt by nature.[8] Taylor upended New England theology, resulting in debates, heresy charges, and a split within the church.

Although the professor went on in detail about the controversy—known as the Taylor-Tyler debate—I got lost in a single line: "Sin is in the sinning." When he quoted Taylor, I looked up from my notes and stared at him. *Sin is in the sinning.* That's what I thought, what I always thought. There is some good in us, however wounded, however damaged, however obscured—an intuition, a whisper, a memory of some other way of being. Sin is not our nature; rather, goodness is. Sin is a choice, the wrong path. I remembered my own conversion, a kind of turning, what scripture referred to as *metanoia*, returning to the deepest part of myself, finding the path again after having lost my way, rediscovering the road I knew I was intended to travel.

I looked around the classroom. Everyone else was taking notes. No one else seemed to hear "sin is in the sinning." I looked back to the professor. "Taylor," he explained, "was not orthodox. Tyler defended the true faith, biblical Christianity." So *sin is in the sinning*—not orthodox. I looked back down, scribbling away: Taylor bad, Tyler good. That would be on the exam. I did not want to be the only heretic in the room. Seminary taught me one thing: ignore the promptings of your own heart; your experience does not matter. Theology is a matter of submission to ideas shaped by men who were smarter than you. Orthodoxy is everything. Keep your head down.

That same semester, I also took a course at a neighboring seminary, not an evangelical one, but a school associated with the long history of New England Congregationalism. Unlike my seminary, it actually had women on the faculty (my seminary had one), and I wound up taking a class on medieval history from the Rev. Dr. Eleanor McLaughlin, an Episcopal priest and noted scholar. One day, the announced title on the syllabus was "Celtic Christianity." Professor McLaughlin entered the classroom and walked past the lectern. Instead of standing in front of us, she knelt on the floor and lit a candle. As she fanned the flame, she prayed:

I will kindle my fire this morning
In presence of the holy angels of heaven . . .
Without malice, without jealousy, without envy,
Without fear, without terror of any one under the sun,
But the Holy Son of God to shield me.

God, kindle Thou in my heart within
A flame of love to my neighbor.[9]

No one at my seminary would dream of starting a lecture in such a way. After the prayer, she said: "This is the Celtic way. Everything is holy, every moment, everything, and everyone. Christ came to reveal the sacredness of all things, to make clear what was hidden, the Light of the world." She went on to say that one Celtic teacher, a monk named Pelagius from Wales, taught the "dignity of our human nature," something that can be seen in the face of a newborn child. She quoted Pelagius: "You ought to measure the good of human nature by reference to its Creator. If it is he who has made the world good, exceedingly good, how much more excellent do you suppose that he has made humanity, fashioned in his own image and likeness?"[10]

Without malice, without jealousy, without envy, without fear, without terror of any one under the sun, but the Holy Son of God to shield me. Whatever this was, it was far closer to what my heart said was true than anything I was being taught at the other place. Savior . . . or shield?

I wanted to jump up from behind my desk and join her on the floor.

I did not. But I did take another course from her—her doctoral level seminar on Augustine. We revisited Pelagius then and the angry fight between the two men. She made us read Augustine's anti-Pelagian writings, explore the alternative argument by reading through the criticism, and take into consideration the political backdrop of imperial Christianity, with its needs for consolidation and control of the Mediterranean world. Eventually, the Roman Church declared Pelagius a heretic (although it took about six tries to do so) and attempted to erase his teachings from the face of the earth.

I wrote a very conflicted paper on the whole business. I so wanted to be orthodox, but I secretly believed Augustine the villain and Pelagius the hero. In the end I toed the party line—total depravity, original sin. I said what I was expected to say, not by Professor McLaughlin, but by the evangelicals at the other seminary, just in case they got wind of my questions. And it was the only B I received in my seminary career.

I would later understand that my sin in the whole affair was not being myself, subordinating the gifts and insight I brought to studying history and theology to what others insisted I must believe (under, I must add, the threat of hell). I allowed myself to be colonized by a system that wanted to silence me and participated in the kind of obedience that slaughters the soul. I found myself in a theological cage, one, sadly, that I helped to build. My sin was *not* pride; I did *not* want to be God. My sin was the negation of my own self, in effect killing myself in favor of the person others told me I must be.[11] Sin does indeed lead to death.

Eventually, I learned that Irenaeus was right when he said, "The glory of God is the human being fully alive." Sin is the rejection of the beauty and goodness of God's image in every person. Jesus lived such fullness perfectly, and he revealed the deep wisdom of that truth; Christ the Word speaks this into the world. The Light of the World, the flame of our hearts. Jesus saves.

The Cross

Scottsdale Bible Church was devoid of image and icon. It featured clear windows high in the ceiling, plain light wood, and folding chairs. The only signal that this was a Christian worship place were the three huge crosses that stood outside the church, harkening back to Calvary, the hill where Jesus died.

Architecture always makes a point: what people care about, how they witness to their story is communicated through their buildings and art. In most Christian churches, the cross is central. Sometimes, it is a simple cross, sometimes a cross bearing the dying Jesus, and sometimes a cross with Christ the King. Crosses are everywhere, above altars and Communion tables, at doorways and exits, on baptismal fonts, atop soaring steeples. If you had no experience of Christianity whatsoever and were touring churches, surely one of the first questions you would ask would be: "What does that symbol mean?" In a solemn tone, your host would reply, perhaps with some minor variation, "Jesus died for our sins."

At Scottsdale Bible, however, the cross was central in a singular way. There were no saints or icons or Bible stories in stained glass to serve as comment on or explanation of the three crosses reaching into the desert sky. As stark as Good Friday itself, they made a theological point about the faith being proclaimed within: everything was about the cross, about salvation.

In Bible study, one of the leaders referred to what happened on the cross as "atonement," a word I had not heard before. "What does that mean?" I asked.

He replied, "Atonement means 'at-one-ment.'"

"At-one-ment?" I queried.

"Yes," he went on. "How we are reconciled with God, how we come into relationship with him, are made 'one' through the cross."

I nodded as if I understood.

For those at Scottsdale Bible, it was simple. If human beings are completely sinful and God is utterly holy, there is an infinite distance between the two. Sin makes it impossible for people to reach toward God. On the off chance that someone did reach out to the divine, God could not reach back, because God is repulsed by sin. God's holiness would not allow any impurity to come into God's presence. What is holy and what is sinful can never, ever touch.

And there is our predicament. We can never be one with God—we cannot even be in the same room, the same house, or even the same universe with God—without some sort of God-initiated "at-one-ment." In the absence of atonement, we human beings would be eternally separate from the Holy One. Sin makes atonement necessary. Impurity makes some sort of divine cleansing imperative.

If I were Jewish, I would have known the word "atonement." I would later learn that Jews have a Day of Atonement—Yom Kippur—first presented in Leviticus 16 as a yearly purification rite. In ancient practice, animal blood was offered as a sacrifice in the Temple to cleanse the sacred precinct and atone for the sins of the people. This was the holiest day of the year. After the Temple in Jerusalem was destroyed in 70 CE, around the time the New Testament itself was being written, the Day of Atonement became a time of reflection, fasting, and prayers during which the Jewish people sought God's forgiveness and assurance of mercy for the coming year.

In the New Testament, Paul took these ideas and developed an elaborate theological argument that connected the death of Jesus on the cross with the Day of Atonement from the Leviticus tradition. Since Paul was a Jew, it is helpful to remember that he is reflecting on a Jewish practice that was being rethought within Judaism itself. In Romans, immediately following "All have sinned and fall short of the glory of God," Paul writes with "grace as a gift" through Christ. How does this gift come to humankind? "As a sacrifice of atonement by his blood," Paul insists (3:23–25), directly appropriating Yom Kippur. In effect, Paul says that Jesus is the final sacrifice, the "Pascal lamb," whose blood covered all human sin once and for all and whose death ended the need for all other sacrifice.

Thus, Paul linked sin, grace, and atonement in a single, lean argument, making the cross the central—and holiest— action of salvation. When Christians meditate upon the cross, when they lift the cross up as the image of faith, they enter into this theological understanding of sacrifice and atonement, somehow seeing God as a sacrificing priest, and Jesus as the offering on the altar or the scapegoat carrying the sins of the people into the wilderness. Good Friday becomes the Christian version of the Day of Atonement, and Easter Sunday seals the deal three days later, when Jesus destroyed even death, the final and most feared consequence of sin.

None of this is easy to understand—neither the history of sacrifice, the arguments over the nature of sin, nor Paul's complex retelling of the atonement from Leviticus. Any first-year seminarian trying to translate Paul's Greek will tell you how hard it is to follow the good apostle's argument and how its implications wind through the rest of Paul's letters and the letters ascribed to him. Paul insists that this is the main thing, the central act of Christianity, this salvific sacrifice that repristinated Yom Kippur, linked it with Passover, and then replaced both with the cross. It is not an entirely surprising argument for an early Jewish convert to make.

At the Bible Church, they loved to tell this story—in Bible studies, in sermons, in hymns. This was the old, old story of a fountain filled with the blood of the Lamb, the rugged cross to which everyone must flee for mercy, the great wonder of a God who killed his own Son because he loved us. Paul was the hero who told the tale, and his words were repeated as the way to eternal life. Jesus took God's punishment for sin; Jesus died for me. Jesus bought and paid for me with his blood.

Despite the fact that my new friends revered Paul and that this rendering of the atonement was the central story of faith, no one seemed to notice that Paul explained the cross in more than one way. In addition to the sacrifice narrative, Paul also wrote of the atonement in relation to the tradition of scapegoat, as redemption, justification, reconciliation, and adoption into a new family. Paul's letters explore six different theological versions of Christ's work on the cross, and sometimes he combines them. Each of these metaphors offers a slightly different angle for understanding atonement—the scapegoat cleansed the community of sin; slaves were redeemed from bondage; justification makes our character right, in line with God's desire; through reconciliation the world is brought back into relationship with God; and by adoption God is revealed as our loving parent.[12] Paul's sacrificial view of the atonement was, perhaps, the harshest of the six and, in the history of Christianity, the one empowered by fear of death and hell, but it is far from the only rendering possible, even in the authentic writings of the great apostle himself.

Yet Protestant Christians, and even a good number of Catholics, are not aware of the multiplicity of images for atonement and are, instead, stuck in the single story of sacrifice. A strange vision of God lies under the story—that God is angry with humankind and must have that rage assuaged. One scholar insists that we secretly think God must be appeased: "Fear is the underlying psychological motivation in sacrifice; life is unsafe, the Deity is not always favorable; he must be won over."[13] It is a primal human worry that God hates us and will do us in. We must do anything to make God happy, to keep God from punishing or getting rid of us altogether. We sacrifice to change God's mind, we offer up to pay off God.

Although it seems crass to put it that way, my friends at the Bible Church would have said this is true. That is the reason God sent Jesus. No offering we could ever make would be enough. Only one offering—God's own Son—was sufficient. The atonement was a sacred quid pro quo. God forgives us in exchange for an offering of blood. Salvation's this for that. In this case, however, God gives both the quid and the quo, and we stand by watching, accepting in faith what God did on our behalf.

Strangely, no one mentioned that this vision of atonement does not appear in the gospels; the books about Jesus's life are largely silent on these ideas. Many scholars agree that the closest the gospels get to Paul's sacrificial atonement theory is

Mark 10:45, a short verse that may not even be original to the text: "For the Son of Man came not to be served but to serve, and to give his life a ransom for many." Even there, however, the larger context is more about equality and service. "If salvation came only as a consequence of his crucifixion," writes New Testament scholar Stephen Finlan, "Jesus certainly forgot to mention this to those people who came to him seeking salvation."[14]

In one of the most well-known gospel passages, a rich young man asked Jesus how to be saved:

> As he was setting out on a journey, a man ran up and knelt before him, and asked him, "Good Teacher, what must I do to inherit eternal life?" Jesus said to him, "Why do you call me good? No one is good but God alone. You know the commandments: 'You shall not murder; You shall not commit adultery; You shall not steal; You shall not bear false witness; You shall not defraud; Honor your father and mother.'" He said to him, "Teacher, I have kept all these since my youth." Jesus, looking at him, loved him and said, "You lack one thing; go, sell what you own, and give the money to the poor, and you will have treasure in heaven; then come, follow me." When he heard this, he was shocked and went away grieving, for he had many possessions. (Mark 10:17–22)

When we read this in Bible study, I was shocked. Jesus did not tell the man to believe in him, to get born again, or pray the sinner's prayer—none of the things a person seeking salvation would be told if they asked someone at Scottsdale Bible. Instead, Jesus asked if he kept the commandments. The man did. And then Jesus said, "Go sell everything you have and give the money to the poor; then come back and follow me." Jesus was concerned for the man's character, what he did. Even more, salvation did not seem to be a single act of confession; rather, it was the result of following Jesus.

The youth pastor carefully explained that although this sounded like salvation by works, it was not. He insisted that Jesus laid down an impossible demand to show that human beings would never be able to follow him without the cross. "Jesus told him he'd have to surrender the one thing he could never give up," he said. "We can never give up enough for God." We took notes or scribbled on the pages of our Bibles.

"The rich young man would come back," the pastor assured us, "when he realized that he needed to be born again." Ah! The story might have a second act! The sad man would understand that his works would never save him. He would return, repent of trying to save his own soul by works, accept Jesus in his heart, get born again, and become a true disciple. Honestly, that sounded like a bit of a stretch.

And it was not just the rich young man who asked Jesus how to be saved. All sorts of people in the gospels got saved *before* Jesus died on the cross. When Jesus healed, they experienced *salvus*, God's salvation. They followed him. Lives were changed, transformed. Disciples did give up riches and goods that they might inherit eternal life. Tax collectors abandoned their jobs and surrendered their social standing to eat with him. Children, slaves, soldiers, peasants, fishermen, farmers, prisoners, the sick, the blind, the lame—when they encountered Jesus, they found salvation, the wholeness, the healing, the oneness with God that had only been the stuff of longing. Every miracle, every act of hospitality, all the bread broken and wine served, everything that Jesus did saved people long before Rome arrested and murdered him.

It was all this loving and healing and saving that got him in trouble with authorities. He was not killed so his death would save people; he was killed because he was already saving them. He threatened a world based in fear, one held in the grip of Roman imperialism, by proving that a community could gather in love, set a table of plenty, and live in peace with a compassionate God. Jesus did at-one-ment long before being nailed to a cross. At-one-ment was the reason the authorities did away with him. No empire can stand if the people it oppresses figure out that reconciliation, love, liberation, and oneness hold more power than the sword. So Rome lynched Jesus: tortured him and hung him on a tree. That is the raw truth under all those sophisticated atonement theories.

Jesus was born a savior, and he saved during his lifetime. "Fear not!" "Peace on earth!" He did not wait around for thirty-three years and suddenly become a savior in an act of ruthless, bloody execution. Indeed, the death was senseless, stupid, shameful, evil. It meant little other than silence without the next act—resurrection—God's final word that even the most brutal of empires cannot destroy *salvus*. This is no quid pro quo. Rather, Easter proclaims that God overcomes all oppression and injustice, even the murder of an innocent one. At-one-ment means just that. Through Jesus, all will be renewed, made whole, brought back into oneness, reunited with God. Salvation is not a transaction to get to heaven after death; rather, it is an experience of love and beauty and of paradise here and now. No single metaphor, not even one of Paul's, can truly describe this. We need a prism of stories to begin to understand the cross and a lifetime to experience it.

The End Times

The best thing about the Bible Church was that I no longer feared dying. The worst thing was that I became terrified about the imminent end of the world! Getting born again meant I would go to heaven. There was something I could actually do to push aside worries of eternal emptiness. But the end of the world? There was literally nothing I could do about that except read the signs of the times and wait for God's plan to unfold. At least that is how they explained it. The Bible Church essentially replaced one anxiety with another. It was fear that opened the door to this new theological world, and it would be fear that held me there.

In the 1970s, Americans seemed preoccupied with beginnings and endings. It is true that human beings are perennially curious about such things. Where did we come from? Where are we going?

In 1968, *Chariots of the Gods* became an international mega-hit, eventually selling more than seventy million copies. It was a nearly perfect creation story for the Space Age, claiming that we humans were the offspring of ancient astronauts. At the other end of the spectrum, *Star Trek* embodied the future we dreamed about. Every day, we were told that the world could end by nuclear war. Yet *Star Trek*, in a spirit of optimism, assured us that the human race would avert disaster and, instead, embark on a peaceful exploration to find meaning and purpose in the universe. As mythology, *Chariots* explained the beginning, and *Star Trek* offered a compelling end.

That conservative evangelicals, like the folks at the Bible Church, would have been interested in beginnings and endings should be no surprise. After all, Jesus said, "I am the Alpha and the Omega, the first and the last, the beginning and the end" (Rev. 22:13). When it came to beginnings, however, they found the mythology offered by *Chariots* as wanting as Darwin's theory of evolution. During these years, biblical literalists revived an old attack on evolution under the guise of "scientific creationism," insisting that Genesis is a factual account of creation and emphasizing the young-earth theory. Creation scientists posited an intelligent and purposeful creator who intervened—and continues to intervene—in human history. In 1968, the American Supreme Court struck down all laws banning the teaching of evolution that remained on the books of some states, and conservative Christians went to legal war in order to get equal time for the teaching of their mythological views on the basis that

Genesis is not a myth at all. Rather, they insisted, Genesis is science.

Thus, "origins" in biblical creationism, an idea that had been pushed to the culture's margins since the 1920s, re-emerged slowly with the growth of evangelical Christianity and the religious right. But it would prove a long process of court cases, writing textbooks, building megachurches, homeschooling, and establishing institutes to gain cultural credibility. The conservative story of the beginning, re-birthed in the 1960s and 1970s, would require a lengthy fight to change the culture.

Not so with evangelicals' story of the ending, however. As tedious as courts and scientific arguments would be in inhib-iting the quick spread of their creation myth, evangelicals had at the ready a story about the ending that was flashier, more in line with the cultural moment, and packed with an emo-tional punch. The world was about to end, and they knew the details. No *Star Trek* optimism there. Just bleak fact: the end of history is upon us; it is God's plan.

In the 1970s, evangelicals did not sugarcoat endings. For baby boomers, having grown up hiding under school desks during nuclear-war drills, the possibility of the end of the world seemed true enough. None of us believed that our grade-school teacher's closing of lead-lined drapes would save our lives in a nuclear holocaust. But that the world would end like that seemed random and purposeless—that someone somewhere would accidently press a button and all human history would come screeching to its bloody conclusion. No heroism, nothing to live or die for, only the stupidest of endings to life. We had reached the last days without much of anything as an escape. We were so young. It was all very sad.

Enter evangelicals with their message: the end is not without purpose.[15] God intended the world to end, ever since the beginning. Jesus himself warned of the last days:

> But in those days, after that suffering,
> the sun will be darkened,
>   and the moon will not give its light,
> and the stars will be falling from heaven,
>   and the powers in the heavens will be shaken.
>   (Mark 13:24–25)

But this would not be a curse to us—because we were saved. Yes, we were sinners, but we were born again, freed from sin, and could expect life with God in heaven. However, we also needed to be saved from the ugly mess of the world, rescued from these evil days.

Christians group sin, atonement, and heaven into a triad of "problem," "solution," and "eternal results," but different traditions do not explain the connections between the three in the same way. Catholics, for instance, talk about original sin and the cross, but emphasize the sacraments and church as the mediators of the work of atonement, promising (at the very least) purgatory to those seeking to follow Jesus. Traditional Protestants emphasize sin, with baptism and faith applying the atonement, and trust that heaven will be open to most (if not all) humankind. Catholics and mainstream Protestants, for all their gloominess about sin and their willingness to motivate sinners with fear, generally believe that those who trust Jesus's work on the cross make the world better—and that their good works demonstrate God's love and shape Christian character, both of which form the soul for eternity. The best rendering of these ideas is that sorrow over sin, trust in the cross, and fear of hell ultimately make for a moral life filled with charity, beauty, and great compassion, and lead to a faithful death.

Evangelicals told a radically different story of sin, cross, and heaven. In their version, sin was so extensive that no matter how many people converted, the world would get worse and worse. The atonement only worked for individual believers who clung to the cross amid the buffeting winds of this evil existence, and the fact that human history was coming to an end. To them, the world ending in chaos was actually a good thing. Increasing evil proved that Jesus's return was close at hand. True believers would always be a minority whose calling was to save as many as they could before that return. At God's appointed time, a truly vile man would arise whom many would mistake for the savior. He would actually be the Antichrist, and under his wicked rule God would unleash seven years of tribulation—including everything from famine to nuclear war—followed by a huge battle between good and evil, called Armageddon. At its height, Jesus would return and establish his earthly reign. After one thousand years, there would be a final judgment, and this world would be replaced with a new heaven and a new earth.

Their version was so much more specific than anything I had ever heard about sin, death, and eternity. And it was frightening, cosmic in scope. This was not just a case of one sad teenager worrying over eternal nothingness. This was a story of the actual end of everything, not just me. There was, however, one remarkable hope: before the Tribulation Jesus would return in secret and snatch believers up to heaven, where we would escape the conflagration of the last days. This was what every Christian wished for—to be part of the generation that would not die, but go straight from this life to Jesus's arms when he returned to take the saints, both living and dead, to heaven. We were not just born again, not just saved from sin—we were going to be saved from physical death to be with the Lord: "Truly I tell you, this generation will not pass away until all these things have taken place. Heaven and earth will pass away, but my words will not pass away" (Mark 13:30–31).

These were the last days. We were the last generation. What a hope! To live and never die. Jesus would rescue the faithful and keep the born again safe from harm while the planet destroyed itself. "Two will be in the field; one will be taken and one will be left," Jesus warned. "Two women will be grinding meal together; one will be taken and one will be left. Keep awake therefore, for you do not know on what day your Lord is coming" (Matt. 24:40–42).

Around campfires and at Bible studies, we sang "I Wish We'd All Been Ready." The tune was plaintive, the words both a threat and a comfort, often punctuated by sobs as we lifted our voices:

> *Life was filled with guns and war*
> *And all of us got trampled on the floor.*
> *I wish we'd all been ready.*
> *The children died, the days grew cold,*
> *A piece of bread could buy a bag of gold.*
> *I wish we'd all been ready.*
>
> *There's no time to change your mind,*
> *The son has come and you've been left behind.*

No one wanted to be left behind. None of us thought we would be, for we were all saved. No one, however, wanted friends or family to be left behind. Occasionally, the song was evangelism, words directed toward the unbelieving parents of someone in our Bible study. But mostly it was a reminder. God would save us from the coming Tribulation. We would be raptured. We would escape the end of the world, watching the earth suffer from the safe distance of heaven with Jesus.

It never occurred to me that the early Christians wanted to escape too. The longing for Christ's return was not unique to 1970s America. There is an apocalyptic thread running through the New Testament, leading some scholars to argue that Jesus was primarily a prophet who truly believed that the end was near—and that the kingdom of God was imminent.[16]

The first generation of Christians fully expected that history was about to reach consummation. Jesus, Savior and Messiah, had arrived to set God's people free from Roman oppression, to defeat the empire and establish the hoped-for "age to come."

Jesus lived at a time fraught with cosmic meaning, when a political tyrant was asserting power throughout the Mediterranean world, slowly acquiring divinity to shore up geographic ambitions and replacing local religions and customs with new cosmopolitan globalist ones. Jesus was born into a Jewish world struggling with imperial colonization, where resistance groups and those willing to be complicit with the colonizers disliked each other. The Jews were an embattled people, a persecuted religious sect doing its best to survive.

"The time is fulfilled," Jesus proclaimed in his first sermon, "and the kingdom of God has come near; repent, and believe in the good news" (Mark 1:15). That must have seemed good news to those longing for divine justice against the Roman usurpers. Not every Jew believed Jesus, but enough did that he and his followers created controversies with other Jews and, eventually, with Roman authorities as well. After three years of public ministry, the Romans killed Jesus, and his followers were both disappointed and confused. They wrapped the story of Jesus's death with the proclamation of resurrection, the proof that sin and death were destroyed and the new age had begun.

But after the Resurrection, Jesus's followers waited—and waited—and waited for him to return in triumph. Months stretched into years, years into decades, decades into centuries. No kingdom, no return. Early Christian thinkers, like Paul, addressed the concern that believers were dying and still Jesus tarried. Later theologians turned Jesus's urgent words into figurative language about the last things. Nobody, of course, wanted to say that Jesus was wrong to have expected the kingdom, or that he had misread the eschatological time line. At the Bible Church, the pastors recognized there was a chronology problem in the New Testament about the last days. They reminded us that a thousand years were as a day to the Lord. Jesus was not wrong. Instead, we did not understand time. What seems a long time to us is only Jesus "tarrying" so that millions more may be born, be born again, and one day be taken to heaven.

My mother never offered up the end times and a coming kingdom when I had cried out at night, afraid of death. She had never heard of the Rapture, did not know that a generation would never die. Learning all this freed me from my childhood fears, but a new anxiety stalked me: What would the Rapture be like? When would it come? Would I really be ready? Was I awake?

I discovered I was not alone in those fears. Quietly, my new friends confessed that they were frightened by these doctrines, obsessed by the possibility that they might not truly be saved and worried that they would be left behind—alone—when Jesus returned and took their faithful parents. Churches showed a film called *A Thief in the Night* at youth events, and its opening scene of a ticking clock and a breaking news report of the Rapture kept me and my peers awake at night.

On top of everything else, we were conflicted. Everyone wanted to be raptured. But few wanted the Rapture to happen before they found true love, married, and had sex (in that order). It would be good for Jesus to come, just not quite yet. We wanted to live. At least a little. We didn't want to tell our parents, but Heaven could wait.

Although the whole business of Jesus as Savior depended upon sin and depravity, a sacrifice to get us to heaven, and the terror of an apocalypse, we still wanted to live. To love, to work, to know passion, to create and procreate, to experience joy. To grow old. Here was an entire, oddly compelling theological system to explain sin and death, yet even we, teenagers who in some way bought into it, longed for something else, a different sort of savior. None of us wanted to look in the face of a lover and say, "You are going to hell unless you accept Jesus in your heart," or declare that our newborn baby was a sinner from birth, or believe that a lynching was God's will and that blood running down a tree made for peace. Would Jesus really come like a thief in the night and snatch us from the Tribulation, only to make us heavenly voyeurs of the mayhem broken loose on earth? Would we cheer the arrival of Armageddon and the destruction of our planet?

We knew it was not true, even when we insisted it was. Whenever we joked, "Wait, Jesus, wait," we were confessing that this whole structure of salvation ran counter to something deeply and beautifully human. Maybe, just maybe, Jesus had more to do with living life than with escaping it. To admit that, however, was heresy.

Christianity has often been given to proclamations of disaster feeding off fear, from visions written down on the isle of Patmos, through apocalyptic visions of Franciscan monks who believed the world would end in 1260, to Americans fleeing to the hills in 1844 confident of Jesus's momentary return. Those with visions of fiery judgment and hell, a faith founded in persecution and fear, had a field day with an entire generation of teenagers who grew up cowering under desks. Even though it made no sense and provided no real hope, the chaos of the days, the anxiety into which we were born, made it oddly believable. In the 1970s, it seemed important to understand our beginning, and most assuredly we needed to know our end. We wanted to be saved.

And, to me at least, Jesus seemed a better Alpha and Omega than the other options.

Forty years after I summoned my mother to my bedside, my sister called me while I was in an airport awaiting a flight to Mexico. She said that our mother was critically ill and that I should get to Phoenix as soon as possible. The airline changed my flight to one headed for Arizona. When I arrived, I went immediately to the hospital.

For the next several days, I spent many hours at my mother's bedside. She was, as the doctors said, "nonresponsive." There were tubes—lots of them—and the one that enabled her to breathe also kept her from vocalizing. The doctors did not really understand what was wrong, but it seemed she was dying. A nurse told me to talk to her, whatever I thought to do, as there was no real telling what a person comprehended in her state. "There are miracles," she said. "I've seen some surprising things."

And so I sat and talked and read to her. On Sunday morning of the vigil, neither my brother nor sister was at the hospital. Mom and I were alone. I recited some prayers to her, mostly from the Methodist hymnal, and repeated Psalm 23, creating an impromptu church service, hoping she might recognize some familiar cadences from her own childhood faith. I noticed that her eyes had opened and were a more brilliant blue than I had ever seen. They were not really registering her surroundings, but seeming to search for something, almost as if pleading, a bit agitated perhaps.

Then I realized what I saw in those eyes: fear. She was afraid. Did she know she was dying? Maybe we both feared dying, a fear she never would have revealed to me sitting at my bedside all those years ago. She taught me to be brave the best way she knew, attempting to comfort me by embracing the dark. Now it was my turn to be brave for her.

Not entirely sure what to say or do, I held her hand, looking steadily into the eyes that had beheld me at my birth, eyes that saw me long before I could comprehend the world. And I sang to her. An old Charles Wesley hymn, one every Methodist knows by heart:

Jesus, lover of my soul,
Let me to Thy bosom fly,
While the nearer waters roll,
While the tempest still is high:
Hide me, O my Savior, hide,
Till the storm of life is past;
Safe into the haven guide;
O receive my soul at last.

She seemed to hold my gaze, for a few seconds at least. "I love you, Mom," I said gently. Maybe she understood, maybe not. Her eyes closed. For a moment I thought she had died.

But she was still breathing, not normally, but breathing. I leaned in close. "Don't be afraid, Mom." I whispered. "Your work is done, you can leave if you need to go. Toward Dad. Toward Jesus. Just walk toward the light."

I kissed her hand, but there was no response. Her breathing calmed.

"Toward the light, Mom," I repeated, "toward the light." And then the words came from some deep place of memory: "Let us pray: Now I lay me down to sleep, I pray thee, Lord, my soul to keep."

It would be easy, I suppose, to imagine this a story of triumph over death, of a victorious Savior who takes the hand of the fearful at life's end, guiding one into heaven where a mansion awaits. A good death, that thing most Christians hope for. It was not that. Instead, it was just two women, one old and one younger, mother and daughter.

Forty years ago, the older one had spoken of salvation. She urged her daughter to accept the dark, to live well with life as it is, to help others and make the world a better place. That was the way past fear; that was deliverance. She had not used the language of Jesus as Savior, but she had a tough assurance that God was with us here and now and that service and compassion made a difference. She had lived it all.

Holding her hand, I thought of all the people she had helped and loved. Even as she aged and fell ill, she busily gave of the little she had so those with less could live with more. For her, salvation came through baptism and potluck suppers. She longed for joy, yet often walked in sadness. She did her best, and that, I can assure you, was more true for her than for most people I know.

That blueness in her eyes? The brightness I had never seen before? There was fear, yes, but also clarity of a sort. I think she saw more than I can guess. Perhaps she saw the light. We forget that light can be even more terrifying than the dark.

The other woman was, of course, me. I took my turn to be brave at the bedside. "Toward the light, toward Jesus," I urged. "Don't be afraid." As I let her go, I realized that I could let go too. One day I would be in the bed and, God willing, someone would be holding my hand, releasing me toward the light, toward Jesus. Salvation meant understanding that life is, indeed, a circle, where living and dying intertwine, where we help one another live fully now and hold hands while passing into the age to come.

Once I had hoped that Jesus would save me from the fearsome eternity of that passing, but now I know better. At the hospital bed, I was aware that we had both—Mom and me—been delivered, rescued, and made whole, but neither as we expected nor as we might have liked. Yet somehow, Jesus had saved both of us—the one who had repaired our shattered hearts, been with us always, and had somehow inspired courage and resilience. We had seen Jesus in one another's eyes and witnessed Jesus in the good work we had done with our own hands.

She never taught me *about* salvation; there was no fancy vocabulary, no born-again experience, no end times rapture. Instead, she had shown me how to live with dignity, persistence, charity, and occasionally joy. For her, salvation was goodness beating back the sin, violence, and injustice of the world, with a kind of quixotic ferocity and always, always, always, trusting that. "Don't be afraid," she had urged. "Fear not," the words of the angel long ago.

Salvation is not really about heaven; it is not an escape. It is about living beyond fear, knowing that death comes for each of us, often in mundane, quiet ways. "It is a characteristic of God to overcome evil with good," wrote the fourteenth-century mystic Julian of Norwich. "Jesus Christ therefore, who himself overcame evil with good, is our true Mother."[17] *Jesus Christ, Savior, our true Mother.*

It was the last time we were together. The doctors moved her to hospice shortly thereafter. A few days later, she died as the late morning sun streamed through her window. The nurse said it was very peaceful. I was glad she had not died during the night.

Lord

Why do you call me "Lord, Lord," and do not do what
I tell you? I will show you what someone is like who
comes to me, hears my words, and acts on them.

—*Luke 6:46–47*

I've decided," I announced one night over dinner, "I'm
going to go to a Christian college."

My mother's face turned red. "What about Duke? Smith?
Or Lewis and Clark or the University of Arizona?" she asked,
reciting all the schools where I had put in applications. She
had not gone to college and wanted me to go somewhere
prestigious, a "real" school, which would give me unlimited
opportunity to succeed in the world. "What are you going to
study? The Bible?"

"Well, yes," I stammered. "There are other subjects too. It's a real liberal arts college."

I actually wanted to be safe and to attend a college of which my church approved. But I also hoped my family would be proud. I knew I needed to leave home, and yet I did not want to distance myself from my new faith that had offered me protection, rescue, and salvation. I was growing up, but I was afraid of the world.

I had found what I was looking for in Jesus, and I desired to know everything possible about who he was, what he taught, and his purpose for my life. Getting saved was partly an intellectual quest, partly a flight from fear, and partly a love affair. "As a deer longs for flowing streams, so my soul longs for you, O God," wrote the Psalmist. "My soul thirsts for God, for the living God" (42:1–2). At eighteen, I could not get enough of God, Jesus, or the Bible. Sin, the cross, the Rapture—they were just the beginning. I wanted to study systematic theology, the scriptures, church history, and apologetics. I did not want to party; I wanted to pray. Had it been the Middle Ages instead of the late 1970s and had we been Catholics rather than Protestants, I am confident my parents, given my inclinations, would have packed me off to a convent.

Instead, in autumn 1977, I found myself at an evangelical liberal arts college in Santa Barbara, California. My parents' worries eased when they saw the campus, hidden on a hillside in posh Montecito, more an elegant estate than a fundamentalist Bible camp. With its manicured gardens and magnificent views of the Pacific, the school embodied a mannered, maybe even vaguely worldly evangelical faith. In the parking lots, expensive foreign cars were marked as Jesus's own with discreet fish stickers on their bumpers. Maybe one could have a piece of heaven here on earth; people joked about finding Eden.

When they dropped me off, Mom and Dad seemed relieved, perhaps understanding that depositing their daughter at a school with required chapel and religion classes might not be such a bad thing during the last days of the counterculture. My mother made me promise to major in political science and go to law school, or at the very least marry a lawyer or an aspiring politician. I agreed. He would have to be a Christian, though.

I dutifully signed up for courses in American government and international politics, but they were dull. The religion classes kept drawing my attention. Who really cared about the Cold War and nuclear policy when you could be learning about arguments between Catholics and Protestants and exegeting the gospel of Luke?

In religious studies classes, we explored the nature of salvation, the work of Jesus, and Christian ethics. We learned about martyrs and saints and great preachers and theologians. We plumbed the secret art of biblical exegesis and the mysteries of hermeneutics and demythologizing and had an entire course on how to argue someone into faith. My intellectual world was aflame with the Holy Spirit. It was heady to discuss things like double predestination and realized eschatology over dinner or converse about Thomas Aquinas and Karl Barth as if they were my best friends. Challenging contemporary books joined the classics: *Rich Christians in an Age of Hunger*, by Ron Sider; *The Politics of Jesus*, by John Howard Yoder; *Agenda for Biblical People*, by Jim Wallis; and *Let Justice Roll Down*, by John Perkins.

One of those books, *Your God Is Too Small*, by J. B. Phillips, accused Christians of having "put God in a box," of constructing a God in our own image and according to our own preferences. During that first year in college, that "box" phrase dogged me. Perhaps the Bible Church was too much of a box, and even if I had only put God there relatively recently, all these classes and books were convincing me that Jesus was far more than a personal savior who would rapture me at the end times and take me to heaven forever.

There was an entire underground industry of radical Christian literature in the 1970s, not only books, but magazines as well—*Sojourners*, *The Other Side*, and *Radix*. The college chaplain was a surprisingly hip guy who wore jeans and casual shirts and had posters of an unkempt Palestinian-looking Jesus on his wall. His office became a hangout for particularly precocious students, where we would sit on beanbag chairs and talk about the Bible, missions, and world Christianity. He invited speakers to chapel who challenged the evangelical establishment—which prompted my friends' parents to write threatening letters to the school—preachers like Tony Campolo, who literally yelled at a full gymnasium about how evangelicals ignored poverty; John Perkins, who shared his experience of being a Black Christian, pretty much called us all racist, daring us to move to and minister in Mississippi; and Ched Myers, a biblical scholar whose Jesus-was-a-pacifist takedown of the American military caused a near riot among the students.

In the avalanche of words, someone in a class or at chapel remarked, "Jesus can't just be your Savior; he must also be your Lord." I was riveted by the idea—Lord, Master of all, a God who cared about justice and peace and things that happened here on earth. Admittedly, the Jesus I had encountered as a teenager could manage to save people from sin and death, but maybe there was more. Maybe Jesus could save the world.

⸎

Around 112 CE, a Roman governor named Pliny reported to Emperor Trajan about the activities of the new religious sect called Christians in his region. Wanting to contain increasing incidents involving those who followed Jesus, the governor sought more information about the group by "torturing two female slaves who were called deaconesses."[1] He told the emperor he had not discovered much, except their "depraved, excessive superstition." Pliny was far more concerned about how the potential spread of Christianity might reflect poorly on him than he was, of course, about torturing a few slaves. The deaconesses, of whom we have no record after this, had most likely been found out through their customary Christian confession "Jesus is Lord."

This sordid bit of history reveals something important between its lines. Early Christians often proclaimed their faith in three words: "Jesus is Lord." Historians refer to it as an early creedal affirmation, but it was really more of a theological slogan. At its simplest level, the Greek term *kyrios*, meaning "lord" or "master," quite literally meant the one who owns you. Slaves called their masters "lord"; students often referred to revered teachers as "master"; and workers might call their employers "lord." In a world where millions were held in slavery and millions of others lived in poverty and powerlessness at the bottom of a rigid social hierarchy, claiming Jesus as "Lord" announced one's liberation from oppression. "Jesus is Lord" made sense in an empire of slaves, as submitting to his lordship amounted to spiritual freedom, especially in the new community called the church where, apparently, female slaves held leadership positions and Roman social status was upended. Baptism was the rite of initiation into this egalitarian community. All Christians were baptized into their new master, Jesus, according to Paul, who includes an early baptismal creed in his letter to Galatians: "There is no longer slave or free . . . for all of you are one in Christ Jesus." (3:27–28).

Everything and everyone in the Roman Empire was, however, owned by a different master—the emperor, who had ultimate authority, power, and control over all. As New Testament scholar N. T. Wright makes clear, "The emperor was the *kyrios*, the lord of the world, the one who claimed the allegiance and loyalty of subjects throughout his wide empire."[2] When slaves and women said that Jesus was Lord, they surely meant that Jesus was now their master, the one who truly owned them, no matter the claims of earthly masters. But because Caesar was Lord of all, saying "Jesus is Lord" also carried political connotations. Especially when those who professed "Jesus is Lord" also refused to say "Caesar is Lord."

And Pliny, like most Roman authorities of the day, found "Jesus is Lord" both confusing and threatening. How could a dead Jew be "Lord"? Proclaiming that precluded those who did so from making sacrifice or swearing loyalty to the emperor. Were they mocking Caesar? Plotting a revolt against the empire? Perhaps this Christian talk of resurrection deflected attention away from a political insurrection. "Jesus is Lord" meant far more than "Jesus is my personal master." It meant, "If Jesus is Lord, Caesar is not." Early Christians moved quickly from the spiritual freedoms they acquired by following Jesus to sedition and treason against the political order.

In addition, "Lord" appears in Jewish contexts of the time. Because the name for God in the Hebrew scriptures, YHWH, was considered too sacred to utter aloud, whenever that term appeared in the text, the word *adonai*, "Lord," was used in its place. In the Greek version of the Hebrew scriptures, the Septuagint, *kyrios* was the translation of the Hebrew word *adonai*. Thus, Greek-speaking Jews referred to the Jewish God as *Kyrios*, "Lord."

Thus, "Lord" held multiple meanings in the biblical world, meanings that were personal, political, and theological, and

expanded as a term to include multiple ways in which believers experienced Jesus. Writers of the New Testament use
kyrios more than seven hundred times, many to specifically
refer to Jesus—making the word seem so common that contemporary readers seem to take it for granted. Yet *kyrios* was
a startling word to describe a wandering miracle-working
rabbi. "Lord," "master," "ruler," "God"—all *kyrios*, each sig-
nifying one who holds dominion over the lives and fates of
those under his sway. "Jesus is Lord" was subversive and em-
powering, a form of submission one could choose in a world
of otherwise little choice, a way of life that resulted in finding
oneself by giving oneself totally and unreservedly to this
crucified Jewish peasant *kyrios*.

Master

A revival broke out during my sophomore year at college. It
started small, with just a few students gathering to read the
Bible, people who longed to live faith in a powerful way,
but soon grew to over seventy of us meeting for study, worship, and prayer. We read the text and asked ourselves where
we were in the story, attempting to remain open to all the
voices and testimonies in the room. There were no trained
leaders, no adult authorities. Together, we interpreted the
Bible, free of oversight and constraint, attempting to make
it make sense in our world. Although we did not know it
at the time, we had started something that Latin American
Christians would call a "base community," a completely

nonhierarchical, lay-led, experiential Bible-reading group. The conveners, Jimmy and John, called it "the radical Christian Bible study." "Radical," they explained, "means going to the root."

Someone in the group had read Dietrich Bonhoeffer's book *The Cost of Discipleship* and shared this quote: "When Christ calls a man, he bids him come and die."[3] Following Jesus was costly, not easy; it meant surrendering everything to Christ's lordship. Suddenly, those words were everywhere, overheard in conversations in dorms, spoken by preachers in chapel, even scribbled on bathroom doors. Cheap paperback editions of Bonhoeffer's book sat atop Bibles in the cubbies outside the dining commons and fell out of backpacks or book bags as students scurried across campus. Hundreds of young Christians, mostly fundamentalist kids or newly converted Jesus freaks, became preoccupied with the idea of dying to self in the here and now. Maybe following Jesus was not about the afterlife. We needed to follow Jesus, to go where he called, to give up our lives for him here and now. More than Savior, Jesus is Lord! Jesus bids us come and die!

Jimmy and John were roommates, both religious studies majors. They had been reading the gospel of Luke together when Jesus's words, on the heels of Bonhoeffer's quote, struck them with fresh urgency: "Then he said to them all, 'If any want to become my followers, let them deny themselves and take up their cross daily and follow me. For those who want to save their life will lose it, and those who lose their life for my sake will save it'" (Luke 9:23–24). They shared with others how our home churches had largely ignored this truth—that few were willing to die for Christ—having accommodated to middle-class southern California values instead.

The pair began the Bible study centered on that verse and, within a few weeks, dozens of classmates crowded in the dorm lounge in a quest to become radical Christians, "rooted" in the confession that Jesus was Lord. Soon it was the buzz of campus. It was, indeed, a revival. But there was no Billy Graham–style altar call, no insistence on being born again. We were already born again, but most of us felt something was missing. It was about following Jesus, really following him, being disciples.

"What would it look like," Jimmy asked me as we walked to class one day, "if we picked up the cross every day? If we died to self? If Jesus was Lord of all?"

I did not know.

By sophomore year, however, I knew I had become equally disenchanted with political science courses and the future lawyers in my classes. I switched to an education major because I wanted to help people—and perhaps become a missionary.[4] On the path, when Jimmy asked the question, I felt in a quandary. I had known the cross as a part of church architecture or as the place called Calvary, where salvation was accomplished. But to pick it up? Every day? An evangelist named Arthur Blessitt was carrying a giant cross around the world, but that did not seem to be what either Jimmy pondered or Jesus meant.

We might not have known, but a group of us realized we would not know until we tried to put it into action. Instead of hauling a cross around, we started a street ministry intended to serve people the way we imagined Jesus might. Santa Barbara had a large homeless population, and many people lived under bridges, on benches, at the beach, and in parks and plazas. Each weekend, our idealistic band, dressed in clothes we had bought at a thrift store—in order to "identify" with the street people—walked about in the city's poorer neighborhoods. We fed people, sat and talked, and took "the poor" to shelters or hospitals as needed. It was not a turn-or-burn type of evangelism. We had no motives to make converts, no tracts to pass out. Instead, we wanted to do what we thought Jesus demanded of us—serve those at the margins of society, following the call of our Master.

We met and befriended a godly and boisterous Black woman named Queenie, who ran a café on lower State Street. We were never quite sure how she made any money, as she gave away more coffee and sandwiches than she ever seemed to sell. When we came in, she would shout, "Praise Jesus!" She let us host Bible studies at her tables and play Christian music to entertain her customers; in return, we often did her dishes and cleaned her floors. Queenie's became the hub of our radical Christian community, and she taught us what she knew of both the Bible and the streets. Under her guidance, we got braver and learned everything from how to get someone who had overdosed to the local rehab to the art of protesting against real-estate developers who were trying to close her café down.

Jimmy, John, and the other male leaders thought it was a bad idea for their sisters in Christ—like me—to haunt the mean streets of Santa Barbara. Except for one thing. We were allowed to minister to other women, and that meant those whom we politely called "ladies of the evening." None of us would have ever thought of referring to these women as "sex workers," for the word "sex" was generally avoided, and it would have appalled us to think of what they did as "work." They were tragic women, victims of men's lust, who, we believed, like Mary Magdalene would jump at the chance to be saved when introduced to Jesus. Thus, I was deployed with a few female classmates to talk with the ladies, whom we would offer to take back to our dorms (that was until college authorities discovered that we were putting up prostitutes on spare sofas on campus) to await transport to a place of moral and physical safety.

One night, I was standing on a corner with some of the ladies when a police van pulled up. I do not remember who my teammate was that evening, but when I looked around, I realized she was gone. It was just the women from the streets and me. The police rounded us up and opened the door of the paddy wagon, when it suddenly dawned on me that I was going to be arrested with everyone else. My heart skipped a beat: I was going to jail. Jesus went to jail. Paul went to jail. Was this what it meant to die to self? To pick up the cross? I wondered how I would explain this to my parents.

Just as I was considering the cost of this particular discipleship, one of the women spoke up. "She's not one of us, fellas," she said as she pushed me away from the back of the van. "Leave her be. She's a Jesus girl."

The cops did as directed, driving off with the women and abandoning me on the street corner with passersby who had watched the whole episode. I walked back to Queenie's.

She's not one of us. She's a Jesus girl.

I felt strangely conflicted. No jail. But maybe this radical Christian thing was not for me. This going to the root of things, this lordship business, scared me, *the Jesus girl*. Jesus hung out with sinners, tax collectors, and prostitutes. He would have gotten in the van, even if someone tried to push him away. Some people would have said I made the right choice to stay on the street corner while the others were rounded up. But it made me feel terrible, sending women off to the police station while I was safe, and I remembered the words of judgment uttered by Jesus: "I was in prison and you visited me" (Matt. 25:36). I wanted to serve, and yet a huge rift opened between them and me. "Lord," asked his disciples, "when was it that we saw you . . . sick or in prison and visited you?" Jesus replied, "Truly, I tell you, just as you did it to one of the least of these . . . you did it to me" (25:37–40). The Jesus girl had failed her master.

These words—and the idea that Jesus was my "master"—make me wince now. Indeed, about a dozen years later, I was in a church Bible study at my Episcopal church, and our group read Romans 6:22: "But now that you have been set free from sin and have become slaves of God, the benefit you reap leads to holiness, and the result is eternal life" (NIV).

Slaves to God? I felt queasy. I begged the others and the pastor to think about how these words had been used throughout history as justification for racism and chattel slavery and how offensive they were to those who had been held in slavery. I confessed that the verse upset me, and I wished for different language to describe what Paul was saying. Could we *not* call ourselves slaves? And, more important, could we *not* think of either God or Jesus as a slaveholder?

"If Jesus were a slaveholder," I insisted, "he would set everyone free."

"But he's a good slaveholder," the pastor insisted. "We are slaves. That's what it says, what it means."

I got flustered. "You don't understand. It's oppressive. It makes everything . . . worse. No thoughtful woman, no Black person . . ."

He interrupted, "We are all enslaved to something. Either God or the devil."

The pastor, a charismatic (as in "Pentecostal," not "personable") Episcopalian, then called me a heretic and tried to speak over me in tongues to cast out my demon of confusion. I excused myself to the bathroom to wait out his attempted exorcism.

By the time I was thirty, I had learned that when Paul spoke of slavery, it was far from clear what he meant, what one scholar calls a "study in diplomatic obfuscation."[5] The apostle seems to have drawn analogies from what was a social reality of his day (and for whatever reason, it was difficult for him to clearly criticize slavery, the "third rail of ancient society") rather than a vision of what should be.[6] And despite the givenness of slavery in the ancient Roman world, in the century after Paul some of the next generation of Christians began to subvert enslavement with stories like the one found of the *Shepherd of Hermas*, where a slave is made "joint heir" with a son.[7] It would take a very, very long time for the words "no longer slave or free" to become more than a spiritual metaphor in my own life, but, more important, for the world.

At nineteen, however, I was completely comfortable with the idea that Jesus was my master and that, in some fashion, Jesus owned me. I would serve my Lord as loyally and faithfully as was possible. I was very sincere, even if naive.

Ruler

If Jesus was Lord, that also meant he was in authority, like a king or ruler, here on the earth.

A favorite passage of our radical Christian group came from Jeremiah 18, where the prophet visits a potter's house. Jeremiah sees a craftsman working at the wheel: "The vessel he was making of clay was spoiled in the potter's hand, and he reworked it into another vessel, as seemed good to him. Then the word of the Lord came to me: . . . 'Just like the clay in the potter's hand, so are you in my hand'" (18:4–6). Jeremiah's words are directed to the people of Israel, but never mind that. We personalized the story to mean that whenever we failed to live up to the Master's expectations, the softened clay of our hearts could be reworked until it became the vessel God intended.

A popular song, often sung in chapel, summed up the kind of tenderness we hoped would keep us spiritually malleable and so of use to Jesus:

Spirit of the Living God, fall fresh on me.
Spirit of the Living God, fall fresh on me.
Melt me, mold me,
Fill me, use me.
Spirit of the Living God, fall fresh on me.

"O Lord, you are our Father; we are the clay," we prayed using words from Isaiah, "and you are our potter; we are all the work of your hand" (64:8). What did it mean to be the potter's clay?

A group of students began to go to Ensenada, Mexico, in search of more challenging ministry opportunities and cross-cultural experiences. Impoverished Baja villages provided plenty of both. Thus was born Potter's Clay, a week of mission work during spring break south of the border, which mostly involved building an orphanage and repairing churches as well as preaching, leading revivals, and teaching Bible classes for children.

The first time I went, as we crossed the border from San Diego to Tijuana, I was unprepared for the poverty of the people and the economic distress of the city. We drove southward, and my friends pointed out villages that had welcomed our group. We navigated up a dirt road to one hamlet where the pastor awaited our arrival. After we parked, I looked around. Much of the tiny community was built out of old tires! Foundations of houses, walls that held back hillsides, and raised garden beds—tires. Tires everywhere—little kids crawling over them, food grown in them. The shock must have registered on my face. Tires were toxic, subject to special handling and recycling as hazardous waste.

"Yes," my friend Gordon whispered to me. "Americans dump tires over the border. And these people live in our garbage." He shook his head, saying angrily, "At least they have a place to live."

As Gordon chatted with the pastor, it was hard to follow in Spanish and I became lost in my own thoughts. What did "Jesus is Lord" mean here, living in a village made from American trash? And what were we doing polluting this country and poisoning these children? As the dust blew in my face, almost as the Spirit, it dawned on me that Jesus's lordship was far more than surrendering control of my own life to God. It had something to do with this place, bringing this under his lordship too. "Jesus is Lord" was not just a personal confession; the implications of the proclamation edged toward politics, toward a reordering of economics, of environment, of power.

Recently, the youngest theology professor at the college had begun to teach us about liberation theology, a relatively new and radical idea from Latin America. A Dominican scholar, Gustavo Gutiérrez, had shaken up the field of religion by asserting that European theology was complicit with un-just social structures, conquest, and colonization. He called for new attention to the dictum to love one's neighbor, and he argued the only way to do so in the now-globalized world was to privilege the poor as God did. Although the young professor in our department was most assuredly evangelical, he was willing to poke the status quo, and soon enough we were reading Gutiérrez, who, like Bonhoeffer, taught about dying to self. For him, dying to self meant being raised to liberation and then liberating others.

This was heady stuff, not the typical curriculum of evangelical colleges at the time (nor probably at this time either), but it made sense of the tire village and the other injustices and inequities we witnessed in Ensenada. We argued mightily about God's preferential option for the poor, and found it increasingly hard to defend its detrac-tors while playing with homeless orphans and cleaning up poisoned streams in Baja.

In California in the late 1970s, we increasingly looked southward to the radical Christian politics being proclaimed mostly by Catholic priests, sisters, and missionaries to try and understand the injustices beyond our ken. Those Christians were standing against oppressive, militarist regimes, especially the one violently controlling El Salvador. That such evil was being perpetrated in the "Republic of the Savior," that a country named for Jesus the Savior was so far from living as if Jesus was Lord, was painful to fathom. The words of El Sal-vador's Archbishop Óscar Romero wended northward, and even we, students at an evangelical college, eagerly listened as he courageously stood with the suffering:

> The church would betray its own love for God and its fidelity to the gospel if it stopped being . . . a defender of the rights of the poor . . . a humanizer of every legitimate struggle to achieve a more just society . . . that prepares the way for the true reign of God in history.[8]

We were not stupid. This was not just a problem for the Catholic Church in El Salvador. We knew that our own churches had not defended the rights of the poor, had failed to work for a more just society in our own communities.

To be fair, the Methodist church of my childhood had, in many ways, attempted to raise some of these concerns and certainly tried to teach a vision of justice to its members, however imperfectly. Indeed, my Confirmation class had traveled to Watts to teach us about racism and brought Latino missionaries to speak. But Scottsdale Bible had eschewed worldly politics in favor of heavenly salvation, preaching imminent escape from the evils of the day. Most of the students at the college came from churches like Scottsdale Bible. Conventional political theology for evangelicals amounted to quoting Romans 13:1: "Let every person be subject to the governing authorities; for there is no authority except from God, and those authorities that exist have been instituted by God." This was often paraphrased as "obey the government" and trust that God has ordained the social order. To hear voices like Óscar

Romero challenge the church for its complicity with injustice and a plea for the poorest of the poor—to imagine the "true reign of God in history"—was an epiphany.

The true reign of God in history. Was that possible? Could Jesus be Lord in history? We discovered what the early Christians had known—"Jesus is Lord" was a political proclamation. Not only was Jesus Lord of our hearts; he was Lord of the whole earth, active in history, working toward liberation and love, and willing to take down empires in doing so.

Although these theological questions excited me, much went on as before, especially with classes and chapel. But I began to see things differently. Despite the growing popularity of worship choruses, we often still sang traditional hymns in chapel, some of which I remembered from my Methodist childhood. One old favorite was "Crown Him with Many Crowns," with its grand vision of Jesus on the heavenly throne in the first verse. The fourth verse, however, one I had never really noticed before, now jumped out at me:

Crown Him the Lord of peace,
Whose power a scepter sways
From pole to pole, that wars may cease,
And all be prayer and praise.
His reign shall know no end,
And round His pierced feet
Fair flowers of glory now extend,
Their fragrance ever sweet.

Jesus was not just Lord in heaven; he reigns as Lord over the entire earth.

The world was less than a decade beyond 1968, a time of chaotic politics and challenging social movements, followed by Watergate and the scandal of a president who lied to the American people. The new president, Jimmy Carter, was an evangelical and seemed a good person, but new crises erupted in the Middle East, there was not enough fuel for cars or heat, the American government supported all sorts of bad political actors around the world, unemployment was through the roof, and interest rates on things like student loans and mortgages soared. Singing "crown him the Lord of peace" about a Jesus who ruled the earth and ended all wars felt more like a protest anthem than a praise song. Jesus as a Christian Caesar seemed a pretty good idea over against Exxon and the American military ruling the world.

Of course, Satan had once tempted Jesus with that very thing, to make him ruler of all the world's kingdoms. "To you I will give their glory and all this authority," he hissed into Jesus's ear, "for it has been given over to me, and I give it to anyone I please" (Luke 4:5–6). The trade was that Jesus had to worship him in order to rule the earth. This text is full of oddities, not least of which is the idea that Satan owns the realms of the world and can distribute them at will, a devilish claim that was not theologically true according to other parts of scripture. The kingdoms were not his to give.

Jesus said no. Even though Jesus resisted this devilish offer, he did not eschew earthly kingdoms for a purely spiritual one. Indeed, Jesus went from Satan's temptation to Galilee, where he proclaimed that the kingdom of God was at hand: "The time is fulfilled, and the kingdom of God has come near; repent, and believe in the good news!" (Mark 1:15).

For centuries, the Jews had looked for the kingdom they called the "age to come," when God's dream of peace and justice would fill the earth. Captives would be released, the blind would see, the oppressed would be set free—the Lord's jubilee would be upon the people of Israel. That kingdom would be real, not a metaphor or some spiritual place in the clouds. Rather, the whole of creation would be transformed and God would rule that dominion, a kingdom that stretched through the heavens and renewed the earth. Jesus taught about it, describing the kingdom in parables, and modeled it by healing the sick and performing miracles. If you hung around with Jesus, it was easy to believe that some sort of political revolution was at hand.

It was not only hymns that sounded different now, but Jesus's words as well, like his own prayer: "Our Father who art in heaven, hallowed be thy name; thy kingdom come, thy will be done on earth as it is in heaven." When his first followers asked him how to pray, he directed them to pray not for a heavenly kingdom, but for an earthly one where all would be fed, there would be no more debt, and peace would reign. Here and now, not there and then. How had I never noticed this before? Jesus was Lord, a kind of alternative Caesar, not one who gave in to Satan's taunting offer of power, but the One who embodied divine authority and had arrived on earth to take back the planet for the Father.

The priorities of Jesus's kingdom would be exactly opposite of those in the world we knew—there holy generosity and true peace would replace capitalism and militarism. "God's Word teaches a very hard, disturbing truth," wrote Ron Sider, an evangelical theologian who also spoke in our chapel. "Those who neglect the poor and the oppressed are really not God's people at all—no matter how frequently they practice their religious rituals or how orthodox are their creeds and confessions."[9] What we did mattered more than right belief? Right treatment of the poor mattered more than doctrine? No one imagined this would go down well with the trustees.

Nor would the week in chapel when a relatively unknown young theologian named Ched Myers debated a military officer on Just War theory. Myers flatly declared that Jesus was a pacifist and that the church had betrayed him. No Christian should ever participate in the military, and no Christian could support a "peace" based on nuclear superiority. Students sat stunned as Myers reeled off verse after verse, quoted both ancient and modern theologians, and criticized the United States's dealings in Latin America. After chapel, dozens of students surrounded him, wanting to hear more. For the three days of his campus visit, Myers was like a pacifist pied piper, sitting in the middle of students teaching peace. Nobody could even remember the army officer's name.

No, the trustees were not going to like this at all. But it did not really matter to us. This theological door had been pushed open, and we barged through as if storming heaven. Blessed are the poor! Blessed are the peacemakers! This was the kingdom of God come among us. Give away everything you have and follow me. Turn the other cheek. It was all so clear, so simple, so . . . so literal.

Jesus is Lord! I had picked up that cross and my Bible and found a very different Jesus from the one who saved me. Years later, my friend actor John Fugelsang described that Jesus as:

> a radical, nonviolent revolutionary who hung around with lepers, hookers, and crooks; wasn't American and never spoke English; was anti-wealth, anti–death penalty, and anti–public prayer (Matt. 6:5); who was never anti-gay; who never mentioned abortion or birth control, never called the poor lazy, never justified torture, never fought for tax cuts for the wealthiest Nazarenes, never asked a leper for a co-pay; and who was a long-haired, brown-skinned, homeless community-organizing, anti-slut-shaming Middle Eastern Jew.[10]

Jesus was all that, and I found him in the least likely of places, a small evangelical college in a ritzy suburb of Santa Barbara. And in a village made of cast-off tires in Mexico.

God

The same theology professor who introduced us to liberation theology also handled more mundane subjects, like the required course Introduction to Christian Doctrine.

"The doctrine of the Trinity is the subject today," he announced. "And the truth of the matter is that this doctrine is not found in the New Testament."

Wait, what?

"Early Christians were Jews, and Jews were strict mono-theists," he explained. "Yet they also worshipped Jesus. So either Christians were bi-theists, or they had to figure out how Jesus and God the Father were related."

I looked around the room. Most students were just taking notes. A couple of others, however, seemed to realize this was important.

"Thus, early Christian writers and theologians had to ex-trapolate the doctrine of the Trinity from a few scriptures and from their experience."

Extrapolate?

"There are only a few texts in the New Testament where Jesus seems to claim he is God." This was getting serious, and I began to feel a little panicked. "Those references," he went on, "are mostly found in the gospel of John."

The professor listed those verses on the board, taking them as literal sayings of Jesus (adding nothing, of course, about the historical context or literary sources of John's gospel), and quickly moved to the heart of his lecture—a creed that appeared nearly three hundred years after Jesus had died in which Christians had "extrapolated" the ideas from stories about Jesus, memories of his message lingering in commu-nity, engagement with Greek and Latin philosophy, and new interpretations of Jewish scriptures in an effort to quash heresies that threatened the young church.

I had never given much thought to "Jesus is Lord" mean-ing Jesus is God. That is one of those things that Christians take for granted. It had never occurred to me that once—a very long time ago—this idea did not exist and that someone, or some group of someones, wrestled to invent it. Christian children do not consider Jesus-Lord-God as weird or strange in any way, having grown up reciting creeds about how Jesus is one with the Father and singing songs praising his divinity. Indeed, in some churches, "Jesus, Lord God" is used as a title in prayer.

If you paid attention in Sunday school, you heard the mysterious word "Trinity." Hardly any Sunday school teacher I ever knew could explain how Christians were monotheists and yet worshipped a God who existed as three, but explaining was not the point. Nearly everybody had a relative who scoffed at the idea, but who served on the local church board anyway. And everyone had a friend, perhaps even one on the playground, who said Trinitarian math did not add up. Nevertheless, it just was. As the Father was God, the Lord of all, so Jesus, the Son, was also Lord. And God.

Caesar: *Kaisar Kyrios*. Jesus: *Christos Kyrios*. To the Romans, but not to the Jews, kings were gods. For the Romans, this was not a big deal, as they divinized human beings all the time. But, as John Dominic Crossan points out, the problem arose with divinizing this particular person: Jesus of Nazareth. A Jewish peasant rabbi was God? Pilate scoffed, "Are you the king of the Jews?" Jesus replied, "You say so" (Luke 23:3). For a Roman governor, the Jewish king could have been divine, but if so, he was both a sacred and a political rival to the emperor and therefore a traitor. Pilate took Jesus's nonanswer as an answer and had him whipped for treason.

Jesus may not have claimed to be God (except for those few verses in John), but he certainly believed he was the Anointed One, the Messiah, in Greek *Christos*, who had come to save the Jews and establish the reign of God here on earth. But God himself? Jews had kings, but none were divine. In Judaism, there was no real expectation that the Jewish messiah would be divine either. This was one of the reasons the Jews hated Rome, and why they would not and could not participate in its religion. Caesar, the Roman emperor, the Lord, was not God. The Lord God, *Adonai*, YHWH, is God alone. Anything else, any other claim, violated the First Commandment: "You shall have no other gods before me."

Yet in the years after Jesus was murdered by Rome and as Christians believed in his resurrection, they followed a Jesus *kyrios* who was as their master, they proclaimed a Jesus *kyrios* as the ruler of this world, and they came to worship Jesus *kyrios* as *Adonai*, the Lord, who forgave sins, was eternally God, and was one with the Father. As my doctrine professor taught that day, this was a bit of a theological process, as one realization led to the next; but, sure enough, in about three or four centuries, this was the theological foundation of Christianity.

When I was in college, I was not terribly worried about the historical or theological implications of what was presented in Introduction to Christian Doctrine (even if I would be later) that day. I took the theological struggle of the early Christians at face value, trusting that the Holy Spirit had guided them to the truth. What occurred to me was that

"Lord" with its multiple meanings demanded something of me—"Jesus is Lord" called me to personal submission of my life and will to God's; "Jesus is Lord" pushed me to see the whole earth as the kingdom of God; and "Jesus is Lord" meant Jesus was God and King whose kingdom needed to be filled with worshipful subjects. It did no good to have a king if there was nobody around the throne.

As it says in Philippians 2:10–11:

> At the name of Jesus
>   every knee should bend,
>   in heaven and on earth and under the earth,
> And every tongue should confess
>   that Jesus Christ is Lord
>   to the glory of God the Father.

The New Testament professor said this was an early Christian hymn inserted into the text by Paul, the letter's author. In rather dramatic fashion, the professor explained how these words echoed what happened at Caesar's throne. There, terrified supplicants entered the royal room backward, their faces away from the emperor's glory. As they approached the throne in this posture, they would periodically bow, fall to their knees, or even go prostrate, as they recited their creed: *Kaisar Kyrios*.

"Paul is saying that Jesus is Caesar, not the Roman Caesar," he said, his voice becoming more insistent, "and one day *every* knee shall bow before him. *Every* knee, whether willingly or not. People will either fall on their knees or be forced to them, because Jesus is the true Lord."

His description was terrifying.

I did not want anyone to be forced. No one should fear Jesus, or face eternal damnation. I hoped for a happy throne-room scene at the end of history, one in which people from all races, tribes, and nations sang joyful praise to the Lord. Our job seemed to be to make plain the kingdom here by engaging in acts of justice, while at the same time ensuring that its eternal subject population was willing and joyful. I would become a missionary.

The Mission

It is hard to explain to outsiders what it means when a young person in the evangelical world feels a call to become a missionary. Missionaries are to evangelicals as saints are to Catholics—heroes of faith to be emulated. There is no real equivalent to this in liberal Protestantism; the closest my childhood Methodism came to spiritual hero worship was revering either social justice activists like Martin Luther King Jr. or theologians like Reinhold Niebuhr. Theologians generally won the day; we swooned when our men in tweed graced the covers of *TIME* magazine. But those pipe-smoking intellectuals could not compete with evangelical missionaries.

Pictures of missionaries hung in classrooms and halls of evangelical churches, often accompanied by maps with pins pointing to the countries where they served. Great evangelical churches had big maps with lots of pins, showing the "reach" of the Good News from its pews to around the world; "Our Missionaries" read the sign above the maps. The pictures in those days were often the same: either single women, whose prettiness was muted by tautly pulled-back hair and high-necked blouses, or happy family groups, showing a studious-looking, clean-cut father and a smiling mother balancing two or three children on her lap.

Single evangelical men generally did not become missionaries; rather, they became pastors. It was deemed too dangerous to send them alone to places where, it was feared, an unsaved woman might seduce them. Single women were stronger, more spiritually resilient. Women, after all, could not preach or teach here in America, but they were allowed to do so in nations where most of the population were heathens.

Although there were plenty of evangelicals who thought that Catholics were not Christians and were fair game for missionary work, the people in my circles eschewed that. Our experiences in Latin America taught us that true Christianity came in many guises (even if we did not particularly approve of certain doctrines). Instead, we focused on two groups we thought most needed the gospel: secular humanists and Muslims. Europe, we fretted, had lost its faith and must be reevangelized. And the great mass of Muslims, who lived in predominately Islamic-governed nations in Africa and the Middle East, had never heard the Good News because they were beyond the reach of conventional mission strategies.

Surely, Jesus wanted Europe back and desired that those who had not heard should come to know him.

Of the two choices, Europe sounded like a far better option to me. I set myself to learning German, struggled with French, and spent one summer working with a mission agency in the Netherlands. The mission was called International Crusades, an increasingly awkward moniker in the days of the Iran hostage crisis. We mostly did door-to-door evangelism, passed out Bibles, and invited the skeptical Dutch back to church. A few took Bibles, none came to worship, and most slammed doors in our faces. (Having doors slammed in one's face is surprisingly good preparation for life, by the way.) We also ran a Bible school for little ones at a seaside resort, a strategy to get weary parents back to religion. No takers there either.

The long-term missionaries knew that the summer teams would not have much success with traditional evangelism, so they had come up with a unique plan to make us feel useful. The Dutch government sponsored workers to go into the homes of the elderly and disabled to do projects and cleaning for those unable to do so. The mission coordinator thought this was a great "opening" to serve and, perhaps, talk with the clients about Jesus.

I was first sent, along with a male partner, to the home of a disabled widower who needed two things—his kitchen cleaned and some windows repaired. I got kitchen duty. I imagined that this work would be like the kind I had read about in a small devotional, *Practicing the Presence of God*, written by the medieval monk Brother Lawrence, who had found his Lord amid the washing up of pots and pans. When I walked into the kitchen, however, I was sorely disappointed. There were no pots and pans. Instead, there was what looked to be a layer of grease and grime over all the counters, the floors, and the appliances, which seemed to date from the Middle Ages. I had never seen anything so horrid in my life.

The man, in a wheelchair, pointed me to a closet with a bucket, brushes, and bleach. I did not spend the time in holy contemplation. I scrubbed and scrubbed and scrubbed, desperately trying to uncover the surface of, well, anything. It was a gruesome archeological expedition. This was not what I imagined when I thought of being a missionary—I had envisioned people coming forward to accept Christ as their Savior, surrendering all to Jesus, and worshipping their sovereign Lord. I could manage a few pots and pans like the cheerful Brother Lawrence, but not scraping grease from a kitchen that was at least twenty years older than I was.

The elderly man wheeled back into the kitchen while I worked. I wondered how I could witness to him. He spoke little English; I spoke little Dutch. Instead, he sat nearby and watched, occasionally saying, *Dank je wel, dank je wel.* At one point, he pulled out a Bible and started reading aloud from the New Testament, and I could pick out a few words and phrases.

And so the day went, me covered with grease and him offering grace. Although I had been angry, there developed an odd companionableness to it all, this harmony of work and words. The counters began to gleam; shoes no longer stuck to the floor. I wanted the room to shine, sparkling like a mansion in heaven. When I left a few hours later, he smiled and handed me a half dozen tulips as a kindness, and it became obvious that I was the one who had been evangelized by his gratitude. Jesus had shown up in an odd reversal of roles, for my heart was probably changed more than that of my host. I knew I had done better work that day than any other in those weeks.

I wrote about it in my journal, reflecting on the tension I felt. Jesus was King and Lord of the whole earth, as I loved to sing in my favorite Isaac Watts hymn:

Jesus shall reign where'er the sun
Doth his successive journeys run;
His Kingdom stretch from shore to shore,
Till moons shall wax and wane no more.

To Him shall endless prayer be made.
And princes throng to crown His head,
His name like sweet perfume shall rise
With every morning sacrifice.

Let every creature rise and bring
Peculiar honors to our King;
Angels descend with songs again,
And earth repeat the loud Amen.

This was the Jesus of my mission hopes, the One to whom all the people of the earth would bow, knowing him as God and King. I got chills singing these words, and my heart would nearly break with longing before this vision of Jesus on the throne of heaven. Mission work meant making sure the King had a kingdom. Yet the most meaningful day of my summer mission had had nothing to do with this. Instead, it was grimy and inglorious, smelling of bleach and rancid grease, in a state-supported elder program. The only knees that had bent were my own, as I reached into filthy corners of that kitchen. What kind of kingdom was this?

I had not brought Jesus to anyone. Instead, my host had brought Jesus to me as he welcomed me and invited my heart to be cleansed along with the kitchen. There was something of me that got saved that day, not the other way around.

None of this matched any theology of missions that I had studied. As a Protestant, I could not tell anyone that I felt I had gotten somehow saved—at least more saved than before—through scrubbing floors. Nothing had to do with proclaiming Christ as Lord, extending his kingdom throughout the world, or worshipping the Lord in glory. The magisterial words, "I believe in God, the Father Almighty . . ." were never uttered. Whatever happened that day, it had more to do with the kindness found in a kitchen than cringing in a throne room.

The Kin-dom of God

Just recently, I saw a thread on Twitter ridiculing the contemporary switch in theological terminology from "kingdom" to "kin-dom." When I first encountered a prayer using "kin-dom," I remember thinking that it was a sort of liberal watering down of the robust vision of Christ the King in glory, diminishing the power of his lordship. The noted theologian Ada María Isasi-Díaz recalls originally hearing "kin-dom" from a friend who was a nun as an alternative to the language of "kingdom," a word fraught with colonial oppression and imperial violence. "Jesus," she wrote, "used 'kingdom of God' to evoke . . . an alternative 'order of things'" over and against the political context of the Roman Empire and its Caesar, the actual kingdom and king at the time.[11]

"Kingdom" is a corrupted metaphor, one misused by the church throughout history to make itself into the image of an earthly kingdom. Indeed, Christians have often failed to recognize that "kingdom" was an inadequate and in-complete way of speaking of God's governance, not a call to set up their own empire. Isasi-Díaz argues that "kin-dom," an image of *la familia*, the liberating family of God working together for love and justice, is a metaphor closer to what Jesus intended.

If that sounds more like contemporary political correct-ness than biblical theology, it is worth noting that Isasi-Díaz's "kin-dom" metaphor echoes an older understanding, one found in medieval theology in the work of the mystic Julian of Norwich. Julian wrote of "our kinde Lord," a poetic title, certainly, summoning images of a gentle Jesus. But it was not that. Rather, it was a radical one, for the word "kinde" in medieval English did not mean "nice" or "pleasant." Instead, in the words of theologian Janet Soskice:

In Middle English the words "kind" and "kin" were the same—to say that Christ is "our kinde Lord" is not to say that Christ is tender and gentle, although that may be implied, but to say that he is kin—our kind. This fact, and not emotional disposition, is the rock which is our salvation.[12]

To say "our kinde Lord" was to say "our kin Lord." Jesus the Lord is our kin. The kind Lord is kin to me, you, all of us—making us one. This is a subversive deconstruction of the image of kingdom and kings, replacing forever the pretensions and politics of earthly kingdoms with Jesus's calling forth a kin-dom. King, kind, kin.

My experience of Jesus as Lord had taught me of this kinship in my enthusiasm to love and serve others and in my hopes that his liberating rule mattered to the poor and oppressed. I had listened to Jesus when he taught that the kingdom was like a pearl, a mustard seed, and the yeast in bread. But these parables slipped away as the word "kingdom" slowly resumed its original meaning. Like millions of other white European Christians before me, I did not understand that "kingdom" was a metaphor, one that needed to be tempered and understood in the context of Jesus's koan-like pronouncements, an oppositional vision of Rome's empire intended to remind early believers what they were *not* supposed to be. Slowly, my youthful imitation of Jesus as Lord on the streets of Santa Barbara gave way to an exalted vision of Jesus as Caesar demanding allegiance of all humankind, a real kingdom with a real king. And I wanted to be both faithful subject and herald.

The kitchen in the Netherlands may well have been the closest I have ever been to the kingdom Jesus preached. There, the Spirit revealed the meaning of kin, of a "kingdom" with a "kinde Lord," of simplicity, solidarity, and service, things I knew but was on the verge of forgetting. Like the night on the street with the sex workers. I was sad to be separated from them, left on the sidewalk instead of being tossed into the paddy wagon together. Or perhaps the day in the tire village. I did not have the language of kin-dom then, or words to put around these experiences.

But they stayed with me, eroding my theological certainty for years to come. The kin-dom of God is like being rounded up with prostitutes . . . The kin-dom is like a house built on tires . . . The kin-dom of heaven is like a woman scrubbing grease from a kitchen counter . . .

The Orderly Lord

Pursuing Jesus as Lord took me beyond the theological box of the Bible Church. Jesus was much more than I had imagined, and his concerns reached from the most intimate places of my own heart, to Mexican villages and American politics, to a vision of divinity that animated the entire cosmos with its glory. Although I still called myself an evangelical, I was increasingly disenchanted with evangelical churches whose worship seemed stuck on Jesus the Savior as the sum total of

Christian theology. What I experienced in church—which in college had become a mash-up of a charismatic worship service that met in a warehouse, a somewhat traditional Baptist service with good preaching, and the school's chapel services—seemed spiritually out of sync with the Jesus I was coming to know. Whenever I went to church, I walked away fuming at either shallow praise choruses or thin theology in the sermons.

The same young professor who taught liberation theology and doctrine also offered courses in early Christianity and Reformation history. Thus, ideas from the church fathers and Protestant thinkers became part of theological conversation with friends. It was not uncommon to sit at dinner and hear, "But Augustine said . . ." or "Luther insisted . . ." in a completely casual and familiar way. We learned to read both sides of any theological argument, but we also learned that our professors had favorites, and those favorites were heavily weighted toward Western Christian beliefs, ideas that had been given the imprimatur "orthodox" by creeds, councils, and clerics over the centuries.

A subtle change kicked in, somewhere in our senior year, from exploring what was interesting and challenging toward getting the answers right in accordance with the church's larger authority. The books on our shelves shifted; the radical Christian authors were slowly displaced by the likes of Karl Barth, C. S. Lewis, J. R. R. Tolkien, and Dorothy Sayers. Although our political views continued to lean left, responsive to the voices of Óscar Romero and Dorothy Day, our theological views began to take on both more romantic and more orderly forms, displaying an interest in tradition. I think we were searching for a justice-oriented politics *and* an authority-laden religion at the same time. Somehow, we wanted a Jesus who could be both a radical and the divine head of an ordered church.

This was about as far out of the Bible Church box as could be imagined. Jesus as Savior did not take sides in political arguments, because it just was not worth trying to change a world that was doomed. And Jesus as Savior opposed the sorts of theologies that wound up with practices like infant baptism or hinted at anything like works righteousness. At the Bible Church, the word "tradition" was thought to be a death knell to true faith, to the immediate experience of being born again. Sure, they said they liked Martin Luther and John Wesley (never, however, John Calvin), but other than saying the two believed in salvation by faith alone, even these two Protestant heroes were relegated to lesser status in favor of more contemporary Bible preachers like Chuck Smith or Tim LaHaye.

When reading Luther for class, I realized that the great Reformer would probably not actually be welcome in most of the evangelical congregations where I had worshipped. And I could not help but think that Luther would find praise choruses cringeworthy and the low-key, hip California Jesus not much like the suffering Lord described in scripture. Maybe I needed to find a different church.

I wandered into a Methodist church in Santa Barbara, only to find its pews occupied mostly by people decades older than myself. The following week, it was the Lutherans, who talked social justice but seemed shy of prayer. Then came the Presbyterians, who, as was true in much of southern California, were mostly well-dressed brainy evangelicals.

After my six weeks of mission work in the Netherlands, I spent time in England. There, I had gone to a small Church of England worship service at Westminster Abbey led by a clergyperson who seemed straight from BBC central casting. I knelt for the Eucharist and recited words from the Book of Common Prayer. I felt as if heaven had descended to earth—it was quite unlike anything I had experienced, except perhaps for a couple of astonishing charismatic prayer services. Same spirit, but orderly—and with good theology! Martin Luther would, I suspected, have approved.

Back in the United States, the Church of England's daughter church is the Episcopal Church. When my search recommenced upon returning to school that fall, I visited All Saints-by-the-Sea Episcopal, a congregation down the hill from the college, and was swept off my spiritual feet. I had found home.

The funniest thing was that it felt like such a personal discovery, a private journey. But several classmates had similar longings. Soon, we had a VW minibus full of evangelical students who, at All Saints every Sunday, stumbled over words of ancient prayers and struggled to learn when to sit, stand, or kneel. We were the world's most enthusiastic converts, more Anglican than the archbishop of Canterbury himself, wanting to know every rule (called "rubrics" in the Episcopal Church), every detail of what it meant to be Episcopalian.

Then we found out that we were not alone. At other evangelical colleges, in places like Wheaton, Illinois, and Wenham, Massachusetts, students and faculty were joining Episcopal churches near their campuses. A group of them wrote a little book about it—*Evangelicals on the Canterbury Trail*. We had a name, and we had a mission. We could hold the radical, egalitarian, justice Lord together with the Lord described and known through common prayer and priestly order. Jesus could be master, ruler, and God and embodied in an ancient church renewed, as Christian orthodoxy and liturgy became our new utopianism.

We were not, however, the only evangelicals to be searching for a Jesus beyond the boxes we had known. We were longing for a deeper experience of Jesus as Lord, something that led us to a Christ who demanded a riskier understanding of obedience; a more politically relevant Jesus whose dominion could be built here and now. The revivals of the 1970s, with their emphasis on otherworldliness and getting saved, had given way to something else. The counterculture slowly morphed into a culture of narcissism and political pragmatism, creating a kind of spiritual vacuum for those seeking alternatives to the new self-centeredness in both religion and politics. With the election of Jimmy Carter, and his Christian concerns for policy and community, evangelicalism emerged from the shadows of American culture newly energized by the revivals, but also dissatisfied with the liberal idealism of the 1960s and 1970s.

In hindsight, it seems obvious that for significant numbers of Americans those two tumultuous decades birthed a rage for order and authority. It was no longer enough that Jesus saved us from the world; we wanted Jesus to fix it. We did not want to go up to the kingdom of heaven after we died (or at the Rapture). Instead, we wanted the kingdom to come down to us. We could build the kingdom here on earth. Thus, Jesus as Savior gave way to a powerful vision of Jesus as Lord, the One to whom our hearts, the earth, and the heavens bowed: Master, Ruler, and God of the New Jerusalem. He would put everything aright, put everything in order, and reward us for our faithfulness.

However much we shared these longings with other Christians, my college friends and I came to opposite conclusions about how Jesus would go about this than millions of others who also called themselves evangelical.

The photo appeared to have been taken in the 1950s. A smiling man, one of some girth, dressed in a suit and tie, stood in front of a crowd of people waving flags in bleachers decorated with bunting. Other than his dark suit, it was a study in red, white, and blue. The picture captured enthusiastic cheers from an audience led by a patriotic choir, their expressions edging toward a sort of religious ecstasy. Not terribly unusual in an election year, one would suppose, except for two things. First, this was 1980, not 1950, and such old-fashioned displays were not particularly in vogue (at least in California!). Second, the crowd had gathered at a town hall, and the flags were accompanied by the cross—on signs they carried, embossed on Bibles they carried, and as a noticeable pin on the man's lapel. The snapshot was not a conventional political rally; it was a gathering of Christians—and the man was the Reverend Jerry Falwell. He had started a political-religious crusade, the Moral Majority, to restore Christ's lordship in America.

A fellow student brought the picture to our religious studies class, a course in the theology and history of American evangelicalism. Most of our classmates laughed—the pastor seemed part buffoon, part charlatan. Some worried. One said that the image bore a resemblance to pictures of Fascist rallies of an earlier time. A few simply could not believe that anyone could take this seriously; the world had moved on.

"These fundamentalists," one said, "are a throwback to the 1920s. I bet they still don't believe in evolution!"

Another said, "Time for a new Scopes monkey trial!" referring to the 1925 Tennessee court case that had discredited conservative Christianity for a half century.

The professor explained that not all evangelicals liked *Sojourners*, some would never entertain listening to Ched Myers, and others thought Óscar Romero was a Communist and heretic. Most, he insisted, were like those in the picture—Southerners, Baptists, politically conservative with nostalgic ideas of God and country. Their Jesus embodied a traditional vision of the nuclear family and sexual purity, and their Jesus leaned right toward retributive justice and anti-Communism. They believed Jesus's lordship must be restored through New Testament church order, based in hierarchy, right belief, and male authority: obey the government (Rom. 13:1); wives, submit to your husbands (Eph. 5:22); and women, learn in silence (1 Tim. 2:11–12). What we knew as evangelicalism, here on the edge of the continent, where the beach was still fertile ground for the Jesus movement and the last of countercultural Christianity flourished, was the exception, not the rule.

I wondered if he was right—that we were the outliers in the evangelical world. I had been home a few weeks earlier. Scottsdale Bible had sold its building and moved to a giant property in North Scottsdale, where it planned a massive new campus for worship, education, and mission. A multipurpose space (really a fancy gym) had recently opened as the first of many buildings to come.

When I drove up to the new campus, the three crosses stood out front—the same three crosses that once marked the entrance to the old, more modest church. But something new had been added: next to the three crosses had been planted a flagpole. In a strong desert wind, Old Glory was fully unfurled and formed a patriotic backdrop to the crosses. As I walked through the parking lot, I noticed that dozens of cars were adorned with REAGAN bumper stickers next to the fish magnets and fading "I Found It" decals. At the door, someone was registering church members to vote.

Had it always been that way? And I just had not noticed? The church that had introduced me to Jesus as Savior had embraced him as Lord—with a political vengeance. And they were busy building his kingdom in the desert. Literally.

Back in class, the professor had us read a new book called *Fundamentalism and American Culture*, by George Marsden, who would go on to become one of America's best historians of religion. The book explained how evangelicalism had emerged in fights over evolution, biblical interpretation, and doctrine.[13] Apparently, evangelicals thought liberals, like my childhood Methodist friends and family, were bad, evil really, not just that our churches were boring. America was in a battle between true and false religion; "real Christians" had been persecuted for the better part of the century, while secular humanism and immorality had spread across the land. America was no longer a Christian nation, and evangelicals were mad.

This seemed far removed from us, from our radical California evangelicalism, where the golden glow of peace and liberation seemed the very light of God's kingdom. We were new wine; they old wineskins. As the Spirit poured itself out, the old wineskins would surely burst, and Jerry Falwell's movement would go with them. We felt confident this would be so.

In November, Ronald Reagan was elected president. Jerry Falwell and his Moral Majority took the credit. A flag-draped cross paraded into Washington, DC, that Jesus might claim lordship over America. Meanwhile, a small band of seniors at an evangelical college in California were left bewildered, devastated. We had not signed up for this. Somehow, Óscar

Romero had been martyred, and Pat Robertson was attending the inaugural ball. We had wanted a Jesus Caesar, and he had arrived. Just not as we expected. We did not understand how this had happened. Ask for a king, and you just might get one.

Way

I am the way, and the truth, and the life.

—*John 14:6*

If you feel like you are in a cage, why not walk out?" asked Gary. "As far as I can tell, no one has locked you in."

The next words did not need to be said out loud, as they hung in the air in silence, like overripened fruit needing harvest: *except yourself perhaps.*

I had seen a different counselor, that socially acceptable moniker for "therapist," a few years earlier, when, in 1989, shortly before my doctoral exams at Duke, I experienced panic attacks alternating with long bouts of sadness. I felt frozen, unable to move. When I first went to see him, a staff counselor in the student health office, he asked, "What department are you in?"

I replied, "Religious studies."

He laughed a little. "Well, I see mostly grad students from the English department, but I think religion may be a close second."

He was wry, funny actually, and called himself a "Rogerian, as in Will Rogers, not Carl." He was the one person who made me laugh in those days. Will Rogers (I always called him that, although it was not his real name) and I met once a week for a few months until I passed those examinations.

We talked about many things, mostly about theology and church, some about my experiences at seminary, the politics of Duke's religion department, and my recent—and increasingly unhappy—marriage. I had never talked with a therapist before, and I quickly realized how much I needed to explore and understand. Will Rogers helped me pick up the pieces, not feel so afraid, and get on with things. At the end of our time together, he said gently, "You've done some really good work. However, don't be surprised if you need to talk to someone like me again in the future." The comment did not seem awkward or wrong, especially when he restated a common theme in our conversations: "You may need to chat more about God."

Three years later, I was back in Santa Barbara. After graduating from college, I had moved east, gone to seminary, gotten married, failed at being a missionary, earned my doctorate, and then, unexpectedly, was hired as a professor at the school where I had once been a student. It had been a strange decade of leaving home and coming back again; I was either a Hobbit returning to the Shire or a poster child for the T. S. Eliot line, "The end of all our exploring will be to arrive where we started and know the place for the first time."

Thus, on a beautiful Santa Barbara day in 1992, I sat in Gary's office, on his stereotypical leather couch, waiting for the next words, "except yourself perhaps," to finally fall to the earth of reality. For months, we had talked about many things: theology and church, some of my experiences at seminary, the politics of the religion department where I now taught, and my impending—and painful—divorce. And, of course, God.

I had been through it all before. At least it felt that way. Maybe less Tolkien or Eliot and more *Groundhog Day*.

We sat in silence. Gary, a priest-turned-therapist with a contemplative demeanor, could hold attentive quiet like a monk. Although I said nothing, my thoughts were racing backward, retracing the spiritual path that had brought me here, and making me wonder why following Jesus now felt like a trap. How had I looked for salvation and found a box? How had I discovered a radical Lord and found myself back in prison?

Here I was, in my early thirties, having given nearly two decades to being the best, most faithful woman I could be, dedicated to renewing the spiritual and intellectual life of evangelicalism itself. I had not used the word "cage"; I said "jail." Gary called it a "cage." That startled me. Box. Jail. Cage. A prison of my own making? I could not take that on.

"They promise that the truth will set you free," I said. "That's a lie. It's conditional. Freedom if you agree, freedom if you accept their rules. Not real freedom."

Just a few weeks earlier, shortly after Christmas, I was sitting in a restaurant on the top floor of an elegant hotel in San Francisco with a colleague. He had grown up in evangelicalism, and he was extracting himself from his childhood faith. I sympathized and shared my own troubles and doubts. Although we were mostly talking about him, he suddenly blurted out: "What do you really want, Diana?"

There was that same silence, the empty space where answers dissolved. I gazed out the windows, looked over the city lights as they seemed to mark the way toward the bridge, like a multitude of stars guiding to the promise of new birth. Epiphany, revelation. God from God, Light from Light. *What do I want?* I sighed, hesitated, and said the only thing I could think of saying: "All the lights of San Francisco."

I wanted to cross the bridge.

"Well, maybe they built the cage," Gary said, interrupting my pondering. "But what is holding you now?" I could think of a million excuses but said nothing. He went on, "Walk out. Just walk out. The door is open."

"I am the door," said Jesus. "If anyone enters by Me, he will be saved and will go in and out and find pasture" (John 10:9, NKJV). The door is open? I had always imagined that the door was a one-way proposition. You went in, and there, inside the sheep pen (that is what Jesus was describing in the story about the door; some versions render it "I am the gate"), you were safe, saved, one of the flock. I never noticed the clause "will go in and out," indicating that the door might swing toward the world as well. Perhaps the spiritual life was not about finding the right box or a bigger cage, but wandering into pastures, following the light, crossing the bridge. Not hemmed in by walls, but walking in the open.

How had I confused a cage with a journey? The door was open. The path beyond, however, was less clear.

Throughout the New Testament, Jesus invites people to follow him, to walk with him, to go on a journey. There is nothing particularly new in this, as the Hebrew scriptures are full of stories of wanderers, pilgrims, exiles, and immigrants. And, of course, in the ancient world, teachers of all sorts—gurus, prophets, healers, mystics—gathered followers, those who embraced the master's message and put it into everyday practice. However, in the gospel of John, Jesus upped the theological ante. He not only taught a way inviting the curious to follow him, but he said *he* was the way: "I am the way, and the truth, and the life" (14:6).

That is a beautiful verse, a poetic and parabolic image of the way and the Way, a beckoning for all who know Jesus to willingly embrace the journey. That is the path, the road of liberation. And it would be freeing but for the next sentence: "No one comes to the Father except through me." Wait, what?

The welcome is pulled back, boundaries are put up, and suddenly the picture shifts, as the call to dance and sing and run through the fields fades into a rather grim image of judgment and exclusion.

This is what is sometimes called a clobber verse. In some Christian circles, if you dare wonder aloud if Jews, Buddhists, or secular people will be in heaven, a concerned friend will pull out this verse, smashing the words into the conversation to shut you up as surely as if wielding a weapon. The emphasis is not of the first half of the verse—"Way, truth, and life"— but the second half, where the weight falls on "no one" and "except through me." The way is not a way at all. Rather, it is a circumscribed sheep pen, with fences of razor wire. There is one way: *in*. The other way—*out*—means hell.

Many Christians cling ferociously to the exclusionary interpretation of this verse. About a dozen years ago, I was leading a retreat based on the themes "way," "truth," and "life." I hoped to shake up attendees by taking the verse out of its typical frame of proof-texting Christian exclusion; instead, I wanted to explore spiritual practices (the way), authenticity and integrity (the truth), and abundance and joy (life). At the first session, I had decided to offer a reflection on John 14:6, inviting attendees to open their spiritual imaginations to hear the words differently. I requested that the event organizer tell whoever was assigned to read the passage to stop after the word "life," to allow the group's attention to rest solely on the first sentence of the verse. We sang and prayed, and then she rose and read:

"Do not let your hearts be troubled. Believe in God, believe also in me. . . ." Thomas said to him, "Lord, we do not know where you are going. How can we know the way?" Jesus said to him, "I am the way, and the truth, and the life." (John 14:1, 5–6a)

I stood up and approached the pulpit to preach. But the reader kept right on going:

"No one comes to the Father except through me. If you know me, you will know my Father also. From now on you do know him and have seen him." (John 14:6b–7)

She looked up from the text and glared at me, still standing, Bible open.

"Well," I said, trying to make a joke of it, "I had wanted the reading to end halfway through verse 6. I guess my message didn't get through."

Still standing, she replied, "Oh no. That was the instruction, but I didn't want to do it. You have to have the second part. Jesus is the only way. That's the whole point." She shut her Bible, pulled it close to her chest as if a shield, and sat down, heaving a contemptuous sigh.

During the retreat, I went on to emphasize that "way," "truth," and "life" are relational words, all things that Jesus says he is. "Way" is not a technique or map, "truth" is not about philosophy or dogma, and "life" is not about going to heaven. In the mystical poetry of John, Jesus uses these terms to explain how he embodies a way of being in this world so close to the heart of God that God can be known in and through Jesus.

This short verse is part of a much longer story, one that takes up four chapters in the gospel of John and begins when Jesus tells his friends that he is leaving them: "Little children, I am with you only a little longer. You will look for me; and . . . where I am going you cannot come" (13:33). You can imagine this was hard to hear, especially by those who had followed him for three years. "You can't leave us! What are we going to do??" Jesus probably saw the fear in their eyes and the confusion on their faces, so he quickly added, "I give you a new commandment, that you love one another. Just as I have loved you, you also should love one another" (13:34).

Jesus's instruction to "love one another" in his stead, however, did not seem quite good enough. Peter says, "Lord, where are you going?" (13:36). And then Thomas adds, "Lord, we do not know where you are going. How can we know the way?" (14:5). They are not worried about people of other religions; rather, they are scared for themselves and losing their friend.[1]

Thus, this whole story alternates between fear and love, worry and trust, abandonment and comfort. The disciples are frightened that their friend and teacher is leaving; Jesus reassures them that, although they cannot follow him into suffering and death, he is present with them through love, trust, and faith *in* him, not in ideas *about* him. "I have loved you; abide in my love" (15:9).

The disciples have an intense fear of separation (no co-incidence the section opens with Jesus referring to them as "little children") from God, from Jesus, and probably from one another as well. They have known what it means to live deeply into God, to have overcome estrangement from the divine. They formed a community, a band of fellow travelers. They cannot fathom losing any of that. If Jesus goes away, will they be banished from God's presence, from the joy they had known together? Is that their fate?

Jesus says no. Fear, estrangement, separation, isolation—these are not the last words. Instead, Jesus invites his followers to dwell in him, even as he dwells in God. And as God has been made known through the works of love Jesus has done, so Jesus will continue to be known through the works of love the disciples will do. This is a dynamic sort of dwelling, not a static thing, rather like a tented God on the journey, instead of one inside unmovable walls. "I am the way . . . and not one of you, my fearful friends, knows God apart from what I have embodied for you; stay close, keep faith." This is not a threat; it is a promise. The very walls that once held back God's presence are about to break, and, through the journey of self-giving love Jesus is about to take, mercy and justice will cover the earth.

As one scholar says, the seemingly judgmental phrase "no one comes to the Father" is "not the last word":

"Except" is like a window that lets light into a closed room. It fits what the Gospel says about Christ coming as

light into a world of darkness and serving as the door . . .
that enables people to enter God's sheepfold. Rather than
restricting access to God the word "except" creates access
to God.[2]

There would be no way *except that* the love of God has made
a way. God would be distant, unavailable, separated from us
except for love. We would be all alone. There would be much
to fear *except* for the way, the way that is wide open to those
who trust. Invitation, not exclusion.

The disciples wanted to cower in fear. They did not want
Jesus to leave. They wanted everything to stay the same. Yet
something was changing; the certainty they had known was
eroding under their feet. Maybe Jesus was not quite who
they had imagined him to be, their friend, teacher, Savior,
and Lord. Some of their relatives did not like Jesus, one of
their own had already left and would betray Jesus, religious
authorities were testing them, and the Romans considered
them all troublemakers.

I am the way, the truth, and the life, Jesus assured them. *Except
for my showing you the way of God you'd get lost.* And, with that,
Jesus set on his own path of suffering and sent his friends on
the way.

Lost

Being a Christian is about finding and getting found by Jesus.
Indeed, the first bumper sticker on my first car proudly

proclaimed: "I Found It!" No words capture that experience better than the lyrics of *Amazing Grace*:

> *Amazing grace! How sweet the sound*
> *That saved a wretch like me!*
> *I once was lost, but now am found;*
> *Was blind, but now I see.*

Being lost is the state of being outside the faith. Lost in sin. Lost in doubt. Lost to the wiles of the devil. No one ever wants to be lost. Faith is about being found.

Yet somehow I found myself lost in the oddest way—while attending seminary. After college, I went on for additional theological education. The plan was to get a degree in theology and history and then get a teaching position in a Christian school overseas, perhaps in Africa. Although many of my classmates went to Fuller Seminary in Pasadena, I had a hankering to go back east. And so, a year after graduation, at age twenty-three, I matriculated at Gordon-Conwell Theological Seminary, north of Boston. And it was there that I started to get lost.

It is a bit of a convention to criticize seminaries. Indeed, the joke is to call them "cemeteries," because students often find their faith dies when they start studying theology. That was not what happened to me, however. I loved the academic study of theology, the Bible, and church history. And, for the most part, I liked my classmates, finding them surprisingly imaginative and idealistic. My fellow students at seminary were not terribly different from my religious studies friends at college. What caused me to get lost was an institutional fight between faculty members, a conflict between orthodoxy and Christian practice.

In the 1980s, the seminary was divided into two groups. One group was made up of those professors who were generously minded, as ecumenical as evangelicals could possibly be in those days, supportive of women, and willing to engage new methods of biblical studies. The other group included those who were concerned with boundaries, purity, order, and orthodoxy, especially as interpreted through the theology of John Calvin.

The first group was open to changes in American culture, wanting to ask new questions of the Bible and theology; the second group was increasingly worried that Western Christianity was being overly influenced by secularism and compromised by sin. The former were mostly mainline Protestants, primarily Methodists and Presbyterians, who had gotten born again in the 1970s; a large number of charismatic Christians; and a surprisingly sizable group of Episcopalians. The latter were mostly Baptists, and Presbyterians from smaller (not mainline) denominations like the Presbyterian Church in America (PCA) and the Orthodox Presbyterian Church (OPC), and they usually just called themselves "Reformed."

Coming from college in California, I had mostly known the open sort of evangelicals. I was, of course, aware of more conservative evangelicals through either Scottsdale Bible or the success of the new Moral Majority. But the conservative Gordon-Conwell professors were different: literate, learned, and politically sophisticated, they were anxious cultural critics committed to Protestant creedal orthodoxy. These professors looked down their noses at Jerry Falwell as much as they did Catholics and liberal Protestants, but when pressed, they admitted they sided with fundamentalists more than they did with liberal or ecumenical Christians. Their real heroes were nineteenth-century Presbyterian theologians, mostly those who had taught at Princeton Seminary, and antebellum Southern thinkers, who, interestingly enough, defended slaveholding.

At the seminary, the generous evangelicals and the Reformed were basically at war—there were heresy trials and faculty firings, all of which had created an atmosphere of distrust, division, and fear. The students became proxies in the fight: the socially aware Jesus-y types of the 1970s versus foot soldiers in a new Reformation to save the soul of American culture and Christianity.

I hate writing about this now, for I am ashamed of how I behaved in this conflict. At first, I easily sided with the familiar group, but the longer I was at the seminary, the more influenced I was by the second. In the struggle between the two, the orthodox Reformed gained the upper hand, and the more open-minded professors were slowly picked off through theological witch hunts and crusades. As power shifted toward the Calvinists, I confess that I gave in.

A few years later, in Gary's office, I learned that it is fairly typical for young women to struggle in their quest for knowledge and not at all unusual for them to draw back toward accepting external (and mostly male) authorities before developing mature voices and critical-thinking skills. As researchers have discovered about women in academia, "The woman [is] nearly always pitted against an authority, usually a professor and usually male. These [are] unequal contests. The teacher wields very real power over the student, although masked with genial camaraderie."[3]

At the seminary, I wanted the approval of authorities; I was willing to go along with them, figuring that they were smarter and better educated than I was, and that they knew more about what was better for the future of the church than I ever could. I would always have internal doubts about the theology and politics being taught, but even my closest friends from those days will testify that I was not terribly forthcoming about them. These lines from poet Marge Piercy well describe both my spiritual and my intellectual life at that time:

Phrases of men who lectured her
Drift and rustle in piles:
Why don't you speak up?[4]

I couldn't. I didn't know how.

I cannot, however, blame my choices entirely on the faculty. There was something exhilarating about being part of a new Reformation, about turning Western Christianity back toward its great age of faith of theological truth and spiritual certainty. I was reaching for my own voice and vocation, however uneven the path toward those things would be. For several years, I sought the safety of Jesus as Savior, and then I leaned into the authenticity of practicing the faith with Jesus as my Lord. At seminary, I had another chance to explore who Jesus was and what he meant.

Slowly I came to the conclusion that the main problem of the age was neither safety nor authenticity—it was authority. At the tail end of the baby boomer generation, the free-flowing Jesus movement began to recede. Radical Christianity would be replaced by sterner views. In an age of Reagan and the time of AIDS, a different sort of gospel emerged. We humans had placed ourselves above God, undoing the natural order of society and creation, rebels for our own cause and not that of Jesus. The same impulses that birthed the Moral Majority were present at Gordon-Conwell too, just in a more sophisticated academic and literary package. But the message was the same: submission to divinely ordained authorities was the way of Jesus. Suddenly, to be conservative was to be countercultural.

In the 1980s, any tension I had felt between Jesus as kin and Jesus as king completely gave way to the latter. Order meant hierarchy and subjugation, and the goal of the spiritual life was to find one's place in God's design. All around us, people were giving up on any sort of common good, as materialistic excess emerged as the new cultural value: *Dynasty*, Jim and Tammy Faye, Donald Trump—lifestyles of the rich and famous. The remnants of older patterns of class and religion were upended and replaced by cash and celebrity. Jesus of the Methodist Sunday school was gone, and the Jesus of Scottsdale Bible had become a television evangelist with big ratings and political ambitions to match.

Against this backdrop, it was easy to see why many serious Christians had begun to wonder what had gone wrong and blamed the problems on the loss of authority. Dying to self no longer meant finding Jesus on the streets or in a Bible study led by one's peers. Dying to self meant obedience to God's way, aligning with an orthodox church, accepting your place in the universe, and being faithful to it.

People constantly quoted from the last chapters of Paul's letter to the Ephesians: "Wives, be subject to your husbands as you are to the Lord. For the husband is the head of the wife just as Christ is the head of the church" (5:22–23); "Children, obey your parents" (6:1); and "Slaves, obey your earthly masters" (6:5). Men, women, children, slaves—that was the divine order of things.[5] Paul continues: "For our struggle is . . . against the cosmic powers of this present darkness" (6:12), which would only be overcome through obedience to God's word.

For good Christian women that meant marrying a good Christian man and having lots of children. Careers were not considered bad or ungodly—if one's husband approved and there was no chance of holding a position of authority in a church—and well-educated women were to use their gifts as teachers, lawyers, doctors, even judges and politicians, to forward the new Reformation and build the kingdom of God here on earth. Lots of seminary men, eager to prove that they were not sexist, said that they did not want wives who were "doormats"; they wanted spiritual helpmates to join in this new godly order. Thus, it was more than possible—indeed, it happened all the time—to be a strong woman, smart and skilled, and yet completely submissive at the same time. Think of Anita Bryant and Phyllis Schlafly, or Serena Joy in *The Handmaid's Tale*.

Thus, I found my place. I got brilliant grades in seminary, and I disappeared into order and orthodoxy, into finding my role as a theologically conservative woman in a world of male authorities. In my midtwenties, I did not think of that as a problem. I was grateful for the support I received from powerful men. It was God's design. If I died to myself, if I disappeared, that was all the better.

Map or Maze?

When we think of a way, we often think of a destination: the way to where? In the case of Jesus, he is the way to the Father, to being with God forever, point A to point B. And between the points, the route is plotted on a map. The map is the journey, not all the things that happen along the way. The destination is the meaning and purpose of the trip, and staying on the road is the most important thing.

The seminary was obsessed with the map. The map was the right way, the one way, what you had to believe in order to arrive. The map was called "orthodoxy."

In college, theology classes were exercises in exploration. We read widely in Christian thought, from the early church fathers to modern thinkers like Karl Barth and Rudolf Bultmann and, at rare moments of inclusion, liberation theologians like Gustavo Gutiérrez and Rosemary Radford Ruether.

At seminary, that changed. Evangelical theology was all that mattered, questions were not welcomed, and thinking correctly about Jesus was a life-and-death concern. Theology was the map, and drawing that map correctly was key to getting to the right destination. No need to be in conversation with creative ideas or liberal heresies. All that mattered was theology, and all that mattered in theology was getting it right. And so the arguments, seemingly endless bouts of explosive outrage, over things that most of the world did not care about—about translations of Greek words, whether to dunk or sprinkle babies or adults, whether the Rapture would occur before or after the Tribulation or even at all, whether hell was a literal place of eternal conscious torment or even existed beyond this life, and whether women were allowed to preach or teach without a male authority "over" them or had to always be silent in church.

The defense of right theology even edged toward violence. A group of men proudly recounted how Nicholas of Myra (yes, St. Nicholas), an ancient champion of orthodoxy, had slapped Arius, his theological opponent. A professor admitted that he wanted to destroy every stained-glass window he could find, like the Puritan army commander Oliver Cromwell in seventeenth-century England. The new Reformation would come with a theological sword, they insisted. Winning counted. Orthodoxy was everything—all that right belief, accompanied by a terrifying certainty.

The students performed as if acting for the professors—those who would write recommendations for denominations and send along approvals for their ordination. Being orthodox was the way, a road guarded by its own gatekeepers, that host of superiors who must be assured that you were worthy to handle holy words and sacraments on behalf of the true church. We were not only taught about hierarchies and submission; we were shaped into both if we wanted jobs or positions as pastors, teachers, writers, or missionaries.

There was a huge bulletin board in the central commons called "Iron Sharpens Iron," based on Proverbs 27:17, "Iron sharpens iron, so one man sharpens another" (NASB), where students who fancied themselves the next Martin Luther posted long rants and screeds, often attacking fellow students or accusing some instructor of heresy. It was sort of a precursor to Twitter, with less iron sharpening iron and more theological Darwinism. Winning an argument on the board proved one's theological rigor. I had one fervent hope in seminary—never to show up on the board. Keep your head down and conform. Or else.

Orthodoxy took a very particular form at Gordon-Conwell, that of a vigorously muscular Calvinism. Although other Christians may have recited creeds or considered themselves theologically orthodox, no group did it with such assurance as the self-proclaimed "manly" Calvinists. John Calvin emphasized a sovereign and distant God dwelling in glory, complete human sinfulness, salvation by faith alone, the primacy of scripture, and ecclesiastical order and discipline. In church history, Calvinism is infamous for double predestination—the doctrine that God chooses some people for heavenly bliss while damning others to eternal punishment.

Over the centuries, Calvinism has been interpreted and reinterpreted in myriad ways, but at Gordon-Conwell the favored versions were those of the English Puritans and the Scottish Presbyterians, both forms that had a historical record of linking Calvinist orthodoxy with blood feuds and a raw use of power to forward God's kingdom. Some of my Southern Baptist classmates adopted Calvinism and wedded it to a new fundamentalist movement to take over their denomination. One professor made a project of converting me to a Calvinist sort of Episcopalianism, a theological tradition strong in England, but one that had never had much influence in the United States. He besieged me with books written by Calvinist Anglicans, providing me with a way to both join the theological crusade and retain my affection for the Episcopal Church.

More significantly, however, I fell in love with one of those orthodox Presbyterians and got married, thus submitting myself to a world of hierarchy and authority where Calvinist certainty was everything and my place in God's good order of the universe was assured. I had followed the way of right belief, the path of salvation—right to the altar.

Within months of getting married, I was miserable. When I quietly confessed this to a Calvinist friend, he replied, "Well, Christian faith isn't about happiness."

Probably the biggest theological conversion I underwent in those days was embracing an increasingly low view of humanity. That was one thing the seminary did really well—prove how bad people could be. I had grown up in a surprisingly optimistic Methodist home, a teen who had cried in agreement upon reading the final words of Anne Frank: "In spite of everything, I still believe that people are truly good at heart." That optimism had carried me through abuse and doubt to the sunny hopefulness and idealism of being a Jesus girl and a vision of serving the poor and saving the world for Christ.

Now, however, the prayers recited around me referred to human beings as worms, as being less worthy than dogs, as miserable offenders who mourned, "There is no health in us." Our very existence was an affront to God—my being an offense. Worship became an exercise in rehearsing sin, begging for mercy, listening to a doctrinally correct sermon, and singing hymns to an all-powerful God who deigned to save. I collapsed into darkness, intellectually convinced that humanity was evil, so far fallen that there was no remnant of good in us, utterly dependent on a God who may—in wisdom—choose to save a few, among whom I fervently prayed to be counted. My Calvinist friends said that they were willing to be damned for the glory of God, because, of course, we all deserved it. *Soli Deo gloria.*

As my theological estimation of human beings fell, so my theological vision of God rose. God became more and more distant, untouchable in glory, surrounded by angels, and dwelling in complete holiness. With a low view of humanity and a highly exalted view of God, a huge gap opens between us, brute beasts that we are, and God. Of course, this is a fundamental problem of Christian theology—how a wayward people can be saved—but it was exaggerated in ways that took on the shape of sin porn.

In classical theology, Jesus overcomes the gap by being born into the world, laying down his life as a sort of bridge between the worlds, and satisfying the debt humanity owes to God's honor. Despite the centrality of Jesus to this, he began to seem more an instrument to an end—a means of paying the debt to God—than a real human being. These Calvinists were, frankly, cold when it came to Jesus, all the love and joy of following him subsumed under the mechanics of salvation. For all the talk about the blood of the cross, this Jesus was bloodless, an impersonal technical fix to the human problem of sin. Following Jesus meant trusting that he had paid the debt for your sins, and from your eternal gratitude you dedicated yourself to obeying his will. It was very transactional.

Yet everything in this orthodox Calvinist world depended on maintaining that yawning gap, the divide between human depravity and divine holiness, which was an uneven dualism at that because God held all the cards. My then husband preached a sermon on Psalm 2: "He who sits in the heavens laughs; the Lord has them in derision . . ." (2:4) This scornful

God is one of wrath: "You shall break them with a rod of iron, and dash them in pieces like a potter's vessel." (2:9) He pulled a cheap pot from behind the pulpit and smashed it to the floor. The congregation gasped, a strange collective snort of shock and approval. "That is what God thinks of those who plot against him," he said. "Take refuge in him before it is too late." For a brief moment, I imagined my heart the shards.

By the time I had graduated from seminary and entered the doctoral program at Duke, my universe was populated with a disparate array: Jonathan Edwards's sinners in the hands of an angry God, Southern theologians and their long tomes justifying slavery, Reformed thinkers who rejected Darwin, critics of the very Protestant liberals who birthed and raised me, women preaching sermons on why women should not preach sermons, and a contemporary writer named Francis Schaeffer, who bemoaned the end of culture and called for a crusade against abortion. It was like falling into a world of theological madness, a horrifying fun house of refracted delusions. The only way to survive was to give in, believing whatever grim apparition appeared in the mirror at the next turn. I had followed the map into this grotesque maze.

The odd thing was that I wasn't the only one to get lost. Jesus disappeared too.

Those mirrors—Calvin, creeds and catechisms, submission, order, and correct polity—distorted Jesus beyond recognition. I discovered that the more I gazed in the mirrors, the more elusive Jesus became. Friend? How childish. Teacher? Liberal moralism. Savior? Only if you are among the elect. Lord? Christ-Caesar, the authoritarian king. The Way? True doctrine and submission will set you free. Or take you to a place you never imagined.

So what did I do? I tried to jump through a window to shatter the glass and find a way out. Maybe Jesus would be in the shards. But my own terror stopped me. Will Rogers proscribed Prozac.

The Less-Traveled Road

"If I hear the word 'journey' one more time, I may scream," Matt laughed. "Jo-or-neey, j-oooo-urrr-nee," he mocked, stretching two syllables to three and then a nearly impossible four.

It was about a year and a half before the window incident. Matt, a seminary friend, sat in our living room in Durham, North Carolina, less than a mile from Duke, where I was a student. He had been part of the Episcopal group at Gordon-Conwell, was working in an Episcopal church, and had stopped by for a visit while traveling. We were not talking about Calvinism; rather, we were talking about the church.

"That's all anyone ever says," he moaned, "'Where are you on your journey? How's your journey?'"

My husband and I laughed, knowing what he meant. "Journey" was the latest buzzword in Episcopal churches, a way to talk about following Jesus without being terribly concrete about theology. "Journey" was liberal, and liberal was bad. The orthodox did not speak of journeys. The orthodox spoke of obedience. "Jo-or-neey," they both intoned, followed by uproarious laughter.

There we sat ridiculing "journey." Or there they sat, as I had been exiled to the kitchen to prepare dinner. I had only been married for three years, but all my husband and I had left was shared certainty of truth and scorn for theologies less rigorous than our own. I joined the mockery out of solidarity; after many quarrels over my vocation, supporting his contempt for what he called "liberalism" seemed a small price to pay for maintaining the tentative truce.

The truth was that I had always liked the word "journey"— and I was not upset by its increasing mention in sermons and in small groups at church. The first book I ever loved was *Little Women*, a book about the spiritual journeys of Meg, Jo, Beth, and Amy to find their own voices, gifts, and loves. Louisa May Alcott had modeled her book on an older classic about a spiritual journey, John Bunyan's *Pilgrim's Progress*. To make the connection overt, Alcott paraphrased him in her epigraph:

Yea, let young damsels learn of [mercy] to prize
The world which is to come, and so be wise;
For little tripping maids may follow God
Along the ways which saintly feet have trod.

My first-loved book was a plea for girls to understand their lives as a journey toward goodness and God. I have no idea how many times I had read it since I was nine, but that well-read copy accompanied me to Duke, where it sat on a shelf next to histories of Puritanism and texts on American religion.

The journey impulse, first nurtured by *Little Women*, has marked my spiritual sense, and I resonate with peripatetic saints of all sorts—from ancient Celtic monks who wandered land and sea for Christ to Dorothy Day, who, while founding houses of hospitality, displayed a restless sense of moving deeper into both the world and God. In 1979, when I was still in college, a professor assigned a book called *Journey Inward, Journey Outward*. No surprise that I loved it. The author, Elizabeth O'Connor, told the story of a Christian community organized around two spiritual journeys—the interior one toward knowing our true self and knowing God, and the one directed outward into the world to enact God's justice and love. These two movements comprise the way of Jesus, a continual flow of breath: in, out; in, out; in, out. "Breathe it all in," writes poet Mary Oliver. "Love it all out." This spiritual dynamism was the wellspring of knowing Jesus, of my inner searching and outward service.

By the time Matt was sitting in my living room, the journey was still calling, but I struggled to hear it. Truth be told, I could barely breathe. In seminary and graduate school, I had learned much about Jesus, but I had forgotten to know Jesus. The little girl in the woods, who had known Jesus as friend, had been domesticated by rules and dogma imposed from outside, reinforced by her own fears.

I was moody, depressed, worried all the time. This was confusing, because others had convinced me that right belief about God led to what Jesus called "abundant life." But the more constricted my doctrine became, the more constrained my heart felt. Right belief may have provided a port of safety in a tumultuous world—and it is worth remembering that the United States and Russia nearly launched World War III in the mid-1980s and that this was a frightening moment in history—but it also stunted my spiritual journey, almost killing me in the process.

My truest self was not the one who mocked the journey or the one who gloried in authority, order, and right belief. Deep within, I was still the child who ambled by streams and through fields, snuck outside to stare at the stars, and felt the magic of falling snow; I could still summon the scent of the roses and lilac that grew in my yard decades ago. There was some sort of wild gene that ran through the female line of my clan, one of seeing and healing and insight, of questions and curiosity, a spiritual disposition that had gotten one of my ancestors hanged as a witch.

I understood the inward journey, the going deep within, to places of interiority that escaped words. This quest is a mapless journey—there is no single road—the only guides to it are nature, saints, poetry, song, and Spirit. When you dare leave the map behind, Jesus emerges as the road itself and the Light that guides. The Quakers refer to this as the "inner light"; medieval mystics speak of Jesus likewise. Of it Meister Eckhart wrote: "There is a journey you must take. It is a journey without destination. There is no map. Your soul will lead you. And you can take nothing with you."[6] Conventional Christianity (of many different denominations) prefers to see Jesus as a directive or destination rather than this path; for them "way" is a noun, not a verb. On the mapless journey, however, all is movement. There is no destination, only the enveloping presence of love.

Years later, when evangelical Calvinism was far back in my rearview mirror, a blog—written by an evangelical Calvinist—derisively called me a "mystic." The blogger hated mysticism, seeing it as the satanic opposite of orthodox religion and believing it was his mission to reveal the dangers of experiential faith to unsuspecting innocents who might be led astray. He did not seem to know that mysticism was a great tradition in Christian history—not Christianity's dominant note, but certainly its minor chord. Flowing beneath the institutional church like a hidden stream has always been the wisdom of the mapless journey (even, oddly enough, when its practitioners, like St. Teresa of Ávila, tried to draw spiritual maps to explain it!), the wordless knowing.

Not all mystics are remembered, many were martyred by their own church, and a few were made saints. Yet for all their diversity and the uniqueness of their experiences, they tend to express what is within through circles and spirals, poetry and revelations, in visions of love rather than dogma. Theirs was the alternative way, unconcerned with worldly power, seeking only to follow a less-traveled path. "Since I gave myself to Love's service, whether I lose or win, I am resolved," wrote the thirteenth-century Dutch mystic Hadewijch of Brabant in language echoing others'. "I will always give her thanks, whether I lose or win; I will stand in her power."[7] For her, love was the energy of an unreachable destination, the way of a "Being beyond all bliss."[8]

To claim to be a mystic is not something one should probably do, for what Hadewijch describes is an intense and, most likely at her level, rare experience. To be called a mystic, however, is quite another thing. Although intended as an insult, I took it as a compliment. My critic correctly recognized that I did not understand faith to be confined to what he deemed orthodox.

Instead, I held forth the way as an experience of Jesus, following what he taught and embodied. The way had more to do with tearing down boundaries between people, in union and solidarity with God and humanity, and finding God so deeply in the world that the kin-dom is birthed. This radical, boundaryless, radiant vision of Jesus surely terrified more than a few conservative Calvinists—and a whole lot of other Christians as well. Yet it remains the silent spring of Christian faith, ever flowing, carrying any unafraid to enter the waters along the way:

> Come, my Way, my Truth, my Life:
> Such a way as gives us breath;
> Such a truth as ends all strife,
> Such a life as killeth death.[9]

Jesus is the creative breath, true peace, and abundant life, all the things I had lost. I wish I could say that I heard this lovely, lilting inner voice while at Duke. I did not. I did, however, begin to hear groans and grief, feeling a gut intuition that something was deeply wrong.

So I went to see Will Rogers. And I also returned to some books that I had read in college in a January term course years earlier on Christian devotional classics. It was an unusual class, its syllabus full of mostly Catholic books, mostly from the Middle Ages—*Practicing the Presence of God*, by Brother Lawrence; *The Imitation of Christ*, by Thomas à Kempis; *The Interior Castle*, by Teresa of Ávila; and *The Dark Night of the Soul*, by John of the Cross.

All of these works had made a difference in my spiritual life, and all still spoke to me, but none quite as strongly as *The Dark Night of the Soul*. When I first read it at nineteen, much of the book's wisdom escaped me—and, I confess, nearly ten years later its depth was still mostly beyond my ken. What moved me was a simple spiritual truth. The journey could be hard, really hard, a descent into abandonment:

In secret places where no other spied
I went without my sight
Without a light to guide
Except the heart that lit me from inside.

The ancient language of journey described the dual way as the *via positiva* and the *via negativa*, the path of affirmation and the path of abandonment. The first way is the experience of the things that God is—love, joy, thanks, grace, beauty— known through prayer, worship, devotion, and awe. The second way is the experience of what God is *not*—unknown, hidden, absent, beyond—entered into purposefully through fasting and meditation or, more often than not, as John of the Cross depicted it, by unwelcome accident, like being thrown down a set of stairs. One is the path of joy, the other of suffering.

Nobody had warned me of this way, except perhaps Jesus. He told the disciples they could not go where he was going, the way to the cross and death. Yet, as countless of his followers know, you might not get to the point where you are the bloodied Jesus at Calvary, but you can get frighteningly close. I had neither fasted nor meditated seeking the *via negativa*, but somehow I had gotten there. I did not like it, and I wanted to get back on the other road, the right one. Slowly, however, I learned that Jesus as way included both joy and loss—they were not separate roads, more like companion routes. The ways of affirmation and abandonment were not easy, but they sometimes merged.

If I was consigned to this journey, I figured I would need some guides. Will Rogers helped. I eventually found a sweet church that helped too. I loved studying church history and threw myself into teaching. That helped. But I was so unhappy, walking the way without any sense of hope. I could not eat. I lost thirty pounds. I was shrinking away. I did not, however, try to jump out a window again. Even so, echoing the words of John of the Cross, "I remained, lost in oblivion."

It was all a bit of a puzzle, a paradox really. It was hard to ponder too deeply, for there were papers to write and preliminary exams to pass. Getting a doctorate was a consuming distraction.

I am the way, and the truth, and the life. I kept walking. Slowly, one step at a time. After all, it was a journey.

Risks

Eight years after the evening with Matt, a companion and I were traveling in England. On a particularly lovely summer day, we went walking in the Cotswolds. We followed a public footpath, one of those old routes through the countryside, worn by generations of people traversing fields and woods to farms and villages.

We were mostly alone on our walk. The landscape was beautiful, with gentle hills and quaint cottages; the conversation was ever better, mostly about books and faith. We came to a fenced pasture at the edge of a farm. There was usually a gate in the fence for public access, allowing pedestrians to continue on their way. This gate was a little hard to find, but when we finally found it, we saw a notice tacked on one of its posts: BEWARE OF BULL.

We looked at one another. "Beware of bull?"

"Where is it?" I asked.

Our eyes scanned the field.

"Over there," my companion pointed. "On the far side." He opened the gate. "Let's go."

I took a deep breath. Really? We were doing this? We followed the path, keeping wary eyes toward the edge of the pasture. We did not dawdle. The bull did not move. And we breathed easier when we arrived at the gate at the other end of the pasture.

Journeys are risky. Sometimes you've got to get past the bull. And on a faith journey, there can be a lot of bull.

When I got to seminary, I was seeking security and certainty, not an unusual desire for someone in her twenties, especially at a time when the surrounding culture is in a reactionary mode. "Believing that we are right about God," says biblical scholar Peter Enns, "helps give us a sense of order in an otherwise messy world."[10] Seminary heightens this sense. Often students are at a stage where their future is uncertain and ideas in flux, but theological certainty almost seems like a requirement for graduation—or job placement! Authorities demand that you know what you think about God—or what the church thinks about God—and you must present those beliefs in convincing ways in papers, sermons, and ministry.

Being thoughtful and well read in theology is a good thing for those in seminary, and frankly for any Christian. It is equally true that, as Father Richard Rohr points out, "Religion has turned the biblical idea of faith . . . into a need and even a right to certain knowing, complete predictability, and perfect assurance about whom and what God likes or doesn't like."[11] I had gone to seminary expecting that it would strengthen my faith; instead, it presented the sort of religion Father Richard describes.

There is a line, often a very thin one, between knowledge and dogmatism, between clarity and certainty—and far too many people fail to distinguish between being able to share the Good News of Jesus and zealous preoccupation with correct doctrine. "Aligning faith in God and certainty about what we believe," insists Enns, "and needing to be right in order to maintain a healthy faith—these do not make for a healthy faith in God." He calls this the "sin of certainty."[12]

I confess: I sinned.

Fear and a need for approval had caused me to go in the wrong gate. Instead of admitting that I had gone the wrong way, and instead of racing through the field to the exit, I stayed put, insisting that I was in the right place and that, no matter what anyone else said, this was the right path. I had confused being right, believing correct doctrine about Jesus, with walking the way in trust and expectation of surprise. The former is pigheadedness; the latter is faith.

And the worst thing? I got angry with those who disagreed with me, an anger verging on a kind of theologically justified contempt. At Duke, I would be challenged with new ideas, but I stuck to certainty, digging in my heels. At least in public. What was going on inside was a different story, hidden from view. Too risky to reveal.

Risk is hard. Some people seem to love risk—athletes, adventurers, artists, actors. Most of us, I suspect, favor a mix of risk and safety, sometimes choosing challenge and other times seeking conformity and comfort. Risk itself is complicated: on occasion we choose it, but sometimes it shows up like an unwelcome guest. I have been willing to risk, yet I have also sacrificed much for safety and tried to avoid challenging choices when possible. Yet as a young woman, when it came to faith, I had become risk-averse.

At seminary, I loved theology and the New Testament, but I had witnessed cruel crusades conducted by men in those fields against their own peers. Their message was clear: theology and biblical studies were risky endeavors. And it was not only in the seminary. In the 1980s, the entire evangelical world roiled with such inquisitions, especially around issues of biblical literalism and the role of women in the church. There was a lot of bull—and bullying. I did not have a taste for theological blood; neither did I want to become others' sacrificial lamb in their quest for orthodox fame.

So I opted to study church history—the historians I knew were irenic and wise with a knack for staying out of trouble. History, I figured, was a low-risk option when it came to Christian intellectual endeavor. In graduate school, I pursued American religious history. I would be safe, on this side of the fence. It never occurred to me that studying the past could upset one's present.

Wrestling

At Duke, all church history doctoral students—whether specializing in the first century or the twentieth—had to attend an evening seminar led by different members of the history department. One month early in my program, Elizabeth Clark, a scholar of early Christianity, presented research. I felt out of my depth, as her field was farthest from my own.

But the topic was interesting: the formation of the creeds, focused on the early Council of Nicaea. She opened her talk by speaking about the extraordinary diversity of Christianity in the Roman Empire, or, as she said, "Christianities," the patchwork of communities, varied practices, and distinctive doctrines that stretched across the Mediterranean. At Gordon-Conwell, professors spoke of early Christianity as a community of martyrs, a successful mission movement, and a bulwark of orthodox theology—a single entity headed by bishops and theologians. No one suggested that there was theological diversity other than right versus wrong.

That diversity, she continued, caused a particular problem when the emperor Constantine converted to Christianity and proceeded to make it the state religion. Constantine was struggling with political divisions and needed to consolidate his power through imperial unity and uniformity. Christianity seemed an ideal vehicle to strengthen his hand, as religion had always sanctified the empire. But there was a problem: Christians did not agree on even basic issues, like the person of Jesus or the nature of the Trinity. If Christianity were to be Rome's official religion, which Christianity would it be? Thus, the emperor convened a council.

According to the conventional story, the bishops discussed the merits of the arguments, while Constantine listened carefully, after which he deferred to the orthodox position as if miraculously directed. Then she said, "How would this be possible? Emperors don't defer to bishops. Power works the other way around."

Her lecture was not about the truth of the content of the creeds. She was talking about the historical construction of orthodoxy amid the diversity of ancient Christianities. The creeds were the result of politics, power, patriarchy, and privilege, part of a larger argument about who would shape the Christian narrative, and not some miracle of the Holy Spirit. It was a conflicted history involving humans with messy motives and much self-interest. Orthodoxy and heresy as products of power was not something I had ever heard of, much less considered.

But she had a point. Who really thinks an emperor is going to act justly? Politics and power have been part of the deal since the beginning. Jesus was killed for political reasons. His followers were persecuted for political reasons. Why wouldn't Constantine privilege a particular form of theology for political reasons? A few years later, I read these words explaining the results of the council: "Christianity, at least in its official version, froze into a system of mandatory precepts that were codified into creeds and strictly monitored by a powerful hierarchy and imperial decrees. Heresy became treason, and treason became heresy." The author referred to this as an "ancient corporate merger" of faith and empire.[13] Such observations would barely faze me a few years hence, but at the time Professor Clark's lecture worried me.

Although it began with a single lecture by a lone professor, further study of history continued to undermine my theological certainty. There were any number of good historians at Duke who recited the creeds in worship, yet still taught the same historical questions and methods, as did Professor Clark, which felt "unorthodox" to me. But I was becoming a good enough historian to understand that theology is not isolated from political, economic, and social realities. Context matters. Witnesses close to events have motives in telling their stories and can be unreliable reporters. The powerful write history. Texts are expressions of the experience of the person or community who wrote them. Evidence is tampered with, documents are destroyed, and arguments of opponents are falsified to prove a point.

These are the concerns of historical inquiry, whether one is a believer or not. And history students, no matter how devout, understand that complex motives have animated Christians throughout the ages, that things like power, privilege, and sin complicate our understanding of the past in church history, theology, and the interpretation of the Bible itself. I remember one classmate moaning, "Once you begin down this path, it isn't really clear where it all stops."

Nearly all of my Christian friends remember a lecture, book, or conversation that made them reexamine what they thought about the Bible, doctrine, the church, or even God. For me, it was Elizabeth Clark's lecture. It was not really the topic, the creeds and orthodoxy, that was revelatory; it could have been about evolution, white supremacy, the authorship of Paul's letters, or any other topic in church history. The point was that she complicated my view of faith and history.

Complications challenge certainty. You do not have to go to graduate school to know that. We live in a complex world, one where, at any given moment, a sound bite or tweet from the other side of the planet can make you stop in your tracks and reconsider what you believe. An unexpected question or upsetting event can throw a life into turmoil in a flash. If you are alive and paying any attention at all in the early twenty-first century, your world is thousands of times more complex than that of your grandparents.

This is why people move to gated communities, associate with only those who think as they do, block critics on Twitter, believe in conspiracy theories, and find safety in watching Fox News. Huddling in our own corner is a respite from complexity, where we might hold on to at least a shred of our certainty. "Sometimes the biggest challenge to our sense of certainty about God," writes Peter Enns, "is just getting out of the house once in a while and seeing that we are just people like everyone else with a limited perspective and not the center of the universe."[14]

Faith often needs to become more complex before it can become clear again. That sounds paradoxical, perhaps, since we typically define faith as surety. Although it took a couple of years and much wrestling, I came to admit that Christianity itself, as a human story, is profoundly flawed, shot through with all the sins Jesus condemned; much of its tradition is an exercise of power, and its institutions are far from perfect. Knowing this, I learned that faith must be cloaked in humility and open to honest criticism about where the church had gone wrong. And, as a historian, I experienced a kind of graciousness that arises from knowing that, in a century or two, we too will probably be shown to have contributed to some great injustice or really stupid idea that is invisible to us now. I let go of the need to be so darn certain about things.

"We lost almost any notion of paradox, mystery, or the wisdom of unsayability," laments Richard Rohr, "which are the open-ended qualities that make biblical faith so dynamic, creative, and nonviolent."[15] I am not sure I had known these to begin with, except maybe when I was a small child, but I knew there had to be a less-worn path.

This sort of modesty is, as an old prayer says, meet and right. Faith, after all, is a sister of hope and love, an aspect of trust, and a way of life. Certainty is a poor imitation of that, like one of the last copies from an old-fashioned mimeograph. Alan Jones, former dean of Grace Cathedral in San Francisco, would often say, "The opposite of faith isn't doubt. It is certainty." An unpretentious faith—paradoxical, really.

Whenever I am challenged by the temptation to certainty, I recall the sign: BEWARE OF BULL.

"I am the gate," said Jesus. Following his way is often a matter of taking the chain off the post and crossing an unfamiliar field. You take the risk.

Love

The great Catholic writer Henri Nouwen, however, might have disagreed with locating the journey in the feet. "Following Jesus," he said, "is moving away from fear and toward love."[16] Nouwen would go anatomically a bit higher—to the heart. But how to move toward love? In my twenties, I had taken a long detour and now wanted to find the road again. The way is the way of love, as Jesus himself said. "Everyone will know that you are my disciples, if you have love for one another" (John 13:35). Love is the evidence and the location finder of the way.

Understanding faith as a way of love seems to be making a bit of a comeback these days—perhaps because it is an antidote to an age marked by intolerance and bigotry. An entire denomination has rebranded itself as "the way of love," and dozens of recent books have been written about a journey toward love. One of my favorites is by Norman Wirzba, professor of theology and ecology, entitled simply *Way of Love*. He reminds readers that Christianity "is not, in essence, a set of teachings, but a way of life. Christian faith is a vision of flourishing that bears witness to God's love everywhere at work in the world." To say "God is love" is neither sentimental nor facile; rather, it expresses the truth that God's love is the "ever-present, ever-active source and sustenance of all reality."[17]

Wirzba does not explain love. Instead, he says that the way of Jesus is revealed in four movements of divine love: creation ("when love becomes flesh, life is created"), fall ("when love is denied, life falls apart"), redemption ("when love goes to work, life is healed"), and hope ("when love is 'all in all,' life is heaven").[18] Thus, he takes four familiar Christian words, ideas that usually describe doctrines about personal salvation, and deepens and extends their meaning to illuminate the journey of faith. He summarizes the way in a paragraph:

> God's love creates a beautiful world, but our distortion and denial of this love lead to life's degradation. God does not give up on us or any creature, and so God works to redirect our waywardness, so that we can participate with God in the healing of all life. The goal of God's love is for it to be fully active in the life of each and every creature. When that happens, life becomes heavenly.[19]

I wish I had had Wirzba's book a quarter century ago when I was moving from certainty to a different path of faith. But, of course, I did not and would have to figure it out for myself. Over the next years, as I sought to reacquaint myself with Jesus, I would rethink each of these four touchstones—creation, fall, redemption, and hope. At the turn of the millennium, however, the central two were the ones that needed immediate attention and the areas where I experienced the deepest transformation of faith.

The traditional interpretations of sin and fall never really made sense to me either biblically or through experience, and I found them increasingly difficult to maintain. You cannot go on a journey if you are destined to fail and the course is predetermined. And you do not have to be a Christian to know that love is a wildly unpredictable course. I could not walk out of the cage until I had some level of confidence that there actually was a path. There has to be a way to travel.

Like other doctrines I took for granted, the word "fall" does not occur in the Bible. It is another of those extrapolated ideas, one with an ancient and contentious pedigree. At Duke, one of my classmates was a former Southern Baptist who had become a Wiccan. "Is there anything you still believe," I asked, as I was curious about her spiritual journey, "from when you were a Christian?"

"I still believe in original sin," she replied. "There's a lot of sin, and much of it is surprisingly original!"

My initial shock must have registered with her, as, joking aside, that was the issue with which I was struggling. But I did tend to agree with her. I understood the pervasiveness of sin, often by being on its receiving end. But something just did not seem right.

In Western Christianity, God created the heavens and earth, including human beings, and pronounced the universe "very good"; in the beginning everything existed in perfect harmony. However, Adam and Eve disobeyed God by eating the fruit of the one tree that was forbidden them. This disobedience destroyed the relationship between God and humankind, thus causing a "fall" from original blessing into sin and violence. This angered God, who cast humans out, because a holy God cannot tolerate impurity.

The old adage "Pride goeth before the fall" sums up the theology neatly—hubris is the source of sin, and because of it our race is now cursed. According to the conventional interpretation, the fall cut us off from God, doomed us to sin and violence, and we were lost until God decided to save us—

mostly because God loves us pitiful creatures, not because we were worth saving. *There is no health in us.* We are all miserable sinners, fully culpable because a first couple (who never existed) got tempted by a talking snake, ate an apple (or a pomegranate), pissed off God, and got themselves and all the rest of us damned. And because of all this, every time we human beings have sex and conceive, we pass the consequences of all of this on to our own offspring.

Most thoughtful Christians—most, but by no means all—understand that this is a story, like an elaborate campfire tale, to answer the question, "Why is there evil in the world?" At neither evangelical college nor seminary did anyone seriously believe in Adam and Eve, a conniving snake, sacred apples, or sin through sex (although they did believe that sex was a sin!).[20] Yet here is the odd thing: although we rejected all these literary flourishes, reading the story mostly as a metaphor, we retained what we considered the deeper meaning of the tale. We were bad, very bad. God was rightly angry with us, and we brought exile, violence, and hell upon ourselves.

As Will Rogers and, later, Gary pointed out to me, I had internalized this grim view of humanity, thinking I was worthless and unlovable, with nothing to give that would make a difference in the world. This bleak reading of human nature dovetailed with the basic facts of having been born female, having suffered abuse as a child, and ending up in an emotionally destructive marriage. Women are taught that we are lesser, somehow dirty because of our bodies, and unfit for work in the world. To believe that Eve was culpable for the fall reinforced the original sin of being female, and I felt this all keenly.

In effect, I had spent most of my life submitting myself to others, echoing words I thought authorities wanted to hear, and disappearing into acceptability. Even after getting born again, I felt that I had caused my own suffering, that I somehow deserved it when bad things happened to me, and shame was a daily burden. Some women rebel against all this; others conform. I was the latter type.

And it is very hard to imagine Jesus's way as a way of love if you do not love yourself.

At Duke, and then when I returned to Santa Barbara to teach, I became acquainted with Jewish scholars and was surprised to learn that the idea of an original fall did not exist for them. How was that possible? We read the exact same story in Genesis!

According to much Jewish thought, the fall was less a tragedy than a kind of unanticipated liberation. Before Eve took the fruit, human beings essentially had no moral freedom. They did as God directed. Yet the tree—the Tree of the Knowledge of Good and Evil—bore the fruit of conscience. The text (Gen. 3:6) clearly says that when Eve was tempted, she desired the fruit because she desired wisdom. She did not want to be like God, to be better than God, or to rebel. Instead, she reached for wisdom, something most human beings might like to have. This was an admirable or at least sympathetic longing.

Once eaten, the fruit "opened their eyes," and the first couple could see that they had both the ability and responsibility of ethical choice. Genesis, insists Rabbi Jonathan Sacks, is not about God and God's anger at humanity; rather, it is how we human beings relate to God's gift of freedom. "That is good news, but also bad," he says. Sacks continues:

> We can obey but also disobey; we can create harmony or discord. The freedom to do good comes hand-in-hand with the freedom to do evil. The result is the entire human drama as Judaism understands it. Our fate does not lie in the stars, nor in the human genome, or in any other form of determinism. We become what we choose to be. Therefore, we don't know what will happen next.[21]

The breadth of sin is enormous because, starting with Adam and Eve's own offspring, humans have chosen poorly and misused their freedom. Indeed, the word "sin" is not used in the narrative of the fall; the word first appears in Genesis 4, when Cain, envious and angry that God seems to like his brother Abel's offering better than his, murders his sibling. Genesis 3 opens the door for the violence of Genesis 4, and murder is identified as the first sin. This is the abuse of human conscience, an abuse that would turn into a raging— and relentless—pandemic throughout time.

Since Jesus was a Jew, it is not a stretch to think that he may have understood Genesis 3 in a somewhat similar way—not in the terms established in the fourth and fifth centuries by

St. Augustine or the Roman Church. Indeed, Jesus appeared to think that children were not particularly sinful and that it was more than possible for them to choose well.

This was helpful to me. As my Wiccan friend's comment had suggested, getting rid of the idea of sin would be a denial of reality. The world is full of sin, and much of it is horrifyingly original. But that does not mean that we humans are trash; it means that we choose badly. And because so many millions have chosen poorly over millennia, we imitate what we see, living in a poisoned environment, where sin has metastasized, making it all the harder to cut the cancer out. We need to be healed. "Sin, at its core," writes Professor Wirzba, "is the failure of love."[22] *For God so loved the world that he gave his only Son, so that everyone who believes in him may not perish but may have eternal life.*

Sin as the failure of love made sense to me; Jesus came to open a way of love. This helped me understand that I was not actually worthless. I had done unloving things to be sure (and still do), but neither had I been well loved. Love had been distorted, disordered, and even denied me by individuals, and by larger systems and institutions as well.

For my entire life, it seemed that people had been shouting at me—telling me what to believe and how to act. I started a journal. Every day I sat on a park bench overlooking the Pacific Ocean, where sounds of wind and wave silenced the shouts as I scribbled my own thoughts and feelings. "There was a new voice," Mary Oliver wrote of the journey of awakening, "which you slowly recognized as your own."

Until my mid-thirties, I did not know that voice. But once I listened, it grew more insistent. A calling, a beckoning, an urging toward love. And, as Oliver said, I "determined to do the only thing" I could do: Save my own life.[23]

I did not know how that would happen. But I was ready to leave the old voices behind. I stared at the cage's open door, and I knew it was time to walk out into the world. I trusted that Jesus would be on the way.

Liberation

One of the best foolish decisions I ever made was when I agreed to teach a course in feminist theology at the evangelical college. I framed the class around Christian feminism, mostly through *All We're Meant to Be*, by Letha Dawson Scanzoni and Nancy Hardesty. Their work on biblical feminism had first appeared in 1974 and become the standard text in evangelical circles for what was then called "women's liberation." The original edition had been a bible to me when I was a college student, and I, in turn, as a professor at the same college introduced it to a new generation of students in the 1990s.

Much had changed, however, in the intervening decades. And my syllabus included books that went beyond the gentle parameters of Scanzoni and Hardesty, including work by Rosemary Ruether, Mary Daly, Elizabeth Johnson, and Elisabeth Schüssler Fiorenza. All these women crafted theological visions of Christian freedom; each challenged hierarchies and patriarchy, arguing that the core claim of Jesus was a new world of equality, in which a new humanity was liberated for love and justice.

I confess that I hadn't read most of these works until I was assigned to teach the class. As I prepared for a discussion, the opening image from Fiorenza's *In Memory of Her* made me gasp. "In the passion account of Mark's Gospel three disciples figure prominently," she wrote. Those three were Judas, Peter, and "the unnamed woman who anoints Jesus." Fiorenza claims, "While the stories of Judas and Peter are engraved in the memory of Christians, the story of the woman is virtually forgotten. Although Jesus pronounces in Mark: 'And truly I say to you, wherever the gospel is preached in the whole world, what she has done will be told in memory of her.'" Yet, as Fiorenza notes, the woman has been largely forgotten; "even her name is lost to us."[24] The women had disappeared to history—the very woman whom Jesus promised would live in memory. I realized that I didn't want to disappear— that I wanted to be seen as fully human, to be remembered as one who loved Jesus, and as a faithful follower. I had lived too long in a theological community that erased women, excluded us from the story, and trivialized our experiences of Jesus. I wanted the disappearing act to end.

The students grasped the radical aspects of all this more quickly than I did. "Now the Lord is the Spirit," they would quote from St. Paul, "and where the Spirit of the Lord is, there is freedom" (2 Cor. 3:17) and ". . . there is no longer male and female; for all of you are one in Christ Jesus."

(Gal. 3:28). The more I taught the students, the more book discussions I led, the more I understood my own constraints, and words like these from Schüssler Fiorenza tugged at my soul:

> A feminist Christian spirituality defines women's relation-ship to God in and through the experience of being called into the discipleship of equals, the assembly of free citizens who decide their own spiritual welfare.[25]

Equal. No submission. No disappearing into someone else's version of Christianity. Free to follow the path of my own spiritual welfare. The feminist theology course upset the powers that be and caused a general ruckus on campus. That was the foolish part. But it finally brought me to the fork in the road. I had to choose. The unnamed, unremembered *her*? Or forward, freely following Jesus?

It was not exactly walking out of the cage; it was more like crawling. My marriage had died. I did not fit at the college. Friends abandoned me. I finally told my parents about the abuse. One Thanksgiving evening, I sat on the cold floor of the garage turned apartment, having had no company, no feast, no table to share, and collapsed into a torrent of tears. I literally let go of everything, but most especially the pain, doubt, and brokenness that had attached to my soul. I felt utterly empty, forsaken, as if there were nothing left. I was so alone.

And then I heard, as if a voice, familiar words: "I will not leave you orphaned; I am coming to you. . . . Do not let your heart be troubled, and do not let it be afraid." I lifted my head from the floor and heard a final call: "Rise, let us be on our way" (John 14:18, 27, 31).

I got up, wiped my eyes. I learned that letting go—surrender—isn't the same as submission. Finally releasing the fear that holds one back is freeing. Liberation, especially the sort woven into the love of God, is not easy. There were no miracles. Slowly, month by month, I walked ahead, being saved by the most unexpected things. "Love's desire," said Norman Wirzba, "always is that all creatures be well and attain the fullness of their being, which is why when creatures are wounded, love gets busy to bring about healing."[26] For everything that had died, some new thing came into being, small green shoots in a barren plot. Endings make room for beginnings. The Resurrection began to be real—"Unless a grain of wheat falls into the earth and dies, it remains just a single grain; but if it dies, it bears much fruit" (John 12:24). The atonement, the *at-one-ment* of the cross, was no longer an abstract theory or long-ago event; it was an organic, daily reality, where salvation grew like a spring garden. Abundant life.

I asked a friend who was a retired bishop in the Episcopal Church if he believed in the Resurrection. He replied, "Believe it? I've seen it too many times not to!" I think I became more evidence for his case.

I started writing for the local newspaper, published some poetry, began to lead workshops, and taught part-time at Santa Barbara City College and UCSB. I found a new church, one that welcomed all sorts of doubters, seekers, skeptics, misfits, and outsiders; that congregation took seriously the call of God's love to heal and renew the world. I asked all the questions I had ever wanted to ask; I read books frowned upon by the evangelical communities I had known. There were new friends, some of whom would prove the most loyal and compassionate people I have ever known.

I attended lectures by Marianne Williamson on love and took a writing class with Sue Grafton. I traveled all over the country, and to England and Argentina, giving talks, and wrote for the *New York Times* syndicate. I walked on the beach at dawn, slept under the stars on summer nights. I went dancing and wine tasting and sailing and to parties at the homes of movie stars who lived in Montecito, and I dated the most fascinating and completely unsuitable men.

I was free. The farther I got from the cage, the more I knew Jesus was with me. I reached toward him, and he reached back, like the image on the ancient icon of Jesus pulling the dead from the depths of hell: Rise up!

And then, on a warm Sunday in February 1996, I met Richard, who had grown up in a liberal Presbyterian family and loved books and ideas and travel. Our brunch extended long into the afternoon, as we talked about Emerson and Transcendentalism, about history, politics, and faith. We even talked about Jesus, with Richard telling me that he felt that fundamentalists had "stolen" Jesus and he wanted Jesus back. I understood. Eleven months later, we got married at the welcoming church, and the minister preached from the Song of Solomon: "Arise, my love, my fair one, and come away; for now the winter is past, the rain is over and gone. The flowers appear on the earth; the time of singing has come . . . Arise, my love, my fair one, and come away" (2:10–13).

In a picture in our wedding album we are standing next to the cake, our heads thrown back in laughter—an image of pure joy. And liberation.

❦

Step by step, my feet traced the prayer path, not a maze but a labyrinth, recently installed at Mount Calvary, a monastery in the foothills behind Santa Barbara. It was June, a month when fog often settles on the coastal city. Today, it had lifted, but the air was still damp, and nearly translucent clouds hung like a sheer curtain veiling the sun. As I walked, I thought I felt a droplet, and then another. On the labyrinth tiny beads of water, like little spatters of grace, began to mark the way. I looked up toward the source, my palms facing upward as if to catch the drops. A rainbow had formed behind the hills and reached toward the ocean, seeming so close I wondered if the drops were actually small jewels falling from its prism of color.

The way of Jesus is the way of love. It is also a labyrinth, a "meandering but purposeful path, from the edge to the center and back again."[27] Although I adore the poetry of Isaiah, poetry repeated by Luke—"Prepare the way of the Lord, make his paths straight. . . . The crooked shall be made straight, and the rough ways made smooth" (Luke 3:4–5; Isa. 40:3–5)—life and faith do not work that way.

Jesus is no interstate to glory, as I had thought in high school, college, and seminary. I had been so certain. Then I was not certain anymore. Everything fell to pieces. And then new life began, and love. The Jesus way is full of switchbacks, spirals, and unexpected turns; mystery, paradox, unknowing, unsaying. Whenever you think you are near the center, the path suddenly veers in a different direction and you find yourself again at the edge of the way. No wonder Jesus says, "Follow me" and "I am the way." But for a guide, you might never find a path, even if sometimes you are only following bread crumbs he left behind.

And so I stood there, having arrived to the center of the labyrinth—hands in the orans position, the most ancient of prayer postures, showered by the rainbow. The baby inside my belly moved, leaped for joy.

Oddly enough, I remembered Gary's comment about the cage. Yes, I had locked myself in. There were lots of reasons why, many excuses. I think I worried that Jesus would not be with me outside its walls. But it had become obvious that the door was open, and I could stay inside or go. I was not sure where I would wind up, but I learned the truth of the words of a Spanish poet, *Se hace camino al andar,* "The way is made by walking."[28] Whatever had conspired to create the cage, I chose differently. I walked. I had lost much, gained more. I was free. And Jesus was with me. The way had brought us here.

The rain stopped, and the sun burned away the last of the fog. And even stranger, perhaps, than remembering Gary's words, especially given the twists and turns of my own theological journey, a line from John Calvin came to mind: "The brightness of the Divine countenance, which even an apostle declares to be inaccessible, is a kind of labyrinth."[29] Step away from certainty and find yourself on a labyrinth of love. And Jesus is there, both the way and the guide.

The idea of quoting John Calvin made me laugh, but I quickly shook off his ironic specter. My hands now cradled my growing baby, as I moved from the center back to the path, toward the waiting world. I thought of a book sitting on my desk at home, one by Maya Angelou: *Wouldn't Take Nothing for My Journey Now.*

CHAPTER

—— 6 ——

Presence

And remember, I am with you always, to the end of the age.

—*Matthew 28:20*

Y ou've talked a lot about church trends and sociology," the
pastor said in an accusing tone, "but I've not heard you
say one word about Jesus. What about Jesus? Where is Jesus?"

The workshop seemed a hard slog that day, teaching about
demographics and the future of church, answering tough
questions, and dealing with the clergy's worries about the
implications of the decline in religious affiliation for their
denomination.

The pastor's colleagues murmured their displeasure. I saw
a few heads shake from side to side and lots of eyes rolling.
He had sat at a table near the back of the room, tight-lipped,

glowering at me the entire time. At events with required clergy attendance, there is always at least one hostile questioner, a pastor who has waited until the very end to undermine the work of the woman who dared speak all day. Like an old joke or a sunny weather forecast in Phoenix, I had grown to expect it, in all its wearying predictability.

"As far as I know, Jesus is here," I responded. "Why do you think he is absent?"

"Because you haven't said his name. Not once." He stood with his hands on his hips, feet apart, facing me down as if he were the "Fearless Girl" statue on Wall Street. "You haven't said his name."

"I have to say Jesus's name for Jesus to be here?" I asked. "I just assumed Jesus would be present in a roomful of clergy."

His colleagues laughed, and then someone called out, "That's not necessarily a good assumption!"

"Point taken!" I replied, laughing along with them. "But I trust that wherever two or three are gathered Jesus is in their midst. Where love is, Jesus is there."

My interrogator thudded down into his seat, unhappy with the entire exchange.

Although his colleagues were embarrassed and a few of them apologized to me after the lecture, it did not particularly surprise me. For several years, my work involved warning faith leaders about the coming tsunami of religious disaffiliation, lecturing mostly on sociology and history and the need for institutional change. I often avoided theology, not because I was averse to talking about it, but because it was not central to such workshops. Pastors, however, press theological questions, especially about Jesus. The exact question had arisen before: "Why haven't you mentioned Jesus?"

My answer had always been the same. "Do you think Jesus isn't here?"

❧

Early Christians had a hard time figuring out who Jesus was, especially those new Jesus followers who were Jews. "Hear, O Israel: the Lord is our God, the Lord alone" (Deut. 6:4) is a central vision of Judaism. There is no other God, no worship of idols. Yet Jesus's first disciples, those Jews who embraced him as their teacher, struggled. Even though they believed he was the Messiah, they wondered how they could worship him. Only God could be venerated. Yet the young Christian community experienced Jesus in ways that seemed to make him equal to God. Did God exist as *two*, as Father and Son? If so, how?

If this was not hard enough, an additional question emerged: What of the Spirit? When Jesus breathed on his friends and gifted them his Spirit? When the Spirit fell like fire from heaven? When the one called the "Comforter" makes her presence known? Was God one? Two? Or three?

These were difficult questions for the early church, not easily answered, and they prompted nearly five hundred years of theological speculation before being distilled into a set of philosophical ideas that, at the very least, framed a doctrinal vision of who Jesus was. The formal answer of the church was that God existed as the Trinity, as three *persons* (from the Latin, a term that has caused great theological woe throughout the ages but nevertheless remains), who are distinct yet—at the same time—completely one. Jesus, the "second person of the Trinity," is fully human and fully divine.

Like most Christians, I have affirmed and recited historic creeds that teach these things. And I have taught these doctrines to college and seminary students—as well as rooms of middle-school children preparing for Confirmation and classes of adults seeking to deepen their faith. I admire the precision of the creeds, the stunning staying power of ideas formed more than a thousand years ago, and their continued capacity to both shape ritual and provoke argument.

Yet I also wonder why it is that words so treasured, ideas fought over to the point of death, somehow fail to communicate the lived experience of millions of Christians throughout these same ages. Every week, I recite words *about* Jesus that actually communicate nothing he taught, lack mention of his passionate love, avoid the fact that he welcomed and fed all sorts of sinners and outcasts, say nothing about the poor (whom Jesus spoke of all the time), leave out the Beatitudes, conveniently omit Jesus's harsh words against Caesar, and studiously avoid the uncomfortable reality that he radically transformed the lives of those who followed him.

It is not so much that I disagree with the creeds or find their teachings intellectually difficult. I bear no ill will toward those ancient thinkers who tried to weave diverse strands of biblical story together with their Greek and Roman culture to create a theology that made sense in their world; nor do I think it bad that they bequeathed that work to subsequent generations. Rather, I cannot believe how much they left out of the story—and how distant they seem from the life I and countless others have lived *with* Jesus.

Living with Jesus is where it gets messy. This is why, I suppose, I became a historian and not a theologian. I prefer fluidity to precision, how we actually live rather than what we should believe. Whatever theological definitions Christians use for Jesus, life typically uproots them. In recent decades, Jesus has often surprised me by showing up where I did not expect him, by redirecting my attention to scripture and theologies I had ignored, and by introducing questions I would rather have avoided. Jesus has become present, with me, with us, with the world, in ways I never expected.

This is why I mention the creeds and the Trinity—with all their clean theological language about coming down from and ascending to heaven, as if Jesus rides a holy elevator between here and there. Truth is, scripture says that Jesus is at God's right hand, and that Jesus is right here. Where does that leave the other person, the Holy Spirit? There is a good deal of doctrinal slippage when it comes to Jesus and the Spirit. Theologically Jesus is here—in the lives of Christians, known as a friend, teacher, savior, lord, or the way—separate from the Spirit, that third and distinct person of the Godhead. But to experience Jesus is the work of active divinity; Jesus is known as the presence of God, made alive to us through the Spirit. God, Jesus, Spirit. You cannot really separate the threads, as much as philosophical theology differentiates. If nothing else, lived experience underscores the confusion felt by the early church. The first Christians experienced Jesus and the Spirit without reference to creedal certainty.

The Spirit empowers Jesus to be continually present in the world, and, it must be admitted, the same Spirit has been fully at work since creation, in the life of Israel, in the Word, and in the world. Indeed, God's Spirit conceives Jesus, initiates his public ministry, and sustains his spiritual life. The Spirit is the driving force, the animating creative life of the entire cosmos, responsible, in particular, for the vision of those in human history most attuned to the heartbeat of God. Even the apostle Peter recognized this as he preached to the Gentiles: "You know . . . how God anointed Jesus of Nazareth with the Holy Spirit and with power; how he went about doing good and healing all who were oppressed . . . for God was with him" (Acts 10:36–38).

To separate Jesus from the Spirit is nearly impossible. Jesus would not exist without the Spirit; Jesus would have been a humble tradesperson sans Spirit; Jesus would not be a continuing presence if not for the Spirit. Christian theology has typically privileged knowledge about Jesus as the way to know the Spirit, but the Christian life works the opposite way. We cannot know Jesus without the Spirit.

In the scriptures, the Spirit is called the *ruach*, *pneuma*, and the *shekhinah*, the "wind," the "breath," and the "dwelling."[1] Theologian Marjorie Suchocki refers to these as God's power, wisdom, and presence. Those three things are the heart of redemption, of experiencing the full life God intends for all:

> God as presence answers alienation and loneliness with love; God as wisdom answers the loss of time with trust; God as power answers injustice with empowering hope. This vision of a redemptive God of presence, wisdom, and power comes from the biblical revelation of God's presence in Jesus of Nazareth, named the Christ.[2]

When Jesus is understood in relationship with Spirit as presence, wisdom, and power, we can experience Jesus as a dynamic figure, one related to God's mysterious activity and one who dwells with us, always present.

Jesus, as a Jew, would have been familiar with the idea of *shekhinah*, the presence of God dwelling with the world. As Amy-Jill Levine says, "Judaism has the idea of the Shekhinah, the feminine presence of God descending to earth and dwelling among human beings." She continues, making the point that the possibility that a person could somehow be the presence, the dwelling among us, was not out of line with ancient Judaism:

> First-century Judaism was sufficiently fluid to allow even the idea that an individual could embody divinity. We know that because the earliest followers of Jesus who recognized him as divinity incarnate—such as Paul or James, the brother of Jesus who's running the Jerusalem

church—still called themselves Jews. Everybody recognized them as Jews.[3]

Was that how Jesus's first followers experienced him? Not with philosophical precision, but as a person inhabited by *shekhinah*? That he somehow was the dwelling place of God, and that there was no real conflict in the mind of his brother and sister Jews between bearing the mystery of the sacred and being fully human? And if that is who he was, is that who he still is? The presence, the wisdom, the divine dwelling with us, the feminine spirit, here and now?

Birth

It was a long birth, more than twenty-four hours of labor, when my daughter finally came into the world. She was born in the evening, and my husband held her while the doctor and nurses did their postbirth business, making more hubbub in the hospital room than I had expected. She was finally placed in my arms, kisses and pictures followed, and then she was taken to the nursery. The room quieted. I was exhausted; Richard was exhausted. He headed home, and I fell asleep alone.

I heard a voice. "Mrs. Bass? Mrs. Bass?" I opened my eyes, blinking in the hospital light. It was the nurse, the same one who had squeezed my hand a few hours before as she said, "Keep going, keep going. Push." Now she cradled the baby, tightly wrapped in a blanket. "Time to feed your daughter."

I sat up, reached out to receive my infant, and drew her close. The nurse, who had been my birthing teammate, smiled and walked out of the room. Two of us remained, the newborn and me. I was not particularly skilled with babies; only once before had I held an infant this young. The nurse had closed the door behind her, and silence surrounded us, as if swaddling mother and child. Except for my own heartbeat, made more rapid by uncertainty about what to do, the only thing I heard was a soft cooing and gentle breathing, like the *ha*, the Hawaiian word for "breath of life."

I nuzzled her—and natal sweetness filled my senses. We were two who had been one, and yet still were one in some mysterious way. And so we remained, fully present to each other, lost and found in a moment of new creation that neither had ever experienced. I glanced at the clock on the wall. More than an hour had passed since the nurse left. I looked down, and the baby opened her eyes, seeming to look up at me. Pure love enfolded us, a hallowing of this intimate world. The room had become a temple.

I had always known birth would be hard. I never knew it would be holy.

A friend of mine, Scottish writer John Philip Newell, often shares the story of being overwhelmed by seeing his newborn grandson for the first time and how profoundly spiritual the experience was. Ancient Celtic Christians believed that infants came from God and that in gazing in a newborn's face, we see the very image of God; and conversely, through the infant's eyes, in some mysterious way, God beholds us. The birthing place is a sort of inner sanctum where we encounter the freshly born presence of God.

No wonder that Christian tradition makes much of the birth of Jesus, the one whose birthplace opens to angels, animals, shepherds, and shamans. It is more than the silent midnight holiness between Mary and her son; the whole cosmos witnesses the birth. More than an image fresh from heaven, the Infant is the very embodiment of the divine. Every birth is echoed in this birth—no wonder the stars fill the heavens, the light shines forth. The presence of God made manifest, the glory of the One from the womb of grace. Darkness of birth, light of the world.

"Very truly, I tell you," said Jesus, "no one can see the kingdom of God without being born from above" (John 3:3). "Born from above" is the phrase that some Christians translate "born again." Back at Scottsdale Bible, it meant saying the Sinner's Prayer and confessing Jesus as Savior. As much as that meant to me at fifteen, I did not really understand Jesus's words until my daughter was born, when the womb opened and water broke forth, and then, in the silence, the breath. Water and spirit. Cradling the image of God so close, the image staring back.

"She [woman] will be saved through childbearing," says one of the letters written in Paul's name (1 Tim. 2:15). Yes, indeed. Women understand this transformation, this new birth, in all its tenderness, the freshness of God's presence come into the world. This was true for me, and mysteriously, painfully true for one of my best friends, Teresa, whose son was stillborn. Even with the sadness of simultaneous birth and death, she felt it too: "God's presence was in the midst of the worst of our lives; they will call him Immanuel, God with us." Years later, we shared our memories of those days. "Birth," she said knowingly, "is so transformative."

"What is born of the flesh is flesh," said Jesus with more than a little irony, "what is born of the Spirit is spirit" (John 3:6). Everyone is born of both, flesh and spirit. The problem is that we forget.

I was born into this world. I had been born again at fifteen. And then, I got born again *again* when giving birth some two decades later. "Do not be astonished that I said to you," Jesus reminded his friends, "'You must be born from above'" (John 3:7). Jesus, the birthed one, is also the ever-birthing presence, calling new life from the womb of God into the world. Not once, but many times.

Bowels

Parenting raises all sorts of issues, including how parents teach faith and religious traditions to their children. When my daughter was born, I imagined imparting wisdom to her, teaching her great theological insights from both my education and my experience. Like most new mothers, I quickly discovered that child-rearing does not work that way most of the time, as the whole business winds up in a strange mutuality where parents most often learn from their children. And thus, my young daughter started to teach me theology.

It started innocently enough, during Lent when she was two. I taught in the religious studies department at Rhodes College, in Memphis. Our family attended a local Episcopal church, and she went to a church day care. Religion, church, preaching, altars, pulpits—this was the stuff of her toddler world. Conversations about God came easily, frequently, and with more than a little passion. One day, as we headed to the store, a tiny voice came from the car seat: "Mama, where is God? Where does Jesus live?"

I replied, "Jesus lives in your heart."

For some children, that may have settled the matter, but not for my daughter. For weeks on end she asked everyone the same question. My husband replied, "Jesus is in heaven." Most of the adults offered similar answers—Jesus is "with you" or Jesus is in heaven.

The answers reveal both a tension and a bit of a theological rift in Christianity. The tension is between what is called "immanence," the idea that God is close by, and "transcendence," the opposite notion, that God is far off. Some churches emphasize one more than the other. The Methodist tradition, my own childhood church, leans toward the former; Presbyterians, however, my husband's childhood church, prefer the latter. When our daughter asked her parents, we each echoed our own childhood theology. Mine: Jesus is in your heart. Her dad's: Jesus is in heaven.

Christian theology does have a formal position on the argument, however. The technical doctrine is that God is both immanent and transcendent, here and there, close and far, completely with us and absolutely beyond imagining. By affirming this paradoxical dualism, the church asserts that Jesus's presence, once embodied as a human being two thousand years ago, is now a great mystery, as intimate as our inner awareness and as far-flung as the stars.

Theology, even the sort shrouded in mystery, often fails miserably the test of reality. As much as Christians have claimed immanence *and* transcendence, humans are notoriously bad with paradox, and immanence has typically been pushed aside for transcendence. The very idea that God is present in and with us, known where two or three are gathered, kicking up whatever dust is in the way, well, that kind of God is wild, unpredictable, and uncontrollable. Who knows what sort of unbalanced humans might think that such a God lives in their hearts or speaks directly to them? What misery would be caused! What chaos! Thus, the institutional church has always preferred a transcendent God, the One in heaven, safely distant from sinful whims and human meddling, and in need of a mediating, sensible, organized polity and an obedient priesthood.

In their desire for order, Western Christians structured the world around the transcendent God. In the three-tiered universe—heaven, earth, and the underworld—God was on the top, evil and impure things resided underfoot, and we poor humans were in the muddled middle, awaiting our eternal destiny in either the good (up) or bad (down) place. The political, social, and economic hierarchies of an up-and-down universe privileged a theological hierarchy as well, and in these mutually supportive hierarchies, shaped by inequities, injustice, prejudice, and oppression, the transcendent God won the day.

Much of this theology first developed in the context of the Roman Empire, when Christianity was still young, and the church saved itself by turning the peasant rabbi Jesus into its alternative Caesar, adjusting and adapting to the surrounding culture in order to survive. Thus, the abiding presence of the simple carpenter from Nazareth morphed into a vision of imperial glory, Lord Jesus Christ, high above the earth and her people. It is really hard to warm up to a Jesus wrapped in robes on a throne at the right hand of God the Father surrounded by an angelic chorus. But the crowned Christ is all-powerful, and who needs a strangely warmed heart after all? If your only options are a wicked hierarchy versus one with an imperial Jesus at the top, the latter might well be a better option. This makes historical sense and can be understood with more than a little sympathy. Much like watching a Shakespearean tragedy, although you suspect it will end badly, you stay for the play.

But children? They simply say what they feel and answer questions in ways congruent with their experience, which is unhindered by the need to conform to a universe of ladders, with authorities ready to kick you down the rungs at will. Thus, that spring, after my daughter had considered all the grown-up answers to her question, she turned to me following Communion and announced: "Mama, Jesus isn't in my heart. He's in my tummy!" Perhaps "heart" is too abstract a concept for a two-year-old, but eating Jesus seemed just right.

As I reflected on this, I recalled my first memory of Jesus, when I was just about her age. I was afraid of the dark and had just been moved to the "big girl" bed. On my bedside table, my mother had placed a glow-in-the-dark figurine, the greenish-yellow kind that absorbed daylight and then gave it off again when the lights were out. It was a manger scene, a plastic version of a picture in the church nursery: Mary, Joseph, and the baby Jesus. I stared at Jesus, this little light in the darkness, until my fears ebbed and I fell asleep.

For weeks, that luminous Jesus kept nocturnal peace. Then, one night my screams woke the entire household. My mother ran into the bedroom, a look of panic on her face. "What's wrong? What's wrong?"

I held out the manger, mumbling incoherently, "Jesus teeth. Jesus teeth."

She took it from me, puzzled. "Jesus teeth?"

I could not stop crying. She examined the manger and then, looking panicked, pried my lips open and said, "Oh no!"

Wedged in my baby teeth was the head of the glowing Savior. I loved baby Jesus so much that I ate him.

Whether in tummy or teeth, both my daughter and I ingested God.

A beautiful prayer in the Episcopal prayer book about the scriptures requests help that we might "read, learn, mark, and inwardly digest" God's word—"Digest," so the word becomes part of us, and we might experience in our guts joy and hope. Archbishop Thomas Cranmer wrote that prayer around 1549, and at the time it was believed that the guts, the "bowels," were the location of the spirit, especially our most tender emotions like compassion, kindness, and desire. In the Hebrew texts, the Psalmist cries out, "I delight to do your will, O my God; your law is within my heart," meaning literally "within my bowels" (40:8). And in what is surely the Bible's most erotic passage, Song of Solomon 5:4, the woman speaks of her beloved's hand "thrust . . . into the opening" (NRSV) and how her "bowels were moved for him" (KJV). Indeed, medieval mystics, especially women, spoke of ingesting and digesting Christ—a reflection of both the piety of the Catholic Mass and a desire for a nearly erotic union with God. Jesus might reside, to use my toddler daughter's turn of phrase, in the tummy. Or, as is otherwise suggested, in our most intimate parts. It is a long and suggestive tradition in Judaism and Christianity, that of a bowel-dwelling God.

For years, I had just accepted the ideas of immanence and transcendence, as do most Christians, not even noticing how thoroughly the beautiful theological paradox had been completely subsumed into a structure of social and ecclesiastical hierarchy that makes the experience of immanence—of the in-the-gut Jesus—nearly impossible. When given the chance, Western Christianity has almost always branded those who celebrate immanence as witches and heretics; the exceptions to this are rare. Yet my whole life experience of Jesus had been one of moving more deeply into the presence within, toward the bowels of knowing. I finally began to understand how profoundly my thinking patterns had been distorted by hierarchies, with their up-and-down, top-is-better-than-bottom dualistic thinking and their inherent injustice and oppression.

So I began searching out how God is *with*, and perhaps, *within* us—the radical immanence of Jesus. In this quest, transcendence does not disappear, because God is also hidden, mysterious, and even Other. Rather, transcendence shifts from "above" to "beyond," like the shimmering light on the horizon. Thus, Jesus is the one who inhabits our inmost parts and yet hovers at the edge of our lives, the ever-beckoning presence in the bowels and just beyond the boundaries.

Body

Becoming a mother is about bowels—and barf and blood and all sorts of bodily functions. Even the most modest, most squeamish of women, which I freely confess to being, has to face the realities of bodies with motherhood—our own bodies, our children's bodies, the bodies of aging grandparents.

Women struggle with their bodies—body images, body issues, changes in their bodies, and the safety and vulnerability of their bodies. I was born into a world where women's bodies were one of two sorts, the modest and moral body or the sexualized and scandalous body—either Doris Day or Marilyn Monroe. There was a third (and unspoken) type as well among the white people of my youth—the untouchable body, women who were desired but forbidden and therefore needed to be controlled, for example, Black women. But for middle-class white girls, church girls, our only real models were of those in the Doris Day category, from June Cleaver and Laura Petrie to Carol Brady and Mary Richards. You could be beautiful, but effortlessly and vaguely awkward about your body, or coy and flirtatious, but never knowingly sexual.

All this changed with the sexual revolution—and that occurred about the time I entered adolescence. Bodies became a battleground in a cultural war about what it meant to be female, to be family, to be human. If it was hard for adults to navigate, it was doubly confusing for children, who learned one set of rules, only to have the entire game change. Understanding, accepting, and embracing my own body have never been easy.

"And the Word became flesh and lived among us" (John 1:14). Jesus had a body. The presence of God, "the image of the invisible God" (Col. 1:15), is embodied in Jesus of Nazareth. The sacred has physical shape, a body that can be touched, held, loved, and treasured—and that body vivifies the whole of creation, including all other bodies. Jesus is not a specter, and not a mere memory; Jesus is a bodily presence, born into the world, broken by its injustice, and reborn through death. These are, of course, the central claims of Christianity.

During adolescence, when I struggled with my own body, I also struggled with the body of Jesus. As a teenager, I did not want an earthy God. I wanted a glorious one, a God who transcended bodies, who existed as pure spirit or pure love on some other plane, a powerful God vastly beyond knowing. Somehow, a God without a body was oddly comforting to my awkward, changing, and wounded one. Bodies were not entirely trustworthy. But a disembodied God and a resurrected Jesus who walked through walls—well, they were compelling.

The evangelicals of my teenage years spoke of the body as a hindrance to faith, as a temptation to sin, and an object whose desires must be controlled. The Christian life was a constant war between body and soul, and bodies were the enemy. Women's bodies were especially problematic. They were needed for purity and procreation (with little explanation how both were possible) and—at the very same time— despised as dirty and deceptive, as the chief source of the fall of men. Women's bodies were soft and nurturing; they were also seductive and threatening.

Theology was used, first, to control the wayward daughters of Eve and, second, to emphasize the parts of scripture that extol the *disembodied* God over and against the world, the flesh, and the devil. Hence, at Scottsdale Bible, there was scant celebration of Christmas but a great hullabaloo about Easter. Stories about an unwed teenage mother giving birth to the Son of God? Or sermons about a resurrected body that is nothing like ours? You can see why they preferred the second over the first.

Bodies are messy. Birth is messy. Unpredictable, dangerous even. You can pretty it up by talking about a virgin birth, thereby undermining both Mary's sexuality and the real physical pain of bringing a baby into the world. But the truth of the matter is that Mary was a real woman, and Jesus a real baby who grew to be a real man; both were flesh and blood, both had real bodies. A woman's body was torn open by a baby forcing its way into the world, a hungry, crying, and helpless infant body to feed, wash, and warm.

Eventually, the mystery of God's glory runs smack into the muck of human bodies; the divine Word became flesh from the same dust and spittle that made us all. Mary's body brought forth the tiny body of God; her water breaking and the bloody birth made possible the water and blood of the cross some thirty years later. "To you is born this day in the city of David a Savior, who is the Messiah, the Lord." We emphasize "Savior," "Messiah," and "Lord," but forget the most amazing word in the angelic proclamation: "born."

When it came to theology and the creeds, I rarely had trouble with the "God" part regarding Jesus. It was the human part, the bodily Jesus that always tripped me up. I did not want the crucifix or the pietà; I preferred an empty cross and no weeping mother. Yet Jesus cared so much about other bodies that he healed them, and even raised one from the dead. Jesus shared our bodily functions and needs, including pain and passion, hunger and rest. That Jesus was present in the flesh reminds us to cherish our own bodies (the New Testament regards our bodies as "temples" of the Lord). The body of Jesus is so central to Christianity that the church understood itself as the extension of his body, and many Christians believe that his bodily presence is still accessible through the bread and wine of the sacrament.

In addition to all these distinctly churchy things, Jesus's body reminds us that all bodies have been caught up in the story of redemption. "The shape of God's body," writes theologian Sallie McFague, "includes all, especially the needy and the outcast."[4] She continues:

> The distinctive characteristic of Christian embodiment is its focus on oppressed, vulnerable, suffering *bodies*, those who are in pain due to the indifference or greed of the more powerful. . . . Jesus of Nazareth has a preferential option for the poor, the poor in body, those whose bodies and bodily needs are not included in the conventional hierarchy of value.[5]

Thus, Jesus's broken body makes possible a community where there is neither Jew nor Greek, slave nor free, male nor female. Through God's body, all bodies are one human body, and through the promise of resurrection, "*bodies*, all suffering bodies, will live again to see a new day."[6] Birth leads to new birth and to rebirth—so many births, so deep God's love of bodies. A born God has a body. Just like us.

Mother

To speak of Jesus as presence, as one filled with *shekhinah*, recognizes the feminine of God. The Hebrew word comes from *sh-ch-n*, meaning "to dwell," which seems to be related to the tabernacle of Exodus, and implies the homeplace of the divine. In Judaism, *shekhinah* is sometimes depicted as "God's daughter," fiery female wisdom.[7] Jesus dwells with us. Jesus is the home for which we have longed.

For several years, I had belonged to a church that used inclusive language, referring to God as Mother in some of the prayers. But Jesus? Jesus was born male, the Son of God. If, however, Jesus is inhabited by *shekhinah*, Jesus brings the divine presence to the world, then, in some way, the man Jesus also embodies the sacred feminine.

What better way to describe that than to refer to Jesus as our Mother? As a new mother myself, I found the image compelling, relatable, and instructive. In the Old Testament, there is maternal imagery for God—including that of a mother bear, an eagle hovering over her nest, a woman in labor, a nursing mother—and verses like this: "I was to them like those who lift infants to their cheeks. I bent down to them and fed them" (Hosea 11:4). In the New Testament, Jesus continues this tradition claiming motherly concern as his own: "Jerusalem, Jerusalem, the city that kills the prophets and stones those who are sent to it! How often have I desired to gather your children together as a hen gathers her brood under her wings, and you were not willing!" (Matt. 23:37).

Although often ignored, there have been important Christian thinkers who have explored the idea of Jesus as Mother. The most notable of these gender-bending reflections came from Julian of Norwich, circa 1390:

And so Jesus is our true Mother in nature by our first creation. And he is our true Mother in grace by taking our created nature . . . He is our Mother, brother and savior.[8]

Julian is a shadowy figure in church history. Her real name and many facts of her life remain unknown. For some reason, this English woman took up life as an anchoress—a solitary nun—walled into a cell at the parish church of St. Julian of Norwich, from which she apparently took her name. On May 8, 1373, when she was around thirty years old, Julian was struck by a devastating illness from which she nearly died. During the sickness, she received fifteen visions of God's love. For twenty years, she reflected on these visions, writing down her reflections in a book called *Showings, or The Revelations of Divine Love.*

The fourteenth century was a particularly trying time in medieval England, complete with wars, pandemic plague, and economic collapse. "Human life was cheap," one historian writes, "and fear of punishment by God ran high. A certain degree of pessimism, fear, and anxiety characterized the darker side of English life."[9] In this context, Julian received her visions of God's maternal love.

According to Julian, this love has its most powerful expression in the Mother God: "the deep Wisdom of the Trinity is our Mother, in whom we are enclosed."[10] To her, "fatherhood" represented God's lordship, a kind of distant rule, while motherhood served as the worldly, sensual, and kind property of God: "in our Mother Christ we profit and increase, and in mercy he reforms and restores us."[11] Only through the Mother God can human beings experience the comfort of the divine:

The mother's service is nearest, readiest, and surest. It is nearest because it is most natural; readiest because it is most loving; and surest because it is truest. No one ever might or could perform this office fully, except only him. We know that all our mothers bear us for pain and for death. Oh, what is that? But our true Mother Jesus, he alone bears us for joy and for endless life. . . . So he carries us within him in love and travail.

Julian continues to explain that Jesus feeds us "with himself," and draws us to "his blessed breast." There, the "tender Mother Jesus" reveals the "joys of heaven, with inner certainty of endless bliss."[12]

Thus, "the fair, lovely word 'Mother'" belongs most truly to Jesus, "the kind, loving mother who knows and sees the need of her child guards it very tenderly."[13] This is the essence of Wisdom, the *shekhinah*, that "precious and lovely are the children of grace in the sight of our heavenly Mother."[14]

Julian was not the only medieval person to delve into the divine feminine. Indeed, maternal imagery appears two full centuries before Julian's *Showings* in the work of noted theologians such as Anselm of Canterbury and Bernard of Clairvaux. In this tradition, motherhood represents nurture, security, and comfort. The mother symbolism was most often expressed in relation to the Virgin Mary, but male theologians also used it to describe Jesus, God the Father, and the Trinity.[15] "Mother" acted as a fleshy metaphor, a sensate comfort, whereby God's love became understandable, personal, and warm.

Therein lay hope. Against a backdrop of pandemic and violence, Julian found assurance, a spiritual surety echoed through her written words, at the breast of the motherly Jesus. When the night was cold and the baby sick, or when I missed my own mother, it was good to know Mother Jesus was nearby.

Quotidian Jesus

During the few years my family was in Memphis, we lived in a big old house that had been built in 1912. Through the decades, residents had added closets and updated bathrooms, but the house had never been renovated. Instead, it was comfortably worn, wooden floors bearing scuffs and scratches of occupants long gone. Odd items—like an old clock, license plates, and yellowed newspapers—were stashed in the attic and basement, and several generations of a raccoon family had established themselves in the garage.

The best part of this rambling old place was the front porch, stretching the width of the house. At the far end, there was the obligatory Southern porch swing, painted white and softened with plump floral pillows. An overhead fan kept the porch comfortable on even the hottest Memphis days. I sat there with the baby, graded student papers, and chatted with neighbors walking by. One of those neighbors, who lived nearby, was Phyllis Tickle, a well-known author who wrote about religious trends and spiritual practices. I loved when she joined me on the porch swing, where we would talk about writing, faith, and the future.

She visited once after returning from a global jaunt, having just covered a story from the Vatican. I felt envious. The porch, for all its charms, was constraining, the view from the swing, limited. I was chaffing to get back to the world. Phyllis understood.

"Life is funny that way," she said. "Sometimes it takes place on a big stage. But most of the drama is in smaller places. The trick is to pay attention, to cultivate awareness right here, right now."

I looked at her quizzically.

"Don't worry. You'll be on airplanes and at conferences again," she laughed. "But it will be different than it would have been if you learn to see the world deeply from this swing."

Not long after, she dropped a small book by my office at the college, *The Quotidian Mysteries: Laundry, Liturgy, and "Women's Work,"* by Kathleen Norris. I groaned inwardly at the label "women's work," but then realized I had no idea what the word "quotidian" meant! "Ordinary," says the dictionary, "everyday, especially mundane, daily." Norris writes: "Our daily tasks, whether we perceive them as drudgery or essential, life-supporting work . . . have a considerable spiritual import, and their significance for Christian theology, the way they come together in the fabric of faith, is not often appreciated."[16]

The world of washing and housekeeping, of cooking and baking, of building a marriage and caring for children—all this was the stuff of everyday liturgy, the prayer of our hands, and it was this, all of "a people's domestic life," that "might be revisioned as the very love of God." That God, Norris insisted, is the one "who cares so much as to desire to be present to us in everything we do."[17]

It was a relief to hear these words. The trajectory of my own faith had gone from the vast to the ordinary. I had felt accompanied by Jesus while rocking a sick infant in the middle of the night, while playing with her on the floor, and while pushing her carriage around the neighborhood. There was lots of laundry and dishwashing in those days.

We attended a church where the priest emphasized domestic faith; she truly embodied the honorific "Mother," a term less common in those days than now. A group of people there hosted a weekly Saturday night dinner and prayer time at a house next to the church. We gathered as families, single people, and lots of children to greet the Sabbath. We laughed and shared and sang, set the table and lit the candles, read the Bible and broke warm loaves of homemade bread.

During the week, I would just drop in—my daughter's nursery school was across the street—and sit on the porch with my friend Cathy, who owned the house. She called the community "Rivendell," after the "last homely house" in *The Hobbit*. It was cacophonous rather than contemplative, and it resembled the description offered by Bilbo Baggins in the story: "a perfect house, whether you like food or sleep, story-telling or singing."[18] When my mother passed on her dining-room furniture to me, I gave my table to Rivendell. It felt like donating an altar to a church. Last I heard they still sit around it, where countless guests have been fed. I sometimes wonder if they recall that I gifted it—and then I remember that I did not. Jesus did.

And thus, those first years unfolded with rhythms of home, work, and church, all within a five-mile radius of our house. It comforted me that half of the Christian year is called "ordinary time," a season of prayers and readings in which not much seems to happen, where holiness is marked by the seasons of nature—summer's growth and fall's harvest. No time of expectant wonder, no miraculous birth, no piercing light, no deep lament, no Resurrection triumph. Instead, these are the weeks when the church reads stories of Jesus teaching, healing, and eating, all that is familiar and the familial—the motherly presence of Christ—just ordinary time.

Ordinary time is not perfect time, however. My father died, not unexpectedly, from the cancer he had battled for two years. For every moment of domestic joy, there were others of frustration and fear. There were bills to pay, plumbing needing repair, and the blistering summer heat of Memphis. There were skinned knees and runny noses, barf and blueberry poop, and toothaches and high fevers. I worried I was not cut out for motherhood and did not know what I was doing. I could not fathom how the human race had survived so long—there must be some secret to this domesticity that I did not comprehend.

It was harder work than I guessed, and I feared I was losing the life I had only just found. I cried when I realized that I had not touched my suitcase or book bag in months; they had been replaced by a breast pump and a diaper bag. My husband surprised me a few weeks later with a new briefcase saying, "You'll need it soon enough." The seasons would turn. Eventually.

I talked to Brother Robert, a friend who was a monk, about my fear that I would never write another column, never speak at another conference, and never write the book I had always wanted to write. He wisely said, "This season will not last forever, but give this time to your home and baby. This moment is a gift, and God is with you."

Ordinary time meant being present to one another, child and mother, husband and wife, neighbor and neighbor, and being present to God in the liturgies of sink and porch swing. I leaned into Brother Robert's wisdom, trusting in the quotidian Jesus. Theologian Grace Ji-Sun Kim puts it well:

The Christian faith is different from what the world teaches. The Christian faith is not "seeing is believing," but rather, "believing is seeing." We must open our eyes and hearts and see Jesus's presence in our lives. We need to see him in the places that we dare not to look and dare not to think about.[19]

For the first time in my adult life, nothing much happened beyond my domestic sphere. I dared to embrace the ordinary. One day, while sitting on the swing, I was reading the gospel of John. In chapter 5, Jesus healed a man he had encountered in a portico. I laughed, unsurprised by the miracle, because I knew that Jesus did some of his best work on porches.

Rock

Some people refer to the rocks as red, but they are only red when the sun rises or sets on the desert. In full light, which, admittedly, is most of the time, the mesas, cliffs, and buttes of New Mexico are rusty-tinted siltstone and sandstone, with layers formed by primeval waters and winds. The landscape itself is history, where time reveals itself in the shape of the sand and rocks, the past visible to human sight.

I stood in the blazing sun in the Zen garden at Ghost Ranch, in Abiquiu, New Mexico, once home to artist Georgia O'Keeffe and now a retreat center of the Presbyterian Church. I had first visited Ghost Ranch when my daughter was two; now, almost twenty years later, I was back. Then, we still lived in Memphis. In the summer of 2000, however, we had moved to Alexandria, Virginia, in the suburbs of Washington, DC. Nothing in Washington is ordinary; the pace is brisk and the people brusque. Domestic rhythms gave way to long commutes by car, train, and plane. Brother Robert was right. The porch interlude was short, and the two decades following were marked by work and change. Life was busy. Things moved quickly. Sometimes I forgot to breathe.

Two decades is nothing, however, at Ghost Ranch, especially when looking up at the Shining Cliffs, a massive formation dating back some 165 million years. "The Lord is my rock, my fortress, and my deliverer," proclaims the Psalmist, "my God, my rock in whom I take refuge" (18:2). The wind was still that day, the creek below, dry, giving rise to an eerie silence all around. God the rock. I leaned down and scooped up a fist of garden pebbles, wanting them to impart their permanence to me.

"On this rock I will build my church," said Jesus, "and the gates of Hades will not prevail against it" (Matt. 16:18). Indeed, scholars argue whether Jesus pointed to his friend Peter when saying this—or to himself. But other verses are clearer. "The rock was Christ," said Paul to the Corinthians (1 Cor. 10:4); and even Peter referred to Jesus as "a living stone . . . a cornerstone" (1 Pet. 2:4, 6). I looked at the pebbles in my hand, considering these verses, when the words from that Larry Norman song of my teenage years came to mind: "He's the rock that doesn't roll." Smiling, I gazed at the small stones, realizing they were a kind of icon of Jesus, and I prayed, eyes shut as if seeking deeper sight, feeling solidarity with the earth and God.

Then, a low rumble followed by a thunderous crash interrupted the silence, quite unlike anything I had ever heard. I looked to the sky, fearing a bomb at Los Alamos had exploded, searching the blue for a nightmarish mushroom cloud. There was, indeed, a cloud. Not in the sky, however, but lower. The Shining Cliffs were shrouded in clouds of red dust. The rumbling continued, and when the dust dissipated, I could see huge boulders tumbling from the top of the cliffs and landing far below, as the sheer face of rock collapsed. The earth literally quaked, not from within, but from massive stones smashing against the ground, as if hurled by angry gods.

When it was over, newly revealed layers of ancient red rock reflected the sun like a bloody gash on the cliff. And, at the base of the mount with its nearby creek, a pile of crushed boulders awaited the next flooding rain, all in anticipation of a watery erosion that would turn them into soil and dust. What came down to earth remade the very earth on which it landed. Christ the rock moves, and indeed Jesus is a living stone—the dynamism of creation, which never ceases its restless, thundering work to make the earth anew.

We humans have a habit of domesticating God. A quotidian Jesus is not the same as a tamed one. Christians turn Jesus into a static figure, the one who is "the same yesterday and today and forever." Perhaps the thundering rock is too much for us. Yet God remains the One who "shatters," as C. S. Lewis once remarked. "Could we not almost say that this shattering is one of the marks of His presence?"[20]

To read the Bible fairly, with open eyes, is to discover a God who is always on the move, the wind across the sands and the watercourses in the desert, embodied in a people who tend toward wandering, whose first prophets, Abraham, Sarah, and Hagar, journeyed from Ur to follow a sacred call. The ancient Hebrew people were not terribly good at settling, their occasional stability interrupted by exile, displacements, and pilgrimage aplenty; they were a people who knew God in the wilderness.

This same restless movement is part of Jesus's story. He was born on a journey away from his parents' home, an immigrant to Egypt escaping political violence. As a man he was chased out of a synagogue by his own neighbors and found himself a peripatetic preacher and prophet. Even his last night and day on earth were not settled; he was tossed from one legal authority to another, and his final journey was a cruel pilgrimage to execution. This God—this Jesus—is met along the paths of spiritual and political upheaval.

The idea that Jesus traveled to meet us is found in words my New Testament professor spoke of so many years ago: Jesus "emptied himself, taking the form of a slave, being born in human likeness" (Phil. 2:7). This short verse refers to the *kenosis*, the "emptying," in which Christ abandoned the fullness of God and joined humankind, even as a slave, as one who had no home. In effect, this is the thunder of theological boulders crashing to earth. Christians may sing of this moment with familiar Christmas carols, but the truth of the matter is that the silence of that night was broken by a shattering quake, as the side was ripped from the ancient butte, revealing the wound of the world. *Kenosis*. Jesus is not far away in the sky, but here. He came here on purpose, surrendering the glories of heavenly realms for this humble earth. Emptying, tumbling down the mountainside, the rubble on the ground.

That rubble, however, is not trash. *Kenosis* creates something new. When the dust clears, what has fallen to earth becomes the stuff out of which new earth will be created.

The rocks wear, their remains carried off by wind or water to make new dirt and soil that will change the landscape forever. The fall, the surrender to gravity, releases energy; the moving thundering rocks, what seemed eternally stable, becomes something new. Indeed, those falling rocks might become clay that winds up on a potter's wheel in the art studio at Ghost Ranch.

This is a *kinetic* process, the sort of movement where energy and material interact and create something that has not existed before. This is the way that the earth births itself over and again. Indeed, this is the very meaning of "Mother Earth." Sometimes we imagine "Mother Earth" as a frolicking figure, a kind of white-robed goddess. However, Mother Earth births in the falling rock, the flooding waters, the winds of the haboob. Rock is not static, not permanent or stable. "Cosmic destruction, disintegration, self-giving, and limitation," writes theologian Catherine Wright, "are inextricably intertwined with cosmic creativity, innovation, self-affirmation, and growth."[21] The self-emptying Jesus, the Jesus who falls from heaven and is born on earth, is also the Jesus whose journey of suffering and death becomes the genesis of the new creation. The emptying, always-moving Jesus is the *kenotic-kinetic* Christ, the birth mother of the cosmos.[22] Rock is generative. As God reminded the people of Israel: "You were unmindful of the Rock that bore you; you forgot the God who gave you birth" (Deut. 32:18).

This might sound arcane, but it really is not. It is the truest meaning of "dying to self," an idea that had compelled me so long ago. Standing at the base of the Shining Cliffs, I understood how my life had been marked by giving up and letting go, and that each release—whether purposeful or unwelcome—had created something new. My story was that of those rocks, when what was precarious on the hillside crashed downward, hurled as if by the gods, and began a process that would yield fertile soil.

We do not build a kingdom; instead, we participate in creation. Jesus is not Lord above the earth; instead, Jesus is earthy lord. Jesus is the birthing one. The rock. All the breaking, falling, and thunder; all the growing, nurturing, and gentleness: all of a piece. The earthquake and the porch swing. Mother God, *shekhinah*. This is the divine presence, the sacredness of a God whose name is Immanuel, "God with us," the one who dwells not in a heavenly mansion but at the potter's studio, always at work on the wheel.

Mystery

The waitress delivered two glasses of wine to the restaurant table, placing one in front of me, the other before my colleague. It had been a long day of teaching at this seminar, and both of us were tired. But it had been several months since we had worked together, and we were anxious to catch up.

"What are you writing?" I asked. Marcus Borg, the noted New Testament scholar, was always writing something, even with more than a dozen bestselling books to his name. Always new ideas, new words.

He smiled, a kind of wry half smile, and hesitated a second or two. "I'm doing something I've always wanted to do," he said. "I'm writing a mystery novel."

I laughed. I knew that, like me, Marcus enjoyed mysteries, including the crime novels of Ian Rankin and the detective fiction of the newly published Julia Spencer-Fleming. We often swapped recommendations.

"I never knew you wanted to write a mystery," I said. I felt bad for laughing. "I've always wanted to do the same. Good for you!" I went on, "I'm not completely surprised. You know, a lot of our religious studies colleagues want to write mystery novels. It's a thing. I wonder why."

"Not so hard to figure out," he replied. "We study mystery all the time."

I raised my glass. "To mystery!"

And Marcus raised his in return, "Yes, to mystery."

Sometimes, the word "mystery" is used as an excuse. "We can't really know that," profess some too lazy to pursue a complex subject. "It's a mystery." At other times, "mystery" is seen as a sort of riddle; if a curious inquirer only works hard enough, the mystery can be solved. In either case, mystery may be ultimately unknowable or a temporarily annoying puzzle, something we give up with a shrug or something we can investigate until we reach a satisfactory conclusion in a matter.

But "mystery" is actually a category in religion. Indeed, there is an entire group of traditions that historians call "mystery religions," mostly secretive cults in the ancient

Mediterranean world. The arcane practices and teachings of these communities remain mostly unknown, and biblical scholars argue as to their influence on New Testament writings, especially the work of Paul, and the development of early Christianity. What is clear is that Paul liked the word "mystery," and it shows up variously in Romans, Corinthians, Ephesians, and Colossians to describe everything from the nature of Christ to the resurrection of the dead, the relationship between spouses, and the inclusion of non-Jews in the church.

Often Christians think of "mystery" in the sense of a puzzle with an answer, as if knowing Jesus is a procedural like an Agatha Christie novel or a game of Clue. If you organize scattered facts, interview the proper witnesses, and discern hidden motives, you can figure out things that are unknown. Far too many read the Bible in this way, and even more treat holy mystery as a problem to be solved. The apostle Paul, however, is not inviting you to his weekend house to discover if Miss Scarlett did it in the library with a knife. The New Testament mysteries are of a different sort.

Indeed, a pair of theologians make a helpful distinction between *investigative* mysteries, based on what is unknown, and *revelational* mysteries, which revolve around what is known:

> The whole fascination of a detective story lies in trying to solve the puzzle, and when one knows the solution the mystery is dissolved—it is no longer a mystery. . . . But

the fascination of many of the New Testament mysteries lies in their peculiar character even after they have been revealed. . . . A revelational mystery excites wonder, awe, amazement, astonishment. . . . This is the way a revelational mystery works: we know, and yet the mystery remains.[23]

They conclude: "Theology is not simply a set of truths to believe; it is a path to walk, or a living vision to pursue."[24]

That path is one of humility and listening. In the life of knowing and unknowing, of a hidden God and God revealed, clouds sometimes obscure the light, and, in the words of one ancient saint, "The quest goes beyond what is visible and is enclosed on all sides by incomprehension, which is a kind of sacred darkness."[25] Or as Paul writes, "Now we see through a glass, darkly; but then face to face: now I know in part; but then shall I know even as also I am known" (1 Cor. 13:12, KJV). Mystery—what is disclosed and yet still mysterious.

It is not terribly unusual to think of God as mystery. In 2014, shortly before he died, Marcus employed the term "mystery" to refer to God: "God, the sacred, the Mystery with a capital *M* that is beyond all words."[26] Yet for all the times I heard him or others speak of the mystery of God, I am not sure I ever heard the phrase, "Jesus the mystery." Yes, Jesus taught mysteries, those parables—yet, at the very same time, he is also, in and of himself, *the* mystery, a parable embodied. The *Catechism of the Catholic Church* teaches that "Christ's whole life is mystery," listing literally every aspect of Jesus's existence as "mystery" (512–70), and that believers are "taken up into the mysteries of his life" (562). It has a point in making such an extensive claim. It is relatively easy to think of God as mystery—incomprehensible as love and spirit—but it is less typical, all apologies to the Catholic Church, to imagine Jesus as mystery.

Yet what is more mysterious than speaking with familiarity about a man who lived two thousand years ago? Experiencing love when serving the least among us, knowing blessing with the poor and with those who mourn? Being angry at the injustice of Pilate's show trial, as if we stood in the room and watched? Weeping with Mary over the cruelty inflicted on her son? These things have been known to millions over the entire planet for two millennia as part of the human story.

A man who taught love was unjustly murdered by an empire committed to eliminating all dissent. This happened, but it remains a source of awe and astonishment that so many *feel* it still, through story, song, and ritual, to the point of *living into* the very life of Jesus as if he walked the earth today. This man, who easily could have been forgotten, who by all creaturely standards would have decayed in the dust long ago, is the one we speak of as friend or brother.

For all the faithfulness of my Jewish, Muslim, and Buddhist friends, I do not know if they experience the sort of profound intimacy with Moses, Muhammad, or the Buddha that Christians regularly assign to their relationship with Jesus— and this is neither criticism nor claim to religious superiority. Rather, it is just an observation that Christians locate revelational mystery in a *person* rather than in Mosaic law, submission, or enlightenment (all of which seem perfectly beautiful and even more sensible ways of knowing the divine!).

Jesus as mystery is, indeed, the Christian faith's greatest spiritual enigma. A human being who is fully God? That is what Christianity proclaims—that beyond our wildest imaginings, the ever-creating Love of the cosmos made its way into our small, hurting world, living and dying with us and for us, and promises never, never, never to leave us alone. Love is in the world, and inside of us, dwelling with us even as we dwell in it.

I cannot explain one bit of that. I once thought I could, like a detective, uncover the mystery and make it clear and plain to the world in various ways, as missionary, teacher, preacher, theologian, writer. But now I understand that what I "know" is also ultimately unknowable. We live the mystery, in ordinary days and extraordinary ones, whether rocking the baby or watching rocks crash to earth. "We come from mystery," insists ethicist Barbara Holmes, "and return to it at the end of the life journey."[27] If we are attentive enough, we might awaken to the reality that everything in between is mystery as well. And for many of us, that mystery bears the name Jesus.

Where is Jesus? Right here.

The Universal Jesus

I am the Alpha and the Omega, the first and
the last, the beginning and the end.

—*Revelation 22:13*

The ballroom at the Parliament of the World's Religions was packed to capacity, about three thousand women. A huge banner hung over the stage: "2015 Inaugural Women's Assembly—Salt Lake." I sat under the sign.

Although this parliament has gathered for more than a century, this was the first time in history there would be a meeting for women in advance of the general assembly. Native women opened the ceremonies by telling stories of the place where we convened, land sacred in their tradition, once inhabited only by their people and great herds of beasts. Women from different faiths offered prayers. One by one, sisters came to the podium, wearing everything from Western business dresses and religious robes to tribal clothing, carrying books and beads, some with hair flowing free and some with heads covered by veils. They spoke prayers of many traditions with words, drums, dances, incense, poetry, and liturgies.

I felt nervous, sitting there on the stage as one of twenty keynote speakers. The organizers had seated me between a Wiccan and a Hindu, one seat removed from a Muslim. Of those on the stage, only two were Christians: a Mormon and me. Only six or so were white. I had spoken to groups of Jews, groups of secular people, and groups of African American clergy where I had been the only white woman or only Christian in the room. But never had I been in a place where Christianity was one religion among many, where white was just one shade of humanity among so many others, and where Christians sat on a stage they did not own and were present with no intent to proselytize. Yet there I was: one of two women representing hundreds of millions of Christian women across the globe, sitting with my sisters.

I was scheduled near the end of the presentations. One by one, the women seated ahead of me spoke. And then it was my turn. I walked to the lectern. I addressed the vast congregation, speaking of spiritual wisdom passed on from my mother and my two grandmothers to me. Then I shared this story:

Last week, I was at my neighborhood coffee shop. My favorite barista was there, a young Muslim woman. I noticed something different about her. She was not wearing her usual black hijab. Instead, she was wearing a bright green scarf edged with sparkling sequins.

"I love your scarf," I said.

She looked pleased. "You know, they told me I had to wear black."

"What?" I asked.

"The rules. They said I had to wear black. But I didn't believe it. So I looked it up myself. I don't have to wear black. I can wear any color I want."

I didn't know whether she was speaking of some religious authority or her boss. But it didn't matter. She had searched the "rules" for herself, not listening to someone else's interpretation, but reading the text on her own: "I looked it up myself."

"I looked it up myself" has thundered throughout history. This is the stuff of what we Protestant Christians call Reformation, of a new spiritual revolution. When the women of the world take on words for themselves, when we seize our sacred texts and search them for truth, for wisdom, for strength. To interpret our traditions for ourselves. Not to submit, but to claim authority and look it up for ourselves, to do that which we know to be beautiful and joyful and just. Women with the power of words can change the world.[1]

The audience roared approval! I looked out over a sea of women whose words and wisdom were remaking all their traditions. It was, quite simply, overwhelming.

I returned to my seat. The Hindu woman smiled warmly at me; the Muslim sister reached out and squeezed my hand. At that moment, an image flashed in my mind of Jesus sitting in a circle with Patanjali, the Buddha, Muhammad, Guru

Nanak, and Confucius; with saints and mystics and seers. *In the circle.* Not above it, not beyond it. *In the circle.* With me, with all of us in the circle.

In a famous quote, the medieval mystic Mechthild of Magdeburg (d. 1282) relates an all-encompassing vision of her own: "The day of my spiritual awakening was the day I saw and knew I saw all things in God and God in all things." And the New Testament often uses the word "all" in connection with Jesus, especially in Paul's letter to the Colossians, where Jesus is depicted as the one in whom "all the fullness of God was pleased to dwell" (1:19), "all things hold together" (1:17), and "all the treasures of wisdom and knowledge" are hidden (2:3). "In him all things in heaven and on earth were created" (1:16), and Jesus is the one through whom God "was pleased to reconcile to himself all things" (1:20). In what is the most mystical of the letter's claims, the ancient author proclaims: "There is no longer Greek and Jew, . . . but Christ is all and in all!" (3:11).

The all in all. Contemporary writers and theologians have turned toward the spiritual inclusivity of Jesus, emphasizing his "all-ness" with many titles: the Cosmic Christ, the Ground of Being, the Heart of Creation, the Universal Christ.[2] "The life of Jesus," insists Catholic theologian Ilia Delio, "sets the pattern of whole-making, which includes reconciliation, forgiveness, peacemaking, and compassion, and . . . this pattern permeates the mass of creation—humanity and cosmos."[3] The story of Jesus unfolds toward unity, toward making all things one, to the ultimate wholeness of healing, peace, justice, and love. "God is unbroken wholeness in movement," Delio continues, "and creation is movement toward God-centered wholeness."[4]

This is the truth of Jesus. That Jesus—the one known intimately as friend and teacher, experienced as Savior and Lord, who guides on the way and inhabits the ordinary—is also the universal Jesus, the welcoming and inclusive Jesus, the Jesus *of* the circle and *in* the circle, the all in all.

Over the years, I have been with Jesus in many circles. Sitting in a Sunday school circle and hearing flannel-board stories about him, singing with others in a circle around a campfire, and praying in a circle in a Mexican village for justice and peace. Teaching students theology seated at round tables, offering Communion in a circle around an altar, dancing in a circle with Sioux women at a protest march in Washington, and being in the circle of faith in Salt Lake City. Circles are dynamic and communal. You cannot be in a circle by yourself. "Where two or three are gathered," Jesus promised to be present.

The cross is, of course, the most familiar spiritual symbol of Christianity. But the circle best illustrates my experience of Jesus—around tables, altars, and campfires; in classrooms and church rooms; at rallies and protests. There have been times in my life when I liked lines, wanted to draw lines, and tried to consign others—or myself—to neat rows of pews or desks. I imagined that life was a straight narrative line, with clear beginnings, happy endings, and solutions to all of its mysteries.

It took some time to understand that the mystery of Alpha and Omega is more like a spiral or the mythical snake that eats its own tail—the circle, that infinite geometric form symbolizing the "all." Despite the hesitations that held me back sometimes, the ever-inclusive Jesus kept inviting me into circles, beginning with the Methodist Sunday school room and extending to the stage at the Parliament of the World's Religions. Encountering Jesus in the widening circles stretched my own heart to love more, embrace more.

Not only has Jesus shown up in these circles, but the circle has become an apt image for my spiritual life. When I was in seminary, someone introduced me to the literature about stages of faith. Based on the work of psychologists like Jean Piaget and Lawrence Kohlberg, James Fowler worked out a trajectory of spiritual development that moved through six stages, from fantasy to logic to belief, then to disillusionment and skepticism, then paradox and, finally, unity.[5] I appreciate the framework that Fowler described—and found it meaningful in understanding my own spiritual journey. However, Fowler seemed oddly committed to spiritual development as a linear process, implying that one finally arrives at "universalized faith" on the journey.

Ultimately, however, he misses an important aspect of faith experience. In the "unitive" stage, I find myself returning to the start, wanting to incorporate the wisdom of the entire journey—all the Jesuses—into my life now. What he depicted as an ending, I've found to be a new beginning. I go back in the spirit of informed wonder, what philosopher Paul Ricoeur called "the second naïveté," reimaging Jesus as my friend, learning from the teacher, thankful for the ever-healing Savior, serving the kind Lord, staying on the way, and mindful of the quotidian presence. To find the wholeness of Jesus on a platform with women from many world religions is one thing. To find wholeness with the Jesuses I have known is quite another. Too often, we find it difficult to embrace our own past, to accept our full experience as sacred. Because of that, we cut ourselves off from our own wisdom. Yet, even as the universal Jesus reaches through the whole cosmos; that same Jesus enfolds all the insights of our hearts, the whole of our story. The Cosmic Christ is also the Jesus of Sunday school memory, the Heart of Creation is found in every crevice of our own hearts.

May the circle be unbroken. By and by, Lord, by and by.

As I reflect on the circle, I consider all the Jesuses I have known, six of whom I have shared here: friend, teacher, Savior, Lord, way, and presence. There are a few Jesuses who were hinted at in different parts of the narrative, but not specifically mentioned in this story—Jesus as Lover, a rich image from medieval spirituality, one who meant a great deal to me when I was going through a divorce and speaks again now that I am in my sixties; Jesus as Word (and the corresponding Jesus as Silence), who shapes my vocation as a writer; Jesus as Wisdom, the feminine Sophia, who breathes and births the world into life; and Jesus as Bread and Wine, the familiar Jesus of Communion, who feeds and sustains me. Perhaps Jesus as Lover, Word, Wisdom, and Sustenance feel almost too intimate to share publicly; or perhaps that is the Jesus who is worming his way into my heart at the moment, making it hard to put the immediate experience into permanent prose. *Who are you?* A question with myriad answers.

We know Jesus through our experience. There is no other way to become acquainted with one who lived so long ago and who lives in ways we can barely understand through church, scripture, and good works and in the faces of our neighbors. In these pages, I have shared six Jesuses whom I experienced through something I call "memoir theology" (*not* theological memoir). Memoir theology is the making of theology—understanding the nature of God—through the text of our own lives and taking seriously how we have encountered Jesus.

In seminary, I asked a professor why we only read theology written by men—books by Augustine, Anselm, Aquinas, Calvin, Luther, and Wesley. He told me that women did not write theology.

I quickly replied, "What about Perpetua? Julian of Norwich? Hildegard of Bingen? Teresa of Ávila and Catherine of Siena?"

He replied, "That's not theology. That's memoir."

I fell silent, unsure what to say.

I stewed over that remark for a long time. It is clear that we call it "theology" when men write of Jesus. But we call it "memoir" when women do? What—other than memoir—are Augustine's stories of stealing pears and weeping over his lost love? Or Luther writing of his fear of death or proclaiming, "Here I stand"? Or Wesley sharing his experience of the heart strangely warmed. Or Karl Barth and Dietrich Bonhoeffer resisting the Nazis? All the "big-name" theologians in church history wrote of Jesus from their own stories; their theologies were born from experience. Without their struggles and sins, their theologies would not exist. Theology is born when we wrestle with God in our lives. Spiritual memoir is theology, and experience is a text of Christology.

Of course, women are not the only ones whose experience has not counted in the making of theology—men and women of color, indigenous people, LGBTQ people, disabled people, working-class people, laity, anyone outside of the academy, the poor and outcast. For centuries, church authorities silenced all these theologies by discounting the experiences of most Christian people, consigning them all to some category of "less than" the few men whose experiences were deemed normative to interpret the experiences of the rest of us. As a result, Christianity has lost the wisdom of millions and millions of faithful people whose journeys with Jesus may have reshaped the faith and perhaps inspired the church to live more justly and compassionately.

The limited notion of theology as one thing and experience as another has been the source of untold pain and incalculable loss, surely something that causes the universal Jesus to weep. Our frame is so narrow, and Jesus's is so wide. If only we knew all the Jesuses who have been hidden from view, all the Christs never heard. Thankfully, more voices count now—the experiences of many are arising to bring every Jesus to light the world.

There is an old Berber proverb: "The true believer begins with herself."[6] Your experience of Jesus matters. It matters in conversation with the "big names," when you argue with the tradition, and when you read the words and texts for yourself. It matters when you hear Jesus speaking, feel Jesus prompting, and sink into despair when Jesus seems absent. It all matters. The Jesuses you have known and the Jesus you know matter.

The oddest thing happened while I was working on this book. My story began with Jesus's words at the Washington National Cathedral, "Get me out of here." During the months of reflecting and writing, the coronavirus pandemic broke out across the world, forcing us to distance and church buildings to close. Christians could not gather in familiar places, their buildings empty and dark, their sanctuaries without prayers and sacraments.

If you wanted to find Jesus in a church, you couldn't. The doors were shut tight.

But as millions have discovered in these many months, Jesus was not confined to a building. Jesus was around our tables at home, with us on walks and hikes, present in music, art, and books, and visible in faces via Zoom. Jesus was with us when we felt we could do no more, overwhelmed by work and online school. Jesus was with us as we prayed with the sick in hospital over cell phones. Jesus did not leave us to suffer alone. COVID-19 forced Jesus out of the cathedral into the world, reminding Christians that church is not a building. Rather, church is wherever two or three are gathered—even if the "two" is only you and your cat—and where Jesus is present in bread that regular people bake, bless, and break at family tables and homemade altars. I did not liberate Jesus from the cathedral; a pandemic did. Jesus is with us. Here.

One day, the doors will open again. Many will not go back to church, mostly because they left some time ago. They did not need help to find Jesus in their lives and in the world. They were already discovering what it meant to follow Jesus beyond the church. Perhaps the pandemic hastened the process, caused them to ask new questions, or renewed their courage on the journey.

But many others will return. And, as before, people will sit close, hug and pass the peace, and share bread and wine. I suspect I will pray again at the altar in the National Cathedral, under the gaze of Jesus. I cannot predict what he might say. I do, however, know what I will say: "Thank you."

Whatever happens, however, I hope none of us will ever forget the Jesus we have met in our own lives, who has been with us in fear and confusion and loss, in forced isolation and the surprising moments of joy, and through the ministrations of our shared human priesthood. It all matters. All of it.

My deepest thanks go to all the friends, teachers, mentors, relatives, classmates, former students, pastors, co-workers, neighbors, and fellow writers whose patience and wisdom show up in the pages of this book. Many are Christians; some are not. I've learned of God from all of them. Most are not named or specifically quoted, but if they read these pages, they will find themselves here. Nothing I have written has given me a greater sense of how much we depend on one another, and how our lives exist in a unique community shaped by mutual experience and shared memory stretching through time and space. If our paths have crossed in real life, if you comforted me or challenged me, know that you have contributed to this narrative. And, for that, I am grateful.

A special word of thanks to Scottsdale Bible Church in Scottsdale, Arizona; Westmont College in Santa Barbara, California; and Gordon-Conwell Theological Seminary in South Hamilton, Massachusetts. These communities shaped my faith life at important junctures of young adulthood. We came to have many disagreements, yet I bear you no ill will. I am grateful for the gifts you gave me when I most needed them, grateful that I've had to wrestle with all our limitations and wounds, and I am grateful that you continue to give your unique gifts to the world. Jesus said, "Whoever is not against us is for us." I take those words seriously and consider that we are not enemies, but are ultimately friends in Christ. I write about my experiences in your precincts mostly from memory—now of some decades ago. So, please excuse any paraphrases or lapses, knowing that memory is a tricky thing and that I am aware we would see some things very differently.

To my friends at the Washington National Cathedral: keep an eye on that N. C. Wyeth Jesus. You never know what he might be saying to visitors.

As always, I thank my friend and agent, Roger Freet, for being part of my life and work for nearly two decades now. To the team at HarperOne, especially my editor Katy Hamilton, Mickey Maudlin, Chantal Tom, Lisa Zuniga, Melinda Mullin, and Ann Moru, along with their artists, book designers, media assistants, and copyeditors, who make putting a book into the world as painless as it can be: I am particularly grateful to you for this project, as we learned together how to do this during a pandemic. I can't believe this is our sixth book! Thank you.

I am deeply grateful to all the churches that have invited me to teach and preach, especially in the last few years as this book took shape. Your hospitality and kind reception have embodied Jesus for me more than you know. Thank you for letting me try out new ideas in your midst and offer challenging interpretations in your pulpits. Some of the insights in these pages came from sermons I first preached in your congregations. And despite the fact that I write honestly about people leaving church, you know that I remain your friend, ever hoping that the world may experience your generous faith in Jesus. I hope that what I've written here honors you. Know that I've missed you terribly in the pandemic.

As always, my family deserves the greatest thanks. This book is dedicated to my sister Valerie, for whom I am deeply grateful. My husband, Richard, my dearest friend and companion, holds my heart, navigates my fears, and sharpens my ideas. While writing this book, my stepson Jonah got married, thus bringing the gift of Hannah to our family. Our daughter, Emma, graduated from university (might I add with distinction in her religious studies major?). And Rowan the dog turned ten—although slower than he once was, he still goes after the squirrels in our yard. In other words, I am thankful that we continue on life's path together, discovering always grace and forgiveness. Without them, I'd be lost. *And now faith, hope, and love abide, these three; and the greatest of these is love.*

Thank you, Jesus.

Introduction: Liberate Jesus

1   Anne Rice, from a Facebook post, quoted in Diana Butler
    Bass, *Christianity After Religion* (San Francisco: HarperOne,
    2012), 20.

2   Wade Clark Roof, *A Generation of Seekers* (San Francisco:
    HarperSanFrancisco, 1994); Nora Gallagher, *Things Seen and
    Unseen* (New York: Knopf, 1998); Diana Butler Bass, *Strength
    for the Journey*, 2nd ed. (New York: Church, 2017).

3   Martin Kähler, *Der Sogenannte Historische Jesus und der Geschichtliche,
    Biblische Christus*, 1892.

4   Barna Group, "What Do Americans Believe About Jesus? 5
    Popular Beliefs," *Barna.com*, April 1, 2015, https://www.barna
    .com/research/what-do-americans-believe-about-jesus-5
    -popular-beliefs.

5   Pew Research Center, "Americans Say Religious Aspects
    of Christmas Are Declining in Public Life," *Pew Forum*,
    December 12, 2017, https://www.pewforum.org/2017/12/12
    /americans-say-religious-aspects-of-christmas-are-declining
    -in-public-life; Barna Group, "What Do Americans Believe
    About Jesus?"; Jeremy Weber, "Christian, What Do You Believe?
    Probably a Heresy About Jesus, Says Survey," *Christianity Today*,
    October 16, 2018, https://www.christianitytoday.com/news

/2018/october/what-do-christians-believe-ligonier-state
-theology-heresy.html.

6   Philip S. Brenner, "Exceptional Behavior or Exceptional Iden-
     tity?: Overreporting of Church Attendance in the U.S." *Public
     Opinion Quarterly* (Vol. 75, No. 1, Spring 2011), 19–41. Also:
     "In U.S., Church Attendance Is Declining," https://www
     .pewforum.org/2019/10/17/in-u-s-decline-of-christianity
     -continues-at-rapid-pace/pf_10-17-19_rdd_update-00-018.

Chapter 1: Friend

1   Sigmund Freud, *The Future of an Illusion* (1927), quoted in
     Robert Coles, *The Spiritual Life of Children* (Boston: Houghton-
     Mifflin, 2000), 2–3.

2   Liz Carmichael, *Friendship: Interpreting Christian Love* (London:
     Bloomsbury T&T Clark, 2004), 41, 221.

3   Sallie McFague, *Models of God: Theology for an Ecological, Nuclear
     Age* (Philadelphia: Fortress, 1987), 160.

4   Dirk Baltzly and Nick Eliopolous, "The Classical Ideals of
     Friendship," in Barbara Caine, ed., *Friendship: A History* (Abing-
     don, New York: Routledge, 2014), 1–64, https://philarchive
     .org/archive/BALTCI-2v1.

5   Char Adams, "Boy, 8, Comforts Classmate with Autism on
     First Day of School in Heartwarming Photo," *People.com*,
     August 28, 2019, https://people.com/human-interest/conner
     -christian-autism-first-day-school-photo-kansas.

6   William Rawlins, quoted in Julie Beck, "How Friendships
     Change in Adulthood," *Atlantic*, October 22, 2015,
     https://www.theatlantic.com/health/archive/2015/10/how
     -friendships-change-over-time-in-adulthood/411466.

7   Dietrich Bonhoeffer, "The Friend," in E. Bethge, *Friendship
     and Resistance: Essays on Dietrich Bonhoeffer* (Grand Rapids, MI:
     Eerdmans, 1995), 99.

8   Based on research by Matthew Brashears, of Cornell University, as reported in numerous articles including Susan S. Lang, "Americans' Circle of Confidantes Has Shrunk to Two People," *Cornell Chronicle*, November 1, 2011, https://news.cornell.edu /stories/2011/11/americans-circle-confidantes-has-shrunk -two-people; and Jeanna Bryner, "Close Friends Less Common Today, Study Finds," *LiveScience*, November 4, 2011, https:// www.livescience.com/16879-close-friends-decrease-today.html. The original study is Miller McPherson, Lynn Smith-Lovin, and Matthew Brashears, "Social Isolation in America: Changes in Core Discussion Networks over Two Decades," *American Sociological Review*, June 1, 2006, https://journals.sagepub.com /doi/abs/10.1177/000312240607100301.

9   Paul Wadell, *Becoming Friends: Worship, Justice, and the Practice of Christian Friendship* (Grand Rapids, MI: Brazos, 2002), 17.

10   Wadell, *Becoming Friends*, 17.

11   Quoted in Brian Edgar, *God Is Friendship: A Theology of Spirituality, Community, and Society* (Wilmore, KY: Seedbed, 2013), 119.

12   Elisabeth Moltmann-Wendel, *Rediscovering Friendship: Awakening to the Power and Promise of Women's Friendships* (Minneapolis: Fortress, 2001), 12.

13   Benjamin Jowett, quoted in Edgar, *God Is Friendship*, 155.

14   Quinton Dixie and Peter Eisenstadt, *Visions of a Better World: Howard Thurman's Pilgrimage to India and the Origins of African American Nonviolence* (Boston: Beacon, 2011).

15   Dorothy Day, quoted in Coles, *The Spiritual Life of Children*, 329.

16   Eric Elnes, "'I Call You Friends,' Part I: Our Savior, Our Friend," http://countrysideucc.org/mediacast/i-call-you-friends-part-1 -our-savior-our-friend.

Chapter 2: Teacher

1 Amy-Jill Levine and Marc Z. Brettler, eds., *The Jewish Annotated New Testament* (New York: Oxford Univ. Press, 2011), 188, 734.

2 Amy-Jill Levine, *The Misunderstood Jew: The Church and the Scandal of the Jewish Jesus* (San Francisco: HarperOne, 2006), 20.

3 John A. T. Robinson, *Honest to God* (London: SCM; Philadelphia: Westminster, 1963), 76.

4 Robinson, *Honest to God*, 114.

5 Robinson, *Honest to God*, 116.

6 Marcus J. Borg and John Dominic Crossan, *The First Christmas: What the Gospels Really Teach About Jesus's Birth* (San Francisco: HarperOne, 2007), 41–42; also Marcus Borg, *The Evolution of the Word: The New Testament in the Order the Books Were Written* (San Francisco: HarperOne, 2012), 214.

7 Levine, *The Misunderstood Jew*, 203.

8 Levine, *The Misunderstood Jew*, 205.

9 Mahatma Gandhi, "The Jesus I Love," *Young India* 13/53 (December 31, 1931): 429; see Robert Ellsberg, *Gandhi on Christianity* (Maryknoll, NY: Orbis Books, 1991), 22.

10 Amy-Jill Levine, *Short Stories by Jesus: The Enigmatic Parables of a Controversial Rabbi* (San Francisco: HarperOne, 2014), 3.

11 John Dominic Crossan, *The Power of Parable: How Fiction by Jesus Became Fiction About Jesus* (San Francisco: HarperOne, 2012), 5.

12 Carol Kuruvilla, "These Zen Buddhist Koans Will Open Your Mind," *Huffpost*, October 31, 2015, https://www.huffpost.com/entry/zen-buddhism-koan_n_563251dce4b0631799115f3c.

13 Peter Enns, *How the Bible Actually Works* (San Francisco: HarperOne, 2019), 5, 10.

14 Josh McDowell, *Evidence That Demands a Verdict* (Nashville: Thomas Nelson, 2017), 196.

15 Marcus Borg, *Jesus: Uncovering the Life, Teachings, and Relevance of a Religious Revolutionary* (San Francisco: HarperSanFrancisco, 2006), 14.

16 Julie Ingersoll, remarks to the AAR on the death of Wade Clark Roof, San Diego, CA, November 2019.

17 Marcus Borg, *Jesus: A New Vision* (San Francisco: HarperSanFrancisco, 1987), 97.

18 My favorite book on this subject is Cynthia Bourgeault, *The Wisdom Jesus: Transforming Heart and Mind—a New Perspective on Christ and His Message* (Boulder, CO: Shambhala, 2008). Inspiring and challenging, it offers truly helpful insights on the life of Jesus and Christian spiritual practices.

19 I suppose, in some way it is a sort of sacred coincidence that my favorite Sunday school teacher was "Miss Jean," as was the little boy's teacher. She was *not* the same Miss Jean, however.

Chapter 3: Savior

1 Marcus Borg, *Meeting Jesus Again for the First Time: The Historical Jesus and the Heart of Contemporary Faith* (San Francisco: HarperSanFrancisco, 1994), 131–32.

2 Borg, *Meeting Jesus Again*, 133.

3 One of my favorite discussions of the words "salvation," "saved," and "Savior" is found in Marcus Borg, *Speaking Christian: Why Christian Words Have Lost Their Meaning and Power—And How They Can Be Restored* (San Francisco: HarperOne, 2011), 35–54.

4 Larry Norman, "The Rock That Doesn't Roll," *In Another Land* (Solid Rock Records, 1976).

5 Marcus Borg, *Evolution of the Word: The New Testament in the Order the Books Were Written* (San Francisco: HarperOne, 2012), 122.

6 Borg, *Evolution*, 121–23.

7 Amy-Jill Levine and Marc Z. Brettler, eds., *The Jewish Annotated New Testament* (New York: Oxford Univ. Press, 2011), 292–93.

8   "Nathaniel William Taylor," in Timothy L. Hall, ed., *American Religious Leaders* (New York: Facts on File, 2003), 356.

9   Alexander Carmichael, "Blessing of the Kindling," in "Celtic Prayers," *Vox Veniae*, February 26, 2009, https://voxveniae. com/2009/02/celtic-prayers.

10   Pelagius, "Letter to Demetrias," in B. R. Rees, ed., *Letters of Pelagius and His Followers* (1991), quoted in J. Philip Newell, *Listening for the Heartbeat of God* (Mahwah, NJ: Paulist, 1997), 14–15.

11   The first theologian to argue the view that our notions of original sin were based in the experience of men and did not account for women was Valerie Saiving. In her ground-breaking 1960 article, "The Human Situation: A Feminine View," she proposed that sin as pride and "original sin" were constructed from male understandings of dominance, and that female "sin" was not pride but erasure, the unwillingness or inability to be whole. Since its publication, the thesis has been refined and reargued, but the basic point stands: sin is a gender-, race-, and class-based construct in Christian history, one that has excluded the experiences of the oppressed and marginalized. "The Human Situation" has appeared in many collections, the most notable of which is Carol P. Christ and Judith Plaskow, *Womanspirit Rising: A Feminist Reader in Religion* (San Francisco: HarperSanFrancisco, 1992).

12   Stephen Finlan, *Options on Atonement in Christian Thought* (Collegeville, MN: Michael Glazier, 2007), 1–42.

13   Finlan, *Options on Atonement*, 31.

14   Finlan, *Options on Atonement*, 87.

15   This idea goes a long way toward explaining why conservative evangelicals will not do anything to address climate change.

16   Bart Ehrman, *Jesus: Apocalyptic Prophet of the New Millennium* (New York: Oxford Univ. Press, 1999).

17   Julian of Norwich, *Revelations of Divine Love.*

Chapter 4: Lord

1   Pliny the Younger, *Letters* 10.96–97, https://faculty.georgetown
    .edu/jod/texts/pliny.html.

2   N. T. Wright, "Paul and Caesar: A New Reading of Romans,"
    http://ntwrightpage.com/2016/07/12/paul-and-caesar-a-new
    -reading-of-romans.

3   Dietrich Bonhoeffer, *The Cost of Discipleship* (NY: Macmillan,
    1963; 1978), 99.

4   Education was the shortest major I ever pursued—one semester.
    I'm very grateful to those who pursue teaching children as a
    career, and I'm equally confident that the world is a better place
    because I did not. I would have been a terrible elementary school
    teacher.

5   Stephen Patterson, *The Forgotten Creed: Christianity's Original Strug-
    gle Against Bigotry, Slavery, and Sexism* (NY: Oxford, 2018), 108.

6   Patterson, *The Forgotten Creed*, 110.

7   Patterson, *The Forgotten Creed*, 115–17.

8   "Romero's Wisdom: Prayers," *U.S. Catholic*, February
    25, 2009, https://www.uscatholic.org/culture/social-
    justice/2009/02/romeros-wisdom.

9   Ronald J. Sider, *Rich Christians in an Age of Hunger*, rev. ed.
    (Nashville: Thomas Nelson, 2010), 58.

10 John Fugelsang, monologue.

11 Ada María Isasi-Díaz, "Kin-dom of God: A Mujerista Proposal,"
    in B. Valentin, *In Our Own Voices* (Maryknoll, NY: Orbis Books,
    2010), 173. See also a good discussion of Isasi-Díaz and the evo-
    lution of the language of kin-dom in Melissa Florer-Bixler, "The
    Kin-dom of Christ," *Sojourners*, November 20, 2018, https://sojo
    .net/articles/kin-dom-christ.

12 Janet Martin Soskice, *The Kindness of God: Metaphor, Gender,
    and Religious Language* (Oxford: Oxford Univ. Press, 2007),
    quoted in Amy Peterson, "Kindness, Kinship, and the Bound-
    aries of Justice," *Christian Century*, January 16, 2020, https://

www.christiancentury.org/article/first-person/kindness
-kinship-and-boundaries-justice.

13   George M. Marsden, *Fundamentalism and American Culture*
(New York: Oxford Univ. Press, 1980). Professor Marsden
would later become my graduate adviser at Duke, where I
earned my doctorate.

Chapter 5: Way

1   See Brian D. McLaren, *Is Jesus the Only Way? A Reading of John
14:6* (2019), privately published at brianmclaren.net.

2   Craig Koester, *The Word of Life: A Theology of John's Gospel*
(Grand Rapids, MI: Eerdmans, 2008), 211.

3   Mary Field Belenky et al., *Women's Ways of Knowing* (NY:
Basic Books, 1986), 106.

4   Marge Piercy, "Unlearning to Not Speak," *Circles on the Water*
(New York: Knopf, 1982).

5   If you ever asked about "slaves," as I did many times, you
would be told that the verse now meant that "workers" or
"servants" were to obey their employers, and to "Render service with enthusiasm, as to the Lord" (6:7).

6   Meister Eckhart, *Book of Secrets*, "Your Soul's Delight."

7   *Hadewijch: The Complete Works*, trans. Mother Columba Hart,
Classics of Western Spirituality (Mahwah, NJ: Paulist Press,
1980), 213.

8   Grace Andreacchi, "Hadewijch of Brabant and the High Palace
of Love," January 29, 2011, https://graceandreacchi.blogspot.com
/2011/01/hadewijch-and-high-palace-of-love.html.

9   "Come My Way" is a hymn text from a poem by George Herbert
(d. 1633), fund in sixty hymnals; http://hymnary.org/text/come
_my_way_my_truth_my_life.

10   Peter Enns, *The Sin of Certainty: Why God Desires Our Trust More
Than Our "Correct" Beliefs* (San Francisco: HarperOne, 2016), 21.

11 Richard Rohr, "All Spiritual Knowing Must Be Balanced by Not-Knowing," *Center for Action and Contemplation*, January 27, 2020, https://cac.org/all-spiritual-knowing-must-be-balanced-by-not-knowing-2020-01-27.

12 Enns, *Sin of Certainty*, 18.

13 Harvey Cox, *The Future of Faith* (San Francisco: HarperOne, 2009), 6.

14 Enns, *Sin of Certainty*, 135.

15 Richard Rohr, "Soul Knowledge," *Center for Action and Contemplation*, January 28, 2020, https://cac.org/soul-knowledge-2020-01-28.

16 Henri Nouwen, *Following Jesus: Finding Our Way Home in an Age of Anxiety* (New York: Convergent, 2019), 45.

17 Norman Wirzba, *Way of Love: Recovering the Heart of Christianity* (San Francisco: HarperOne, 2016), 35.

18 Wirzba, *Way of Love*, 41–42.

19 Wirzba, *Way of Love*, 42.

20 It is important to note that, although I happened to attend an evangelical school where there was a recognition of literary genres in the Bible and in my circles it was rare to find anyone who embraced literalism regarding Genesis, it is not at all uncommon for other evangelicals to believe fully in Adam and Eve, the snake, the apple, and physical exile from a garden called Eden. In certain ways, the biblical criticism of elite evangelicalism, especially in university settings, does not particularly diverge from that in more liberal branches of Christianity. But in most evangelical churches and on the ground in popular evangelicalism, literalism is normal.

21 "The Chief Rabbi on Genesis," *The Jewish Chronicle*, November 10, 2009, https://www.thejc.com/judaism/books/the-chief-rabbi-on-genesis-1.12309.

22 Wirzba, *Way of Love*, 96.

23 Mary Oliver, "The Journey," *Dream Work* (New York: Atlantic Monthly Press, 1986): 38–39.

24 Elisabeth Schüssler Fiorenza, *In Memory of Her: A Feminist Theological Reconstruction of Christian Origins* (New York: Crossroad, 1992), 349.

25 Schüssler Fiorenza, *In Memory of Her*, xiii.

26 Wirzba, *Way of Love*, 145.

27 Lauren Artress, *Walking a Sacred Path: Rediscovering the Labyrinth as a Spiritual Practice* (New York: Riverhead, 1995), xii.

28 Antonio Machado, https://en.wikiquote.org/wiki/Antonio _Machado.

29 John Calvin, *Institutes of the Christian Religion*, 1.6.3.

Chapter 6: Presence

1 An excellent book on "Shekhinah Christology" is Michael E. Lodahl, *Shekhinah/Spirit: Divine Presence in Jewish and Christian Traditions* (Eugene, OR: Wipf and Stock, 1992). Much of my discussion in this section was informed and inspired by Lodahl's work.

2 Marjorie Hewitt Suchocki, *God, Christ, Church: A Practical Guide to Process Theology* (New York: Crossroad, 1989), 87.

3 "A Jewish Take on Jesus: Amy-Jill Levine Talks the Gospels," *U.S. Catholic*, September 24, 2012, https://www.uscatholic.org /church/2012/09/jewish-take-jesus-amy-jill-levine-talks-gospels.

4 Sallie McFague, *The Body of God: An Ecological Theology* (Minneapolis: Augsburg Fortress, 1993), 164.

5 McFague, *Body of God*, 164; emphasis hers.

6 McFague, *Body of God*, 174.

7 Amy-Jill Levine and Marc Zvi Brettler, *The Bible With and Without Jesus: How Jews and Christians Read the Same Stories Differently* (San Francisco: HarperOne, 2020), 85.

8 *Julian of Norwich: Showings (Classics of Western Spirituality)*, eds., E. Colledge and J. Walsh (Mahwah, NJ: Paulist Press, 1977), 296.

9 Shawn Madigan, ed., *Mystics, Visionaries and Prophets* (Minneapolis: Fortress Press, 1998), 191.

10   *Julian of Norwich: Showings*, 54, excerpted in Madigan, *Mystics, Visionaries and Prophets*, 200.

11   *Julian of Norwich: Showings*, 58, excerpted in Madigan, *Mystics, Visionaries and Prophets*, 202.

12   *Julian of Norwich: Showings*, 60, excerpted in Madigan, *Mystics, Visionaries and Prophets*, 204.

13   *Julian of Norwich: Showings*, 60, excerpted in Madigan, *Mystics, Visionaries and Prophets*, 204.

14   *Julian of Norwich: Showings*, 63, excerpted in Madigan, *Mystics, Visionaries and Prophets*, 206.

15   For a full exploration of maternal imagery for God, see Caroline Walker Bynum, *Jesus as Mother: Studies in the Spirituality of the High Middle Ages* (Berkeley: Univ. of California Press, 1982).

16   Kathleen Norris, *The Quotidian Mysteries: Laundry, Liturgy, and "Women's Work"* (Mahwah, NJ: Paulist, 1998), 76–77.

17   Norris, *Quotidian Mysteries*, 22.

18   J. R. R. Tolkien, *The Hobbit*, chap. 3.

19   Grace Ji-Sun Kim, *Hope in Disarray* (Cleveland: Pilgrim, 2020), 47.

20   C. S. Lewis, *A Grief Observed* (London: Faber and Faber, 1966), 52.

21   Catherine Wright, *Creation, God, and Humanity: Engaging the Mystery of Suffering Within the Sacred Cosmos* (Mahwah, NJ: Paulist, 2017), loc. 2308, Kindle.

22   Wright's is the only sustained theological work drawing together these two terms; *Creation, God, and Humanity*, chap. 8.

23   Steven D. Boyer and Christopher A. Hall, *The Mystery of God: Theology for Knowing the Unknowable* (Grand Rapids, MI: Baker Academic, 2012), 6–7.

24   Boyer and Hall, *The Mystery of God*, 43.

25   Gregory of Nyssa, *Life of Moses*, quoted in Boyer and Hall, *The Mystery of God*, 233.

26   Marcus Borg, *Convictions: How I Learned What Matters Most* (San Francisco: HarperOne, 2014), 41.

27 Barbara A. Holmes, *Race and the Cosmos: An Invitation to View the World Differently*, 2nd ed. (Albuquerque, NM: CAC, 2020), 19.

Conclusion: The Universal Jesus

1   This version is based on my handwritten notes (scribbles, really) from the event. I believe there is video of the assembly, and my remarks may have been somewhat different in presentation than what I saved in writing (and that is not unusual for my speeches—I often leave the text when I am preaching or teaching). Whatever the differences between my notes and the video, however, the point of the Muslim barista's story remains the same: women with words can be the source of spiritual revolution. This story also appears in Diana Butler Bass, *Strength for the Journey*, 2nd ed. (New York: Church, 2017), 287–90.

2   The titles are from Matthew Fox, Paul Tillich, Rowan Williams, and Richard Rohr, respectively.

3   Ilia Delio, *The Emergent Christ: Exploring the Meaning of Catholic in an Evolutionary Universe* (Maryknoll, NY: Orbis Books, 2011), 68.

4   Delio, *The Emergent Christ*, 33–34.

5   See James Fowler, *Stages of Faith* (San Francisco: HarperSanFrancisco, 1981). Over the years, Fowler has been criticized for bias, especially in failing to bring the experiences of people of color, the disabled, and women to bear in his work. Fowler was popularized by M. Scott Peck in *The Different Drum* (New York: Touchstone, 1987). Although I have found Fowler helpful, the work in women's spirituality, such as Mary F. Belenky et al., *Women's Ways of Knowing* (New York: Basic, 1986), and Nicola Slee, *Women's Faith Development* (New York: Ashgate, 2004), and theories of spiral dynamics, like Don Edward Beck

and Christopher C. Cowan, *Spiral Dynamics* (Cambridge, MA: Blackwell, 1996), can supplement and correct some of the shortcomings in *Stages of Faith*.

6   Quoted in Joan M. Martin, "Re-imaging the Church as Spiritual Institution," in *Church and Society*, May/June 1994, 53.